P9-BIS-561

IN THESE PAGES . . .

. . . you'll meet Sam Douds, a brawling, hate-filled sea captain whose healing of intestinal cancer set the love in him free . . . Elaine Saint-Germaine, an actress whose downhill course into drugs and Satanism was miraculously arrested . . . Dr. Harold Daebritz, whose wife was healed in seconds of a back injury that had defied 20 years of specialists' treatments . . . and many, many more.

Wondrous, authentic and immensely moving, these unique stories are irrefutable testimony to the awesome transformation God can bring to anyone who seeks Him out.

NOTHING IS IMPOSSIBLE WITH GOD

Kathryn Kuhlman

SPIRE BOOKS

Fleming H. Revell Company   Old Tappan, New Jersey

All photographs of Kathryn Kuhlman are by Doug Grandstaff

NOTHING IS IMPOSSIBLE WITH GOD

A SPIRE BOOK
Published by Pillar Books for Fleming H. Revell Company

Spire Books edition published March 1976

Copyright © 1974 by The Kathryn Kuhlman Foundation

SPIRE BOOKS are published by Fleming H. Revell Company
Old Tappan, New Jersey 07675, U.S.A.

Contents

FOREWORD

Kathryn Kuhlman

a Tribute

I should think that everybody knows her by now. For nearly a quarter of a century, she has been a vessel of God that allowed healing and restoration to flow into the lives of thousands.

She is loved and admired by millions and maligned only by those who are down on divine healing or who have made no effort at all to understand her or what she stands for. But I have seen her behind the stage, before she stood in front of a multitude to express her unlimited faith in God, and watched her carefully. Over and over again she cried:

> Dear God, unless You anoint me and touch me I am nothing. I am worthless when the flesh gets in the way. You get all the glory or I cannot go out there and minister. I won't move without You!

And suddenly she bursts on the scene. It's explosive and almost unbelievable. It's not so much what she says—because that's always as clear and simple as the preaching style used by Christ Himself. I don't understand it, nor does she, but when the Spirit begins to move upon her—and she feels suddenly compelled to challenge Satan's power in Jesus' name—miracles begin to happen. People everywhere—even the most staid and dignified—fall prostrate on the floor. Catholics and Protestants raise hands and worship God together—all decently and in order. Holy

Spirit power rolls over the audience like waves of the ocean.

Those in the television media soon learned she was not a phony or a fanatic. People they had known had been helped by her ministry. They were no match for her wit and godly wisdom.

She is not wealthy, nor is she hung up on materialism. I know! She personally raised and gave to Teen Challenge the money to build a place on our farm to reach and rehabilitate hopeless addicts. Her prayers have brought in the money to build churches in underdeveloped countries around the world. She has sponsored the educating of underprivileged children and other talented youth who were recipients of her love and concern.

She has walked with me into the ghettos of New York and laid loving hands on filthy addicts. She never winced or withdrew—her concern was genuine.

And why this tribute from me? Because the Holy Spirit bade me do it! She owes me nothing, and I ask nothing more of her than that same love and respect she has shown me over the years. But all too often we pay our tributes only to the dead.

Now then, to a great woman of God who has so deeply affected my life and the lives of millions more—we love you in Christ's name!

History will say of Kathryn Kuhlman

Her living and her dying
Brought glory to God.

David Wilkerson ———— Author of

THE CROSS AND THE SWITCHBLADE

ONE

The Latecomer

TOM LEWIS

*Tom Lewis, a retired Army Colonel, is one of Holly-
wood's best-known film producers. His list of credits
in* Who's Who in America *covers as much space as did
the ribbons on his chest. He was the founding producer of the Screen Guild Theatre; the founder of the
American Forces Radio and Television Service, of
which he served as Commandant throughout World
War II; and the creator and executive producer of* The
Loretta Young Show. *A regent of Loyola University,
he holds numerous awards for excellence in television
productions, both at home and to the American
Forces throughout the world. A devout Roman Catholic, he is now numbered in that rapidly growing
group who call themselves Catholic Pentecostals.*

Last winter my son—a young film director—and a producer of his own age were contemplating a TV special on the
"Jesus People." I agreed to their request to write the presentation, but reluctantly. Since the Jesus Kids were also
young, I thought my son and his associate should staff the
whole project accordingly.

My preliminary research on the young people I was trying to learn about generated my interest and respect. Many
of them had come back from the hell of drug addiction by
way of a reborn faith in Jesus Christ. At this point I had
not probed into the religious motivation of the movement.
On the human side, however, I could not help but be as im-

pressed with the Jesus Kids' sincerity as I was startled and puzzled by their familiar manner of speaking about Jesus—as if He were right there with them.

I had always thought of myself as a reasonably religious man who enjoyed the sacramental life of the Roman Catholic Church. I didn't go around referring to Jesus Christ as if I met with Him frequently and personally. As a matter of fact, I seldom mentioned Jesus by name. I thought it better taste to shun a more personal approach and preferred the more reserved reference "My Lord" or "the Good Lord."

As a part of my task, I was asked to look into the ministry of one Kathryn Kuhlman, a person highly thought of by the Jesus People. Miss Kuhlman, it appeared, came to the Los Angeles Shrine Auditorium once a month for a Miracle Service. I asked for two seats, in the center row on the aisle near the front. It appeared, however, that this was not how tickets were obtained. One waited in line and took his chances. The capacity of the Shrine Auditorium is 7,500 people, and I was told sometimes twice that many tried to get in. I was amazed, and my amazement didn't wear off for four or five months, I fear, because it took me that long to drive down there and get in line.

The day I did so, I recall, was unseasonably warm for March, even for sunny California. I turned off the freeway at Hoover Street to gauge the traffic situation around the auditorium. Normally that downtown area would be all but deserted on Sunday. But as I approached the Shrine, every parking space on the street and in the huge lots appeared to be taken. Bus after bus drove up to the main entrance to discharge its passengers. Some buses were marked "Charter" and others bore the name of their point of origin. I remember one marked "Santa Barbara," another "Las Vegas." To my astonishment, one travel-soiled bus read "Portland, Oregon"—quite a little trip just to attend a Kathryn Kuhlman Miracle Service. I was wondering what Miss Kuhlman gave away in there. It couldn't be dishes, there were too many people. Nor could it be Bingo—how could one manage 7,500 Bingo cards?

A long line of wheelchair patients was moving along Jefferson Street toward a side entrance, to gain immediate admittance. So, too, did many men and women carrying hymn books—choir members apparently. There were also many Roman-collared men and somberly dressed women, and I wondered what the priests and nuns were doing here.

I found a gas station where I parked my car and then joined the thousands waiting at the main entrance of the Shrine. My watch showed eleven o'clock. The doors were to open at one. Normally I wouldn't wait that long for anything, including the Second Coming. But that proved to be a rash reflection.

More and more people piled in back of me, and I found myself near the center of a huge crowd. This gave me a slight feeling of claustrophobia, so I concentrated on taking mental notes from which I could construct my presentation: big crowd, orderly; quite a few young in the category of the Jesus Kids.

These young people tended to stick together, forming islands in a sea of bodies. They sang while waiting—not loudly, not necessarily for others, not even acting too aware of one another. They sang in a rather quiet, meditative way. I thought it unusual and peculiar. It reminded me of a group of Coptic Christians I had once seen in Rome, praying audibly yet not in unison, independent of each other yet together.

Now, the crowd had grown very large indeed and someone inside took pity on us. The doors were opened some twenty minutes before one o'clock. People in back of me surged forward and I was carried past the closed box office. This surprised me, because I had my hand in my wallet pocket ready to pay for a ticket.

A lady right behind me noticed it and laughed. "Money won't get you nowhere here," she said. "But if it burns a hole in your pocket, there'll be a free-will offering sometime later."

That was the tone of this great crowd: orderly, not festive like a crowd at a ballpark, rather quiet, not very communicative with each other although friendly if conversation was called for.

I found a seat quite far back and to the side on the first floor of the auditorium.

The bright, harshly lit stage was full of activity. Men and women carrying hymnals were finding their places in a bleacherlike arrangement that filled the stage. Two concert-grand pianos flanked the choir. There seemed to be hundreds in the choir, yet here too, as out front, there was no disorder, no confusion. Despite the constant movement due to late arrivals in the choir, singing went on as if in a silent cathedral. The conductor, a slight, aristocratic-looking white-maned man, led the rehearsal with precise, unquestioned authority.

A lovely-looking older lady sat on my right. For all the attention she paid me or the thousands around her, she could have been alone in the Lady Chapel of St. Patrick's Cathedral. She had an opened Bible on her lap, and now and then she read from it silently.

A Bible seemed standard equipment for many of those present. Two young men behind me carried them, but they weren't reading. They hummed or sang the words of the hymns being rehearsed on the stage. I didn't like that. I have never liked the audience-participation type in theaters, concert halls, or movie houses, especially when the audience participation is not specifically solicited. But I was to hear more from these young men.

Meanwhile the harsh lights on the stage were dimmed and softened, and color was added to them. The many pastel colors in the street dresses of the women in the choir made a pleasing contrast to the blue cycloramic curtain surrounding everything.

The rehearsal phase was over, and the choir was singing in earnest now. Most of the hymns were old and familiar and well-loved: *How Great Thou Art, Amazing Grace.* The singers were excellent—drawn, I learned later, from churches of every denomination throughout the Los Angeles basin.

Without pause, the choir went into *He Touched Me.* I

felt a taut air of expectancy take hold of the audience. A spotlight hovered over an area in the wings on the audience's right. The audience stood, and here and there people began to applaud. Miss Kuhlman, a slight and fragile figure in a lovely white dress, came on the stage, singing with the choir. She crossed to a beat-up-looking music rack right of stage center, picked up from it a necklace microphone which she fastened around her throat, and, without pausing, led the people in several rousing and one diminuendo chorus of *He Touched Me*. Then, without a word of explanation, she followed with *He's the Saviour of My Soul*. The audience and Kathryn Kuhlman seemed to agree that these hymns were special to her. Again, without explanation, she began to pray aloud. The audience stood, heads bowed, following her prayer silently.

I knew right then what had been different about the singing of those islands of young people outside the auditorium; what was special about the singing of the large chorus up there on the stage. They were singing, yes, but they were singing *plus*. They were not performing, they were worshiping. And the people in the audience here were reacting with a difference. They weren't an audience at all, they were a congregation. They sang as one with the choir when they were moved to do so. They prayed as one with Miss Kuhlman. This wasn't a show, it was a prayer meeting. I don't know how I felt about this at the time—impressed probably, and pleased with myself that I had made an interesting discovery.

I soon discovered something else, however, and it shocked me. Now and again the young men behind me would give vent to loud "Amens" and "Praise Gods," seemingly in response to a prayer or a statement. Many throughout the house were doing the same thing. Many were holding up their arms in a supplicating gesture that I related to the stance of those Biblical figures one sees in stained glass windows. No telling what this will lead to, I thought, and looked around automatically for the nearest exit.

One young man high up in the choir was particularly

disturbing to me. His arms were lifted high most of the time. This must be the Miracle of the Miracle Service, I thought. No circulatory system can withstand the strain of a posture like that for long. Those arms are going to fall right off.

But I forgot him; I forgot them all. Like the lady beside me, I might have been in a remote chapel, alone except for a Presence one does not normally find in such a huge auditorium.

Yes, that was it. There was a Presence here, and that was why this crowd of many thousands was at times so silent I could hear the sound of my own breathing. That was the reason for the order here, the consideration among so many people. That was why one lost track of time. There was something different here: there was love, specific and actual. Yes, and more than love, there was this *Presence*. I remembered the words of a Jesus Kid's song: "They will know we are Christians by our love, by our love. They will know we are Christians by our love."

The "healings" began—two in the row quite near me. I saw them before they were called by Miss Kuhlman. I saw the amazement of those healed, then unbelief, their realization and their happiness.

There were many, many healings on the stage now. People left wheelchairs. A crippled nun walked, who had not walked in years. I saw gratitude among those healed, thanksgiving so palpable one could almost reach out and touch it. Drug addicts were delivered, and by the evidence of transformed, incandescent faces, I saw interior rebirths and moral regenerations.

I lost track of what I saw, for at some point unknown to me, I ceased to see and began to feel. I *felt* to the depths of whatever consciousness I possess.

I became aware that I was carrying on a conversation, the most astonishing, nakedly honest conversation of my life. I was talking to God. Somewhere within myself I was telling God things I never knew before, or could not or would not admit.

Against the evidence of my flesh, against the visible and

apparent facts of my busy life, the love and companionship of my sons and their friends, my own many friends, my worldly interests, my hobbies—against that evidence I was telling God that I was restless and lonely. Deeply, desperately lonely—and not for people, and not for things. I had those in abundance. I told God I was very empty. Next, I was taken over by the strongest emotion I have ever known: hunger—raw, stark, primeval hunger.

I became aware that people were crowding the aisles now and filling the stage. Miss Kuhlman was inviting those who wanted Christ in their lives to step forward, acknowledge their sins, accept Jesus as their personal Saviour, and surrender themselves utterly and irrevocably to Him.

I followed them. I was among them. *I*, the nonaudience-participator, the self-made sophisticate. *I* was making *my* commitment, and with the most awesome realization of the scope and responsibility of it. I asked God to keep me from fear of it. He has.

That night, driving back alone to my little town of Ojai, I wept. All the way back, I wept. I felt neither happy nor sad. I felt—cleansed.

During the night I awoke with an instant and full realization of what had happened. I recommitted myself to Christ, noted that I neither doubted nor feared my commitment, and fell soundly and dreamlessly asleep.

Late next morning I walked into the little town of Ojai from my home in the country. I felt very well, rested, and at peace, the emotions of yesterday far behind me. I passed my parish church, a small Spanish colonial chapel on the main street. This was the season of Lent. The time was somewhere around 11:30, and I knew there must be a Mass going on inside.

There was. I was in time for the Eucharistic Celebration that we commonly refer to as Holy Communion. I went to the altar automatically, and because there were only six or eight persons present, we received the Holy Eucharist in both species, bread and wine. Instead of returning to the rear of the chapel, I knelt, for convenience, at the first pew.

It was well I did. What I had taken into my body was

not bread and wine, not a symbol, not a memento. It was the Body and Blood of Christ, and the result in me was a most profound knowledge of the Real Presence of Christ. It was an experience of great and unspeakable joy, and my body shook violently with my effort to contain it.

Jesus, the Christ, was there with me, and every cell of my body was witnessing to His reality. I rested my head on my arms and time was suspended for me for a while.

God lives. God truly lives, and He moves among us, and He breathes out his Holy Spirit upon us. And through the merit of the Blood shed for us by His Divine Son, He is preparing us for whatever lies ahead in this troubled world —and beyond.

Praise God!

TWO

No Shortage in God's Storehouse

CAPTAIN JOHN LEVRIER

*I remember well the first time I came face to face with
Captain LeVrier. Every inch a policeman, and every
inch a Baptist deacon, he had reached the end of his
rope. In desperation he had flown from Houston to
Los Angeles. He was dying. But let him tell his story.*

I have been a policeman since I was twenty-one years old.
Back in 1936 I started with the Houston Police Depart-
ment and worked my way up to the rank of Captain of the
Accident Division. In all those years I had never been sick.
But in December, 1968, when I went in for a physical ex-
amination, things changed.

I had known Dr. Bill Robbins ever since he was an in-
tern and I a rookie cop. He used to ride with me in my
prowl car when I first started on the force. Following what
I thought was a routine physical examination in his office in
the Saint Joseph's Professional Building, Dr. Robbins
pulled off his rubber gloves and sat on the end of the table.
He shook his head. "I don't like what I find, John," he said.
"I want you to see a specialist."

I glanced at him as I tucked my shirt in my pants and
buckled my gun belt around my waist. "A specialist? What
for? My back hurts some, but what cop's back——"

He wasn't listening. "I'm going to send you right on up
to see Dr. McDonald, a urologist in this building."

I knew better than to argue. Two hours later, following
an even more thorough examination, I was listening to an-

other physician, Dr. Newton McDonald. He minced no words. "How soon can you go into the hospital, Captain?"

"Hospital?" I detected a tinge of fear in my voice.

"I don't like what I find," he said deliberately. "Your prostate gland should be about the size of a hickory nut, but it's the size of a lemon. The only way I can tell what is wrong is to run a biopsy. We can't wait. You ought to be in the hospital no later than tomorrow morning."

I went straight home. After supper, Sara Ann put the three children to bed. John was only five, Andrew seven, Elizabeth nine. Then I broke the news.

She listened quietly. We'd had a happy life together. "Don't put it off, John," she said evenly. "We have too much to live for."

I looked at her, leaning up against the edge of the kitchen counter. She was so young, so pretty. I thought of our three beautiful children. She was right, I *did* have a lot to live for. That night I called my daughter Loraine, who is married to a Baptist minister in Springfield, Missouri. She promised to have her church begin praying for me.

Three evenings later, after extensive examinations (including the biopsy), I sat propped up in my bed at the hospital, eating dinner. The door to my room opened. It was Dr. McDonald and one of the doctors on the hospital staff. They closed the door and then pulled up chairs beside my bed. I knew busy doctors didn't have time to chat socially, and I felt my pulse begin to throb in my throat.

Dr. McDonald didn't leave me guessing long. "Captain, I'm afraid we have some distressing news." He paused. It was hard for him to get the words out. I waited, trying to keep my eyes focused on his lips. "You have cancer."

I saw his lips move and form the word, but my ears refused to register the sound. Over and over I could see the word on his lips. Cancer, just like that. One day I'm as strong as an ox, a veteran of thirty-three years on the police force. The next day I have cancer.

It seemed like an eternity before I could respond. "Well, which way do we go? I guess you'll have to take it out."

"It's not that simple," Dr. McDonald said, clearing his

throat. "It's malignant and too far advanced for us to handle it here. We're referring you to the doctors at the M. D. Anderson Tumor Institute. They're known all over the world for their research in cancer treatment. If anyone can help you, they can. But it doesn't look good, Captain, and we would be lying if we held out any hope for the future."

Both doctors were sympathetic. I could tell they were moved, but they knew I was a veteran police officer and would demand the facts. They gave them to me as frankly, yet as gently, as they could. Then they left.

I sat looking at the cold food on my tray. Everything seemed lifeless—the coffee, the half-eaten Swiss steak, the applesauce. I pushed it away and swung my legs over the side of the bed. Cancer. No hope.

Walking to the window, I stood looking out over the city of Houston, a city that I knew better than the back of my hand. It was cancerous, too, filled with crime and disease like any big city. For a third of a century I had been working, trying to stop the spread of that cancer, but it was an endless task. The sun was just setting, and its dying rays reflected against the church steeples rising above the rooftops. I'd never noticed before, but Houston seemed to be filled with churches.

I was a member of one of them, the First Baptist Church. In fact. I was an active deacon in the church, although my personal faith didn't amount to much. Some of my friends at the department used to kid me and say I was the same kind of Baptist that Harry Truman said he was, the bourbon-drinking, poker-playing, cussing type. Even though I had heard my pastor preach some mighty sermons on salvation, I'd never had any victory in my personal life. I was a deacon by virtue of my position in the community rather than because of my spirituality. Now here I was, face to face with death, groping for something to stand on. But as I put my feet down into the water, there was no bottom. I felt like I was sinking.

I looked down from the ninth floor. It would be easy just to go out the window. I'd seen men die of cancer, their bodies eaten out by the disease. How much easier it would be to simply end it now. But something Sara had said stuck with me: "We have too much to live for. . . ."

I walked back to the bed and sat on the edge, staring into the gray-black dusk that seemed to be closing in on me. How would I tell her, and the kids, that I was going to die?

The next day the doctors from the M. D. Anderson Institute came in. There were more tests. Dr. Delclose, the doctor in charge of my case, really got honest with me. "All I can tell you is you had better be prepared to see an awful lot of doctors," he said.

"How long do I have?" I asked.

"I can't give you any hope," he said frankly. "Maybe a year, maybe a year and a half. The cancer is very extensive in your entire lower abdomen. The only way we can treat it is with massive doses of radiation, which means we'll have to kill a lot of healthy tissue at the same time. However, if we are to prolong your life at all, we must get started."

I signed a release, and they started cobalt treatment the same day.

I believed in prayer. We used to pray for the sick every Wednesday night at the First Baptist Church. But we prefaced our prayer for healing with the words, "If it's Your will, heal. . . ." That's the way I had been taught. I knew nothing of praying with authority—the kind of authority that Jesus and the apostles had. I certainly believed that God was able to heal people, but I just assumed that He wasn't in the miracle-performing business today.

Thus, when I went into radiation, my body shaved and marked off with a blue pencil like a side of beef ready for the butcher's cleaver, the only prayer I knew to say was, "Lord, let this machine do what it was designed to do."

Now that's not a bad prayer, for the machine was designed to kill cancer cells. Of course, the doctors were trying to keep the radiation from affecting the rest of my organs, so I was marked off to the millimeter. The cancer was in the prostate area and had to be treated from all angles, so the huge cobalt machine circled the table, the radiation penetrating my body from every side.

The daily treatments lasted for six weeks. I was released

from the hospital and allowed to go back to work, coming in each morning to receive the cobalt.

Four months had passed since my illness had been diagnosed. Easter was approaching, and Sara mentioned that it looked like it would be happier than Christmas. Maybe the cobalt had done its job. Or even better, maybe the doctors had made a mistake. Then, just 120 days after the first diagnosis, the pain hit.

It was a Friday noon. I had promised to meet Sara at the little restaurant where we often met for lunch. She had already arrived. I grinned, laid my policeman's cap on the windowsill and slipped into the booth beside her. As I sat down, I felt like I had been stabbed with a white-hot dagger. The pain surged through my right hip in excruciating spasms. I was unable to speak and just looked at Sara in mute agony. She grabbed my arm.

"John," she gasped, "what is it?"

The pain slowly subsided, leaving me so weak I could hardly talk. I tried to tell her; then, like the tide moving in over the salt flats, the pain returned. It was like fire in my bones. My face beaded with perspiration, and I pulled at my collar to loosen my tie. The waitress who had come to take our order sensed something was wrong. "Captain LeVrier," she said with concern, "are you all right?"

"I'll make it," I finally said. "I've just had a sudden pain."

We decided not to eat. Instead, we went straight to the hospital, and Dr. Delclose immediately set up more X rays. As they were preparing me, I put my hand on my right hip and could feel the indentation. It was about the size of a silver dollar and felt like a hole under the skin. The X rays showed it up for what it was: The cancer had eaten a hole all the way through my hip. Only the outer skin was covering the cavity.

"I'm sorry, Captain," the doctor said with resignation. "The cancer is spreading as expected."

Then in measured tones he concluded, "We'll start the cobalt again and do everything we can to make your time as painless as possible."

The daily trips to the hospital began all over again. Sara tried to be calm. She had worked in the police department before our marriage and had been exposed to death many times. But this was different. I didn't know it at the time, but the doctors had told her that I probably had no more than six months to live.

I kept on working, although I was growing weaker and weaker. It was hard to determine whether it was the cancer or the cobalt. One afternoon Sara picked me up from work and said, "John, I've been thinking. I've been out of circulation a long time. What would you say if I went back to work?"

"You've *got* a job," I kidded her, "just taking care of those three children. I'll earn the bread around this house. I've still got a lot of mileage left in me."

"Still the tough cop, aren't you?" she said. "Well, I'm tough, too. I'm going to enroll in business college."

It began to dawn on me what she was doing—getting things in order. It was time for me to do the same thing. But before I could, a new development took place. Surgery.

"It's the only way to keep you alive," the woman surgeon said. "This type of cancer feeds on hormones. We are going to have to redirect the hormone trend in your body through surgery. If we don't do this, you are really going out fast."

I agreed to the surgery, but within another 120 days the cancer reappeared on the surface, this time in my spine.

I first noticed it on a Saturday afternoon in June. Sara had taken the children to a vacation Bible school picnic, and I was at home, trying to set out a little potted plant in the flower bed. By now I was so weak I could hardly bend over, but I thought the exercise would help. I had dug a small hole in the ground, and when I bent over to pick up the potted plant, a pain like a million volts of lightning surged through my lower back. I fell forward into the dirt.

I never dreamed such pain could exist. No one was around to help me, so I dragged myself—partially on my hands and knees, partially on my stomach—up the steps and into the house. Then, for the first time, I let myself go.

Lying on the floor in that empty house, I wept and moaned uncontrollably. I had been holding back because of Sara and the children, but this afternoon, with the house empty, I lay there crying and moaning until the pain finally subsided.

There followed another series of cobalt treatments with more hopeless looks from the doctors. I had received the death sentence.

Cancer takes you apart from the inside, and I wasn't the only one in my family who had been hit. My two sisters' husbands, who also lived in Houston, had died of it. Both of these men were in their early fifties, my own age bracket. I was next, it seemed. It was time to finish getting my things in order.

I had always wanted a big old car. I splurged and bought a three-year-old Cadillac. As the summer ended, we packed the family into the car and set out on what I thought was to be my last vacation. I wanted to make it a good one for the children. Years before I had traveled through the Pacific Northwest, and I wanted Sara and the children to see that part of the world which had meant so much to me: the Columbia River Drive, Mount Hood, the coast of Oregon, Lake Louise, Yellowstone, and the Rocky Mountains. The children didn't know, but Sara and I both believed it would be our last summer together as a family.

I returned to Houston and tried to patch up loose ends. But when life is frayed beyond splicing, it's impossible to pick up the strings. All you can do is let them dangle and wait for the end.

One Saturday morning in the early fall I walked into the den and turned on the TV. Our pastor at the First Baptist Church, John Bisango, had a program called *Higher Ground*. John had come to Houston from Oklahoma, where his church had been recognized as the most evangelistic church in the Southern Baptist Convention. What had happened in Oklahoma was beginning to happen in Houston, as this dynamic young pastor began to turn that huge church right side up. I was thrilled with his ministry.

Too weak to get up, I sat slumped in the chair as the

program ended and another one began. "I believe in miracles," a woman's voice said. I glanced up. I wasn't impressed—very few Baptists are impressed with a woman preacher. But as the program continued and this woman, Kathryn Kuhlman, talked of wonderful healing miracles, something inside me clicked. Can this be for real? I wondered.

The show closed, and the credits were flashed on the screen. Suddenly I saw a familiar name. Dick Ross, producer.

I knew Dick, had known him since 1952 when he was in Houston working with Billy Graham producing *Oiltown, USA*. In fact, I had played a bit role in that movie and as a result had become a good friend of Billy Graham and his team, remaining in charge of his security detail whenever he came to Houston. Now, here was Dick Ross's name associated with this woman preacher who talked about healing miracles.

I had kept in contact with Dick through the years. Whenever I went to California on police work, I always looked him up. I had visited in his home, even sat in on his Sunday school class at the Presbyterian church. I picked up the phone and called him.

"Dick, I've just watched the Kathryn Kuhlman show. Are those healings real?"

"Yes, John, they're real," Dick answered. "But you'd have to attend one of these meetings at the Shrine Auditorium to believe it for yourself. Why do you ask?"

I hesitated, then spoke it out. "Dick, I have cancer. I've already had it break out in three areas of my body, and I'm afraid the next time it will kill me. I know I sound like I'm grasping at straws, but that's what a dying man does."

"I'm going to have Miss Kuhlman call you personally," Dick said.

"Oh, no," I objected. "I know she's far too busy to deal with a policeman in Houston. Just tell me where I can get her books."

"I'll send you the books," Dick said. "But I'm also going to ask her to call you, as a personal favor to me."

In less than a week, she did call, at my home. "I feel like I know you already," she said, her voice sounding just like it did on TV. "We're putting your name on our prayer list, but don't put off coming to one of the meetings."

Although Sara and I both read her books and became avid watchers of the TV program, I did put off attending a meeting. "Where have we been all our lives?" Sara asked. "She's world famous, but I've never even heard of her before."

Like so many other Baptists, we simply didn't realize there was anything going on in the Kingdom of God outside the Southern Baptist Convention. Now our eyes were being opened, not only to other ministries but to the gifts of the Spirit and the power of God to heal. It was all so new, so different. Yet I realized that it was Biblical. Despite my ignorance of the supernatural gifts of God, I had been trained to accept the Bible as God's Word. As we began to see all these references to the power of the Holy Spirit, references we'd never been exposed to before, our hearts grew hungry—not only for healing, but to receive the filling of the Holy Spirit.

In February I knew my time was running out. Sara and the children knew it, too. "Daddy," Elizabeth said, "you go to California, and we'll stay home and pray. We believe God will heal you."

I looked at Sara Ann. Her eyes moist, she nodded and said, "I believe He's going to heal you."

On Friday, February 19, I flew from Houston to Los Angeles. Old friends in Los Angeles loaned me their car, and I found a motel in Santa Monica. As a policeman and a Baptist, I wanted to size up Miss Kuhlman before I attended the meeting on Sunday.

I learned she usually flew in from Pittsburgh the day before the service at the Shrine. I also checked around, using my know-how as a policeman, and found out where she stayed. Soon I had all the information I needed.

Early the next morning I was at her hotel. Being a policeman, I found it easy to get acquainted with the security officers and pump them for information. Before long, they told me what time Miss Kuhlman usually arrived.

I took a seat in the lobby and waited. An hour later the door opened and she walked in, looking exactly as I had pictured her. I knew I was brazen, but I intercepted her on the way to the elevator. "Miss Kuhlman," I said, "I'm that police captain from Texas."

She broke into a wide grin and exclaimed, "Oh yes! You've come to be healed."

We chatted for a few moments, and I said, "Miss Kuhlman, I'm a born-again believer in Jesus Christ. I know I don't have to be healed to be a believer, because I'm already a believer. But you speak of something in your books that I want as much as I want physical healing."

"What is that?" she said, her eyes searching my face.

"I want to be filled with the Holy Spirit."

"Oh," she smiled softly, "I promise you that you can have that."

"Well, I'm mighty sick, but I'm still strong enough to get to the auditorium and get in line. I've read your books and know the plan for the services. I'll be over bright and early in the morning to get a good seat." I started to excuse myself and turned away.

"Wait!" she said. "I've got a feeling about this, and I have to be obedient to the Holy Spirit. You meet us here in the morning and we'll drive over together. You can follow us in your car."

I hesitated. "Miss Kuhlman, I've been a policeman so long, and I've cut so many corners to get into places, this time I don't want to do anything that might hinder my healing. I'll just go and stand in line with the others."

Miss Kuhlman's voice bristled, and her eyes began to glitter. "Now let me tell you something," she said with deliberation. "God is not going to heal you because you're good. He's not going to heal you because you're a police captain. He's certainly not going to heal you because of the way you get into that meeting."

She had to say no more. The next morning I followed her from her hotel to the Shrine Auditorium. We arrived at

9:35 A.M. Although the meeting wouldn't start until one, the sidewalks in front of the huge auditorium were already packed with several thousand waiting people.

We went in through the stage entrance, and Miss Kuhlman said, "Now, you just feel free to roam about this place until you see me meet with the ushers. When I meet with them, I want you with me."

I agreed and wandered off through the vast auditorium. Hundreds of ushers, who had driven for many miles to volunteer their time, were busy setting up chairs for the five-hundred-voice choir, roping off the section for the wheelchairs, seating those who had come on chartered buses, and preparing the room for what was about to take place. Even as I walked through the auditorium, I could almost taste the expectancy. It was like electricity. Everybody was whispering in hushed tones, as if the Holy Spirit was already present. How unlike my experiences in church services! I was feeling it, too, and suddenly I was no longer a policeman, no longer a Southern Baptist deacon. I was just a man filled with cancer, needing a miracle to live. If one was ever going to happen to me, I knew this was the place.

One of the men introduced himself as Walter Bennett. I recognized his name immediately. I had read his testimony in *God Can Do It Again*. His wife Naurine had been healed of a horrible disease. He took me around to the stage door where she was standing guard. Just seeing her in such radiant health, and knowing that she had been dying, gave me new hope and faith. I felt like I wanted to cry.

"John," Walter said, "we have something in common. You are a Baptist deacon, and I was a Baptist deacon, too. Let's go have a cup of coffee."

We slipped out the side door and found a nearby café. "After you're healed," Walter said, "there's a chance that your fellow Baptists might not want to have anything to do with you." He grinned knowingly. He spoke with such faith, as if he knew I was going to be healed.

"I don't care what anyone thinks about me if I'm healed," I said. "Just as long as God touches my body."

Walter smiled. I felt such love for this new friend. "Well,

one thing we can be sure of," he said softly. "God hasn't brought you all this way for nothing. You're going to return to Houston a new man." Having this fellow Baptist deacon speak with such faith filled me with excitement. I could hardly wait until the meeting started.

Back in the auditorium, Miss Kuhlman was meeting with the ushers for last-minute instructions before the doors opened. I joined them on stage.

"We have with us today a man who is a captain with the police force in Houston," she said. "He has cancer throughout his body, and I'm going to pray for him at this time. I want each of you men to bow in prayer as I petition the Lord in his behalf."

I realized this was something special. I knew that Miss Kuhlman's ministry was simply reporting what God was doing as the great miracle services got under way—and that she had no particular gifts of healing herself. She motioned for me to come forward and stretched out her hands toward me.

Even though this was the moment I had waited for, I hesitated. From reading her books, I remembered that often when she prayed for people, they fell down on the floor. I had thought that falling was all right for a few Pentecostals, but it wasn't for a Baptist, and it certainly wasn't for a police captain. But I had no choice. I stepped forward and let her pray for me.

Bracing my feet in my best judo stance, I waited as she touched me and prayed for my healing. Nothing happened, but as I started to relax, I heard her say, "And fill him, Blessed Jesus, with Thy Holy Spirit."

I felt myself reel, and thought, "This can't be!" I reaffirmed my footing, one foot behind the other, and I heard it the second time: "And fill him with Thy Holy Spirit."

It felt like someone had his hands on my shoulders and was pushing me to the floor. I couldn't resist, and crumpled to the stage. I struggled to regain my feet just in time to hear her say it the third time: "Fill him with Thy Holy Spirit." And I was down again.

This time I remained down for several minutes, like I

was soaking in a bathtub full of love. Someone helped me to my feet, and I heard her say, "Now find yourself a seat. We are going to open this place, and in just a few minutes every seat will be taken."

I should have listened, for moments later the doors were thrown open and the people came pouring down the aisles like lava down the sides of a volcano. I fought my way up the aisle, pausing to look at a whole section filled with people in wheelchairs. I couldn't get my eyes off their faces. Some of them were so young yet so twisted. I wanted to cry again. "Oh, Lord, am I selfish to want a healing when there are so many people here, some of them so young?"

As I stood looking, I heard, for the first time in all my life, God's inner voice saying, "There's no shortage in My storehouse."

With new strength I made my way to the back and slowly, painfully, climbed the stairs to a seat in the first row of the balcony.

There was still time before the meeting started. The huge choir had taken its place on the platform and was doing some last-minute rehearsing. I spent my time sizing up the various people sitting around me, and I introduced myself to the man beside me. "I'm Dr. Townsend," he said.

"Are you a medical doctor?" I asked, astonished that medical doctors would attend a healing service.

"Yes, I am," he said, pulling out one of his business cards. "I come because I get a great blessing. I just like to see the mighty working power of God." Then he introduced me to his family. "I've brought my dad here from out of state," he said. "This is his first meeting."

Sitting across the aisle was one of my favorite TV actors. "Well, how about that," I mused silently. "Doctors and movie stars way up here in the balcony! They haven't come to be recognized, just to be a part of the meeting." I was impressed.

The service started. A beautiful girl, a fashion model whose face I had often seen on the cover of Sara's women's magazines, shared a brief testimony of what Jesus Christ meant in her life.

I had been in many evangelistic meetings, but this one was unusual. Maybe it was the sense of expectancy, maybe the sense of awe. Whatever it was, this was different from any other meeting I had ever attended.

Miss Kuhlman was speaking from the platform. "You know, I have been asked to set this Sunday aside for young people, but people come from such great distances, and I just don't have the heart to say, 'Young people only.' However, since there are so many young people here today, I must speak to them."

Her message was brief and geared to youth. She talked about the love of God and then gave one of the most challenging invitations I'd ever heard. Now if there's anything that impresses a Baptist, it's numbers and movement. And when I saw almost a thousand young people leaving their seats to go forward and make decisions for Jesus Christ, I was impressed. Unlike most revival meetings I had attended, this meeting had no fanfare, no tear-jerking stories. Just a simple invitation from this tall woman who said, "Do you want to be born again?" The kids responded, many of them literally running down the aisles to accept that challenge.

She seemed to forget the time as she dealt with them on the stage, praying for many of them individually. Finally they filtered back to their seats, but the congregation was sensing something else about to happen.

"Father," she was whispering, so low I could hardly hear it, "I believe in miracles. I believe that You're in the healing business today like You were when Jesus Christ was here. You know the needs of the people here, all over this huge auditorium. I pray that You will touch them. In the name of Jesus, I ask it. Amen."

Then there was silence. I could feel my heart pounding in my chest. I became aware of each cell in my body and could almost feel the spiritual warfare taking place as the forces of the Holy Spirit did battle against the forces of evil over my body. "Oh, God," I prayed, worshiping. "Oh, God."

Suddenly Miss Kuhlman was speaking again, her voice coming rapidly as she received knowledge of what was happening in the auditorium. "There is a man in the upper balcony, on my extreme right, who has just been healed of cancer. Stand up, sir, in the name of Jesus Christ, and claim this healing."

I looked up. She was pointing to the opposite side of the balcony. It was phenomenal. I could only stare in amazement, as I felt the excitement building inside of me. This was real. I knew it was.

"Do not come to the platform unless you know God has healed you," she emphasized.

I glanced around and saw the personal workers moving up and down the aisles. They were interviewing people who thought they had been healed, making sure only those who were genuinely healed came forward to testify.

The healings she was reporting seemed to be mostly in the balcony. They moved across from the right to the left:

"Two people are being healed of eye problems.

"A woman is being healed right now of arthritis. Stand up and claim your healing.

"You are seated right in the middle of the balcony," Miss Kuhlman said. "You came today to receive your hearing. God has restored it. Take your hearing aid off. You can hear perfectly."

I looked. A woman in her forties was rising to her feet, pulling hearing aids out of both ears. One of the personal workers was standing behind her, whispering. I thought the woman was going to shout as she raised her hands above her head, praising God. She could hear. The doctor sitting next to me was weeping and saying, "Thank You, Jesus."

The healings were coming in my direction across the balcony. "Lord, don't let them run out," I prayed. Then I remembered what He had whispered to me on the floor below: "There is no shortage in God's storehouse."

Suddenly Miss Kuhlman was pointing at the left balcony, right where I was sitting. "You have come a long way for your healing from cancer," she said. "God has healed you. Stand up in the name of Jesus Christ and claim it."

It was so far from the stage to the balcony! She could

have had no idea I was up there. But her long, slender finger was pointing in my direction.

"Oh Lord," I said, "of course I want to be healed. But how do I know this is for me?"

Instantly that same inner voice, the one I had heard downstairs when I was looking at the people in the wheelchairs, said, "Stand up!"

I stood. Without feeling of any kind, I simply stood in obedience and faith.

Then I felt it. It was like being baptized in liquid energy. I had never felt such strength flowing through my body. I felt like I could have taken the Houston phone directory and ripped it to shreds.

A woman approached me. "Have you been healed of something?"

"I have," I declared, wanting to leap and run all at the same time.

"How do you know?" she asked.

"I've never felt so gloriously well. I hardly had enough strength to get to this seat, and now I feel so good!" All the time I was stretching and bending, doing things I hadn't been able to do in more than a year. "I feel like I could run a mile."

"Then run right on down to the stage and testify," she said.

I started. But on the way I began to wonder. What if there's someone here from Houston? I'm going to bound up there on the stage, and Miss Kuhlman's going to put her hands on me, and I'm going to hit the floor. What will they think?

Then I realized that I didn't care. Moments later I was standing beside Miss Kuhlman on the stage. She just walked over to me and said simply, "We thank You, Blessed Father, for healing this body. Fill him with the Holy Ghost."

Bam! I was on the floor again. But this time, because of the new healing energy surging through my body, I bounced right back to my feet. The next time she didn't even touch me. She just prayed in my direction, and I heard her say, "Oh, the power . . ." And I was on the floor again.

I stayed there this time, luxuriating once more in that tub of liquid love. But even there, Satan attacked me. He came on like a roaring lion. "What makes you think you've been healed?"

Miss Kuhlman had already turned her attention to someone else. I rolled over and came up to my knees, my head in my hands, praying, "Oh, Father, give me the faith to accept what I sincerely believe You've given me."

Across the years I had taken numerous Baptist study courses. My mind had been thoroughly exposed to the Word of God, and in that moment a verse came to me: Prove me now herewith, saith the Lord of hosts.

I thought of all those twisted bodies I had seen. "Father, let me see a visible sign so my faith will be made strong."

I opened my eyes, and coming to the platform was a little girl about nine years old. I had never seen anyone so happy. She was running and skipping, barefooted. She danced all the way across the stage, right by Miss Kuhlman, who reached out to catch her but missed. She turned and started back. Again Miss Kuhlman reached for her, but she danced out of reach. By that time the child's mother was on the platform. She was holding a pair of shoes with heavy steel braces.

Unable to catch the dancing, skipping child, Miss Kuhlman turned to the mother. "What do we have here?"

"This is my little girl," the mother was sobbing. "She had infantile paralysis when she was a baby and has never walked without these braces. But look at her go now!"

The huge congregation broke into a mighty roar of applause.

"How do you know God has healed her?" Miss Kuhlman asked.

"Oh, I felt the healing power of God going through her body," the mother almost shouted. "I took the braces off, and she began to run."

Right behind her was another mother, holding a two-year-old child. "What's this?" Miss Kuhlman asked.

"God has just made my baby's foot whole." The mother's voice was shaking so hard she was difficult to understand.

Miss Kuhlman reached out and took the baby's foot in her hands. "Was this the foot?"

"Yes, yes, it was," the mother blurted out.

"But I see no difference between this foot and the other."

"But look at this," the mother said, holding a built-up shoe. "This child was born with a clubfoot. There have been many operations. Had you been massaging her foot the way you are rubbing it now, she would have screamed in pain."

"On the platform with me are a number of doctors," Miss Kuhlman said. "They know me. Is there a doctor in the audience who doesn't know me and doesn't know these children? Would you come up and examine them?"

A man stood up.

"Are you a practicing physician, sir?" she asked.

"I am," he said.

"Where do you practice?"

"St. Luke's Hospital here in Los Angeles."

"Would you please come up and examine these children?"

The doctor came to the platform. "The first thing I say is that this little girl, running and jumping on these toothpick legs, is a miracle. Without a miracle she couldn't even stand on them, much less jump with joy." Then he took the infant's feet and held them together. "Miss Kuhlman," he said seriously, "I can see no difference between this child's two feet. I think this mother can throw away the therapeutic shoe."

I needed no more proof. I staggered backstage, found a telephone, and called Sara in Houston. The line was busy. I asked the operator to break in.

"I can't do that unless it is a matter of life and death," she said.

"That's exactly what it is, operator. And you can listen in if you want to."

Suddenly Sara was on the phone. I tried to talk, but all I

could do was sob. I've never cried harder in all my life than I did while I was holding the phone and standing backstage at the Shrine Auditorium. Sara kept saying, "John, John, have you been healed?"

I finally got the message through. I was healed. Then she began to cry. I hoped the operator was listening. The call was about life, not death.

I made my way back to the edge of the stage and watched. Five Catholic priests, one of them a Monsignor, were sitting in the front row on the stage. The Monsignor was on the edge of his chair, taking it all in. As Miss Kuhlman passed him, she saw how intent he was. "Wouldn't you like this?" she asked.

He knew exactly what she was talking about, because he stood to his feet, his robes flowing, and said, "Yes."

She put her hands on him and said, "Fill him with the Holy Ghost." Down he went. She turned to the other priests and said, "Come on." Each of them had the same falling experience.

Hippies being saved. Twisted limbs straightened. My own cancer healed. Catholic priests being filled with the Holy Ghost. I left in a daze and drove back to the motel. It was more than I could comprehend.

In the motel I did all kinds of exercises—sit-ups, push-ups, things I hadn't been able to do in more than a year. And I did them with ease. Even without a medical examination, I knew I was healed. All that night I kept waking up, not to take pain pills (for I had stopped all medication that morning before going to the service) but so I could say it out loud in the darkness: "Thank You, Jesus. Praise the Lord!"

Then came the reunion with Sara and the children. They were waiting at the Houston airport when I arrived. I rushed to them, hugging Sara so tightly I literally picked her off the floor. She gasped at my strength. Then I grabbed the boys, first Andrew, then John, picking them up and holding them over my head. I hugged Elizabeth. We were all talking at once.

"Your face, John," Sara kept saying. "It's full of color and life."

"I knew you would be healed," Elizabeth was saying. "I prayed for you every day at nine, twelve, and six."

"Us, too, Daddy," little John piped up. "Us little guys been praying, too. We knew God would heal you."

It was too much, and this veteran police captain stood in the middle of the Houston airport and cried.

Shortly afterward, I returned to the M. D. Anderson Institute for a physical examination. I had an appointment with two doctors there on the same day.

The first doctor to see me was the one who had recommended the surgery. I carried her a copy of Miss Kuhlman's book, *I Believe in Miracles*. She glanced at the book, listened as I told her my story, and then looked at me like I was crazy.

"Let me tell you something," she said. "The only miracle that has happened to you is a medical miracle. That's all. The only thing that's keeping you alive is your medication. Quit taking it, and see how long you'll live."

I smiled. "Well, I haven't had any medication since the twentieth of February, more than a month ago."

She was shocked and angry. "You've done a very foolish thing, Mr. LeVrier," she snapped. "It won't be long before that cancer breaks out someplace else, and you'll be gone."

Such a strange attitude, I thought, for a scientist!

I left and went to the office of Dr. Lowell Miller, chief of the Department of Radiation Therapy at Hermann Hospital. I hoped his reaction would be more positive, but after the last encounter, I was determined not to tell him a thing about the miracle. He could just find out for himself.

His nurse asked me to go in the dressing room and prepare for a physical examination. That's when I noticed a strange thing. Like many long-time policemen, I had developed a bad case of varicose veins in my legs. In fact, I wouldn't wear Bermuda shorts in public because I was self-conscious about the knots on my legs. Of course, you don't worry about varicose veins when you're dying of cancer, but in the bright light of the examination room, I looked at my legs for the first time since returning from Los Angeles. Not only had the Lord healed me of cancer, He had healed the varicose veins also. My legs were as smooth as a young teenager's. By the time Dr. Miller came into the room, I was bubbling over with praise.

Unaccustomed to seeing his cancer patients in such a joyful spirit, Dr. Miller stepped back. "My! What in the world has happened to you?"

That was all I needed to launch into the whole story of how Jesus Christ had healed my cancer.

"Now, look," Dr. Miller said. "I'm a Christian, too, but God has given us enough sense to look after ourselves."

"You'll get no argument from me on that," I said gleefully. "That's the reason I'm here to be examined. I'll submit to any exam you want. But I'm telling you, you won't find anything wrong."

"Okay," the doctor said, "let's go." And what followed was the most thorough physical examination I had ever had.

When he finished he said, "You know, I wish my prostate felt as good as yours." Then he went down my spine, beating on me, vertebra by vertebra. "Remarkable," he kept repeating. "Remarkable."

He sent me to X ray, and then said, "I'll call you in a day or so after I've compared these pictures with your old ones. But from all indications, you've been healed."

Three days later the phone on my desk in the second-floor office in the Houston Police Department rang. It was Dr. Miller. "Captain," he said, "I have good news. I can find absolutely no trace of cancer. Now, I want to ask you one other question. Do you ever give talks?"

"You mean about my police work?" I said.

"No," he said, "not about police work. I want you to come out to my church and tell the people what God has done for you."

That opened the door. Ever since, I've been traveling all over the nation, telling hopeless people about the God who has no shortage in His storehouse of miracles.

THREE

Walking in the Shadows

ISABEL LARIOS

Christmas is such a joyous time of year. I receive thousands of cards from priceless friends all over the world. I read each one. My most precious cards, however, come from the children. Children are so open, so honest. When a child tells me, "I love you," I never doubt it.

That is why, when I received a simple little card from a sweet Mexican-American girl in California, I knew she meant what she said. She wrote to thank me for making another Christmas possible. Lisa thanked me, because she could see me. But I know what she meant. And God knows. It wasn't Kathryn Kuhlman, it was Jesus. Lisa Larios was dying of bone cancer before Jesus healed her at the Shrine Auditorium.

Lisa's mother and stepfather, Isabel and Javier Larios, live on the second floor of a modest apartment complex in Panorama City, California. Isabel was born in Los Angeles but grew up in Guadalajara, Mexico. Javier, who spends much of his time at an artist's easel in his apartment, is a respected waiter in the Casa Vega in Sherman Oaks, one of the area's finest restaurants. Besides Lisa, they have two other children, Albert and Gina.

"It's just growing pains, Lisa," I said, as our twelve-year-old daughter complained of pains in her right hip. I was sitting on the side of the bed in the semidarkness, rubbing her back and hip with liniment. Lisa was growing fast. Already she had the body of a fifteen-year-old and seemed to be the picture of health.

Yet here in the gathering gloom of evening, rubbing her smooth skin, I sensed this particular pain was something more than the normal muscle aches experienced by growing girls. Lisa sensed it, too. There was fear entering the room along with the darkness.

"Mamma, turn on the light when you leave," Lisa whimpered. "I don't want to stay here alone in the dark."

Javier had gone to work at the restaurant. The other two children were already asleep. I patted Lisa's back and pulled her pajama-top down. "There's nothing to be afraid of," I said.

"I don't like the shadows," she replied, her head buried in her pillow. "They scare me."

I switched on the light in the hall and left her door open. Then, for a moment, I stood outside her door looking in. Where had this fear come from all of a sudden? Lisa never used to be afraid. Now I could sense fear hanging all around the room, like a net fastened to the ceiling and draped over the bed. Did Lisa suspect something that I couldn't feel?

The next day was one of those rare, beautiful days in the Los Angeles basin. It was the last of March, and a heavy rain just before dawn had washed the air, leaving it clear and clean. The sun was shining brightly, the sky was brilliant blue, and we could see the snowcapped mountains clearly along the eastern horizon. Javier had risen to eat breakfast with the children before they left for school. Then the two of us drove over to Van Nuys to go shopping. I was looking for a sweater for Lisa, and Javier wanted some charcoals to finish a drawing he had on his easel. When we returned, just before noon, the apartment door was ajar. Lisa was inside, lying on the sofa in the front room, crying.

Alarmed, Javier knelt beside her and brushed the hair away from her eyes. "What's all this, Lisa?" he asked gently, the musical sound of his rich Mexican accent soft in her ear.

"It's my hip, Daddy," she sobbed. "It started hurting worse, so a neighbor came and picked me up from school."

Lisa handed me a crumpled note from one of the Sisters at Saint Elizabeth School. "Please look into this. Lisa is having great difficulty walking. We think she should see a doctor."

Javier nodded. "Call Dr. Kovner," he said. "We shouldn't wait any longer."

Dr. Kovner was a friend of the family. He had treated us before, always remarking that Lisa was his favorite patient. His nurse made an appointment for the next afternoon.

The doctor took X rays and did a preliminary examination. Then he called me into his office. "Mrs. Larios, this could be one of several things. We'll just have to start with the most obvious and work from there. I'm going to admit Lisa to the hospital where we can run additional tests."

There were more examinations at Van Nuys Community Hospital. Lisa tried to be brave, but in constant pain, spending the night away from home in a strange place, surrounded by strange people, it wasn't easy for her. Each morning I would get the children off to school and then drive to the hospital, crying all the way, wondering if the people who passed me were aware of the great pain in my heart. At the hospital I was all smiles, but it was just a front. Inside, I was falling apart.

"There is a possibility the pain could be coming from an enlarged appendix pressing on a nerve," the doctor said. "We're going to take the appendix out and see if that solves our problem."

But the pain remained after Lisa returned from surgery. No one seemed to know what to do next. She came home from the hospital on May 12. She was supposed to remain on crutches. There were more visits to the doctor's office.

"This has me stumped," Dr. Kovner said, examining the X rays again. "I think we should call in a specialist."

Dr. Gettleman, a surgeon, was very methodical. He took more X rays and conducted his own examination. "Keep

her on crutches for another week," he said. "Bring her
back in next Thursday."

In spite of the crutches her pain grew worse. Unable to
go to school, Lisa hobbled around the house on crutches,
crying and trying to act brave. Mostly she stayed in bed. At
the end of the week she was back in the hospital, this time
Saint Joseph's in Burbank.

"We're going to have to operate again," Dr. Gettleman
said. "We've seen something on the X rays. It might be a
bag of pus that is causing the pressure. However, it could
be a tumor. There are two kinds of tumors, good and bad.
If it's a good tumor we won't have any trouble. However, if
it's malignant it could be very serious."

Although we belonged to a Roman Catholic church and
our children attended a Catholic school, neither Javier nor
I was very religious. We seldom attended Mass, and almost
never went to confession. Still, I had always felt very close
to Jesus, and the little cards that Lisa's school friends kept
sending her, telling her they were praying for her, helped
me too as I turned to God in prayer.

The night before the operation, I was home alone with
Albert and Gina. They went to bed early, I went into our
bedroom and lay across the bed in the shadows. It seemed
my whole world was crumbling. I had carried Lisa in my
body for nine months. I had been willing to lay down my
life in childbirth that she might live. I had nursed her, held
her in the dark nights, laughed with her, run through the
fields with her, protected her, cried and prayed over her.
And now the doctors told me she might die. I had cried
until my tears were all gone. It all seemed so hopeless, so
futile.

As I lay on my back across the bed, looking up into the
shadows on the ceiling, I began to pray. "Dear God, Lisa
really isn't mine, is she? She's Yours. You've just let us
have her to raise, feed, teach, and love. One day she will
leave us, marry, and raise her own children. If You want to
take her sooner, I give her back to You and thank You that
we've had her this long to bless us."

It was a simple, unemotional prayer. But I meant it. I dozed off, still looking up at the shadows.

In a dream I was sitting in a small, dark room. Javier was beside me, holding my hand. A door opened before us, and coming down a long hall were two men dressed in surgical gowns. One of the men, a doctor, was weeping and could not talk. The other stood before us and said, "Your daughter is very ill. She has cancer."

I awoke, startled. It was past midnight, and I was still lying on my back on the bed. The house was quiet. Only the light in the hall filtered into the bedroom. I got up and checked the other children. They were sleeping peacefully. Then I walked into the darkened living room and sat on the edge of the sofa. Was the dream from the Devil? Was he trying to scare me? Or was it from God, warning and preparing me? How could I know?

When I heard Javier's steps on the stairs outside the door, I slipped down the hall and got in bed before he reached the bedroom. I didn't want him to know the depth of my concern. Lisa would need us both to be strong when she faced surgery in the morning.

Javier and I sat, holding hands, in the small waiting room outside the surgery wing of the hospital. It was natural that both of us should pray, and we did, silently. Doctors kept coming in, giving reports to others who were waiting. "Your dad's great. We didn't even have to operate. . . ." "There's nothing to worry about, your wife's in fine shape. . . ." "You can take your son home this afternoon. . . ."

At two o'clock in the afternoon I looked up and saw two doctors coming down the long hall. One of them was Dr. Kovner. His face was gray. The other was Dr. Gettleman. Javier jumped up and met them at the door, but I stayed seated. I knew what was coming, and my legs were like rubber. It was the same scene I had lived through in my dream.

"We found a tumor," Dr. Gettleman said. "It is inoperable. If we had cut, we would have had to cut her entire leg off."

"Is it cancer?" Javier choked out.

"I'm afraid so," he answered. "She's a very, very sick girl. Her hipbone is like butter. If I'd had a spoon, I could have just dipped it out. The flesh around the bone is like Swiss cheese, full of holes. The lab has already run a test, and it is the worst type of cancer. All we could do was sew her back up."

"Isn't there anything you can do?" Javier pleaded, his face drawn and haggard.

"Nothing right now. After she recovers from the operation we'll start her on cobalt. We can talk about that later."

"But she will get well, won't she?" Javier asked.

Dr. Gettleman hung his head. "The best I can say is that we'll try to prolong her life. I can promise no more."

I looked at Dr. Kovner. Although he said nothing, his face spoke volumes. His eyes were brimming with tears. Lisa was dying, and there was nothing any of us could do about it. I had given her back to God, and He had accepted my offer.

The doctors agreed we should not tell Lisa about her condition. Two weeks later we brought her home in a wheelchair, determined to give her the happiest summer of her life.

Dr. Kovner disagreed with our plans to take Lisa on an extended vacation. "We need to start cobalt treatment at once," he said.

"If we sign the release and let you give her the radiation treatment," I asked, "what can you promise?"

"We can promise nothing," he said. "But you'll never know whether it will help unless you try it."

"What will happen if we don't let you treat her?"

"I don't like to answer questions like that," Dr. Kovner said. "But even with treatment, the most we can offer you is six months. And she will be very, very sick before she dies."

I promised to talk the matter over with Javier. Both of

us felt it would be cruel to take the remaining months of Lisa's life and subject her to the radiation treatment.

On June 9 Lisa was admitted to the Children's Hospital in Los Angeles. It was her third hospital in three months. Dr. Higgins, the woman physician in charge of her case, told us there were three ways the cancer could spread: to her liver, her chest, or her brain. Any of them would prove fatal. It seems that cancer in growing children spreads rapidly, and the only possible way to save her life would be through cobalt treatments and chemotherapy.

We finally consented to the preliminary treatment, and they began a series of injections. Lisa reacted violently. I sat with her throughout the night while she vomited and cried, "Mamma, what's the matter with me? Why am I so sick?"

It was more than I could take. Javier and I talked again and decided that her last days should be spent at home, with us, rather than in the hospital. We would take her home.

The priest from Lisa's school had heard of her condition and was making nightly visits to the hospital, bringing her Communion. We talked to him about our decision to withhold the cobalt. He agreed with us. "If she is dying, then she should spend the last days of her life as happily as possible."

"Lisa has absolutely no chance of recovery without the radiation therapy," Dr. Higgins objected when we told her.

The other doctors agreed. "If she stays in the hospital, maybe we can learn something that will help some other little girl in five or ten years."

"I'm not interested in my child becoming a medical experiment," I told them, honestly. "I just want her healed. Can you promise me that?"

"I'm sorry, Mrs. Larios," the doctors said. "The medical profession can promise you nothing."

The next day we took Lisa home to die.

We spent the rest of the summer trying to make her happy. We went deeply into debt, taking her on vacation trips along the coast, buying her things she wanted—tape recorders and other material things. Yet it all seemed so pathetically empty. It wasn't right that we should sit around smothering her in gifts, waiting for her to die.

One afternoon in the middle of July there was a knock at the door of our apartment. I opened it to see our neighbor, a young bachelor named Bill Truett, standing in the hall.

"How is Lisa?" he asked.

"Not good," I answered. "She's gotten worse since we took her out of the hospital."

Bill smiled faintly and looked me straight in the eye. "She's going to get well," he said confidently.

I shrugged. "I hope so."

"No, you didn't understand me," he said seriously. "She *is* going to get well. Have you ever heard of Kathryn Kuhlman?"

"Well, I've seen her a couple of times on TV but I never paid much attention."

"This coming Sunday she's going to be in Los Angeles at the Shrine Auditorium," he said. "I want to take Lisa to the meeting."

I hesitated. I really didn't know Bill that well, and I had heard the meetings at the Shrine were very long. Bill was insistent, though, and I finally agreed that Lisa and I would go with him, just to get him out of my hair.

After I had told him yes, I closed the door and leaned against the kitchen table. Javier was at his easel near the window overlooking the courtyard. Several of his drawings hung on the wall of our apartment. I knew he was interested in developing his talent, but I also knew that painting was an escape for him. When he was busy with his sketches he didn't have to think about Lisa. I watched him, his face like chiseled stone, concentrating on his charcoals. I felt my fingernails biting into the flesh of my hand as I clenched my fist and tried to hold back the flood of tears. Javier was lost in his art. Bill was making crazy suggestions. But I was Lisa's mother, and I had to face reality. I could not let myself escape into art, or be drawn off on Bill's wild-goose chases about miracles. I had to face things the way they were. Lisa was going to die.

Bill was back the next morning, reminding me of my promise to go with him and take Lisa. "Bill, I don't want to dampen your enthusiasm," I argued, "but the doctors have told me Lisa cannot be cured. There's nothing anyone can do."

"Then let's see what God can do," he said simply.

I wanted to back out. I felt Bill was pressuring me. Besides, I hated to get up so early on Sunday morning and drive all the way across the city just to stand in line for hours.

Bill refused to be discouraged. "I know she is going to be healed. My mother is very, very close to this ministry. She has known many people who were healed."

I had no faith whatsoever. I was just thankful that Lisa didn't know how serious her condition actually was.

Unknown to me at that time, though, Lisa did suspect something. At least she knew her leg wouldn't hold her weight. A few days before, she was visiting with a friend in an apartment across the hall and tried to test her leg without the crutches. Her hip bent in like a wet sponge and she fell to the floor. Although she didn't know what it was, she knew something was seriously wrong with her hip.

Saturday afternoon Bill was back, knocking on the door again. "Remember, tomorrow's the day. Lisa is going to receive a miracle."

"Okay, Bill," I said, closing the door. But inside I knew there was no way. They weren't making miracles anymore, at least not for the likes of us. If miracles did happen, they were for the rich, the pious, the saints in the church. We were just poor Mexican Catholics who didn't even go to Mass very often. How could we expect a miracle?

Early the next morning, July 16, Bill rang the doorbell. "Just let me finish my coffee," I shouted. Inwardly, I wished he would leave without us.

Bill and his girl friend Cindy were waiting with a wheelchair. They helped Lisa down the stairs, around the swimming pool in the patio, down the long narrow sidewalk to the street, and into the car. Soon we were out on the Harbor Freeway, heading south toward Los Angeles and the Shrine Auditorium.

Lisa sat in her wheelchair while I waited on an old army blanket, leaning up against the side of the Shrine Auditorium, wondering when the doors would open. It all seemed so stupid, spending all Sunday morning sitting on a sun-drenched sidewalk waiting for nothing.

Finally we were allowed inside. Bill rolled Lisa into the wheelchair section and I sat down beside her. He and Cindy found seats in another part of the auditorium. I was awed by the size of the crowd and the warmth, friendliness, and love I felt in that place.

The meeting started with the choir beautifully singing *He Touched Me*. Kathyrn Kuhlman, dressed in a flowing white dress, appeared on stage. Lisa pulled at my arm. "Mamma, if you squint your eyes when you look at her, you can see a halo all around her." I shrugged her off, without trying to see the halo myself.

Then Miss Kuhlman preached a little sermon which I didn't listen to. I kept shaking my head. All this was nice, but why were we wasting our time here?

Then, without warning, things began to happen. Miss Kuhlman pointed up to the balcony. "There's a man who is being healed of cancer. Right now. Stand up, sir, and accept your healing."

I turned around in my seat and tried to see into the balcony. But it was too far away. All I could see were faces, stretching up and back into the darkness.

Yet there seemed to be light up there also—not the kind of light you can see, but the kind you can feel. It was all through the building. Light and energy, as if there were tiny flames dancing from one head to another. I was electrified. Miss Kuhlman kept designating other places in the auditorium where healings were taking place.

Then she was pointing down at the wheelchair section, right where we were sitting. "There's cancer right here," she said softly. "Stand up and accept your healing."

I looked at Lisa, but she didn't move. Of course. How would she know she had cancer? We had kept it from her.

I was torn inside. If I told her that Miss Kuhlman was talking to her, and if she stood up, her hip and leg might buckle. What should I do?

Miss Kuhlman shook her head and turned away from our section, calling out healings in other parts of the auditorium. My heart sank. Had Lisa's time passed us by? Was it too late?

Then Miss Kuhlman was looking back at us, pointing down into our section. "I cannot get away from this," she said. "Someone right down here is being healed of cancer. You must stand up and accept your healing."

"Mamma," Lisa moaned, "my stomach feels hot."

We hadn't eaten since early morning, and I fumbled in my purse to find a piece of candy.

"No, it isn't that kind of hot," Lisa said, refusing the candy. "It's something different."

Miss Kuhlman continued to point at us. I looked around. No one else was standing up in our section. I knew Lisa must be the one who was being healed, but I was afraid. What if it wasn't Lisa? What if she stood and fell? Or, even more frightening, what if it *was* Lisa—and she didn't stand?

When I thought I would die from the uncertainty, the wondering, Lisa leaned over and whispered, "Mamma, I think I should go up on the stage. I think I am being healed."

"Whatever you think," I said, feeling great relief that she had decided for me. But I dreaded her trying to stand without her crutches.

One of the personal workers in the aisle sensed something was happening to Lisa. He leaned toward us. "I think I feel better," Lisa whispered to him. "I want to go on stage."

He helped her out of her wheelchair. I held my breath as she stood up. Once I thought she was going to collapse, but suddenly I was aware of something else. That same fire I had sensed dancing from one head to another—now it was resting on Lisa. I could almost see new strength flowing into her body.

The usher let her lean on him, and they started down the

aisle. Slowly, then with more confidence, they walked to the base of the stage where a woman talked with them briefly. Bill Truett met them there, and after a brief conference, they took Lisa up on the platform.

Miss Kuhlman listened as the woman shared a few details. Then she reached toward Lisa. Lisa backed away a step, then slumped to the floor. I gasped, thinking her leg had given way. But Lisa climbed back to her feet.

"I dedicate this child to the Lord Jesus Christ," Miss Kuhlman said, as Lisa stood before her, her face covered with tears. "Now let's see you walk." Lisa began running back and forth across the stage, and all the people began applauding, praising God. Then, as though it were the angels singing, the choir began singing, softly, "Alleluia! Alleluia!"

"I want you to have this healing verified," Miss Kuhlman said. "I want you to go back to your doctor and have him examine you thoroughly. Then come back to the next meeting and testify to what God has done for you."

I glanced at Bill. He was exuberant, as if it were his own sister who had been healed. I would learn later that in the family of God, we are indeed brothers and sisters. But right then all I could think about was Lisa. She was running back and forth across the stage, still limping some, but stomping her foot. I bit my lip. I knew her hipbone was like butter and would give way at the slightest pressure—but it didn't. Could it really be? Was she healed?

I was afraid to let myself believe. I had been hurt once, so deeply, when the doctor had told us there was no hope. To believe now, only to find out later that it was just a false hope, would be more than I could bear. It was safer not to believe at all.

Javier was just leaving for work when we got home. We told him what had happened. "Then we shall begin to hope," he said. "That is something we have not had before. We have had much love for our little girl. Now we have hope. Maybe sooner, maybe later, God will give us faith also—faith to accept this wonderful thing He is doing." It was a wise word from my wonderful husband.

Bill and Cindy followed us into the apartment. "Take away the crutches," Bill said, as I tried to hand them back to Lisa. "Don't you understand? She's been healed!"

For the rest of the evening Lisa limped around the apartment. I watched her every step, fearing she would collapse. But she never did. In fact, it seemed she was growing stronger right before my eyes.

The next morning, the first question Javier asked was, "Where is Lisa? How is she?"

I had been up earlier, so I took Javier to the window. "Look," I said, pointing down into the courtyard. There was Lisa, riding her bicycle around the swimming pool, laughing and playing with the other children from the apartment.

When Javier turned away from the window, his face was lined with tears. Whether I believed or not, it made no difference. He did.

The following week I took Lisa back to the Children's Hospital. Following a series of blood tests and extensive X rays of the hip and chest, the technician said, "We'll phone you as soon as we know something."

Javier's eyes were dancing when he met me at the door of the apartment. "Well, what did you find out?"

I explained the situation and told him we'd just have to wait. He insisted I call Dr. Higgins.

"I was just going to call you," the doctor said when I finally reached her. "But I've been in consultation with seven other doctors about Lisa's case. I just don't know what to tell you."

I swallowed into the phone. "You mean something's wrong?" Could it be true that this was just a cruel trick, my hopes being raised only to be dashed to pieces?

"I don't know how this can be," the doctor continued, as though she had not heard me. "We all see the same thing on the X rays. The tumor has greatly reduced instead of spreading. There is evidence of healing."

Of course she knew nothing of the Kathryn Kuhlman meeting, but she had said "evidence of healing." How much more would it take to convince me that God had touched Lisa's life?

"Doctor, do you have a minute?" I said. "I want to tell you something. I know this will sound odd to you, but we took Lisa to a Kathryn Kuhlman meeting. Ever since then she's walked without crutches, she's been running, riding her bicycle, swimming, and acting normal. We think God has healed her."

There was a long silence on the other end of the line. "I want to get this straight," the doctor finally said. "You haven't given her any medication, have you?"

"None," I said.

"You refused to let her take chemotherapy and the cobalt treatment, didn't you?"

"Yes," I answered.

Again there was a long silence. "Well, it could be that her body is building up some kind of resistance and throwing this off, which doesn't seem natural. Or it could be your Kathryn Kuhlman. Whatever it is, the tumor is disappearing. And to my knowledge, it is the first case in medical history where this has happened."

I was crying. I remembered reading, long ago, the story of Thomas in the Bible. He finally believed that Jesus was raised from the dead when he saw the nail prints in His hands. How much like him I was. Yet, even so, God had allowed me to see His miracle in my daughter.

"I'll tell you something else," Dr. Higgins said, her voice soft on the other end of the line. "There will be great rejoicing in this hospital over what has happened to Lisa, for this is one case we had given up on."

Lisa reentered school in the fall—without crutches. A month later I took her back to the doctor. The tumor was continuing to reduce in size. It was going away. Lisa was almost back to normal.

"How do you explain this?" I asked.

"We have no explanation," the doctor said. "There has never been a case like this healed before. If we had given her the cobalt treatment, and the tumor had receded, we would have called it a medical miracle. But without any treatment whatsoever . . . well, what can we say?"

Our priest had something to say, however. "God has many ways of doing things. Surely this is of Him."

Now that Lisa is totally healed, many of our friends ask, "Why did all this happen?"

I think God allowed this sickness to come into our lives to draw us closer to each other and closer to Him. In my Bible I found a story that explains it all. One day Jesus was walking down a road and saw a man blind from birth. His followers asked Him, "Master, why is this man blind? Is it because he sinned, or because his parents sinned?"

The Master answered, "No, neither one. But rather he is blind so God can be glorified through his healing." Then He touched him, and he could see.

I feel Lisa was sick so God could be glorified through her healing.

Giving God the glory isn't something one learns from books. It has to be learned by walking with Him through the shadowed valley. If one lives on the mountaintops all the time, he gets hard and leathery, insensitive to the finer things of life. Only in the shadow of the valley do the tender crops grow.

I have stood for long moments watching Javier at his easel. He loves to work with charcoals, blending shadows. "Sunshine brings out detail," he says, "but shadows bring out the character."

It was only as we walked in the shadows that we learned to praise God for the little things. It was there we learned Lisa wasn't really ours, but God's. In the darkest time we gave her back to the Heavenly Father. There, in the valley, we discovered the secret of relinquishment. Yet when we gave her up, He was merciful to give her back—healed.

Lisa no longer fears the shadows. Like us, she has found that even in the valley He is with us, His rod and staff comforting us, causing our cup to overflow with His goodness and mercy.

FOUR

The Day God's Mercy Took Over

RICHARD OWELLEN, PH.D., M.D.

Dr. Richard Owellen is an old friend. I met him when he was singing in our choir in Pittsburgh and studying at Carnegie Tech for his Ph.D. in organic chemistry. After two years of post-doctoral study at Stanford University, he enrolled at Johns Hopkins University in Baltimore, where he completed his M.D. degree in three years. Following a year of internship and another as a resident in internal medicine, he was appointed to the staff at Johns Hopkins. Since 1968 he has been an assistant professor of medicine at the University, dividing his time between cancer research, patient care, and teaching.

While I was working on my Ph.D. in chemistry at Carnegie Tech, I began to attend the Kathryn Kuhlman meetings being held every Friday on Pittsburgh's Northside at the old Carnegie Auditorium. There, for the first time in my life, I sensed the power of God at work as people came together to worship. Before long I volunteered to sing in the choir, and it was there I met Rose, who had literally grown up in the Kathryn Kuhlman ministry.

Rose and I dated, fell in love, and in April, 1959, Miss Kuhlman performed our marriage ceremony.

One year later little Joann was born. Rose had a normal pregnancy and delivery, but when we brought the baby home from the hospital, we noticed a large bruise across her buttocks. I questioned the doctor about it, but he assured us it was no indication that anything was wrong.

However, both my parents and Rosie's sister noticed something strange about the baby's behavior. She was extremely fussy—too fussy, my mother said. She cried and whined constantly and wouldn't eat, often pulling away from the bottle, vomiting and screaming if we happened to move her during her feeding. Besides this, we noticed that one leg was always bent and pulled up toward her body, with the knee and foot rotated outward, sometimes at a 90-degree angle. It was impossible to make both her legs stretch out straight at the same time.

When we took her back to our family doctor, he checked her legs and hips. "Yes, there is something definitely wrong with this right leg," he said. "I'm not sure what it is at this time, but let's wait for a while. Sometimes things like this will straighten out on their own."

We waited for several months, but nothing straightened out. Instead, it got worse. Joann continued to be very fussy, often crying when we touched her. When she was drinking her bottle, she frequently stopped to cry. Both of these were signs that she was in extreme pain. But what? And where?

At the end of three months, when Joann should have been picking her head up off the mattress, she was unable to do so. With growing concern, we took her back to the doctor again.

As he examined her this time, he motioned for me to come and stand beside him. Little Joann was on her back on the examining table. The doctor took her right foot in one hand and put his other hand under her knee. He began gently to turn her foot inward. She screamed out in pain. "The leg will not turn in at all," he said. "Now look at this." Gently he began to rotate the leg in the other direction, outward. I gasped and then held my breath as the leg turned in his hand, not only upside down but in almost a complete 360-degree turn or rotation. Only when it had made a complete circle in his hand did she begin to whimper in pain.

The doctor carefully placed the leg back in its original position. Next, he pointed to the creases on the skin along the inside of her thigh. "This is one of the things a doctor looks for," he said. "Notice there are two creases on this side, but only one on the other leg. A normal child will have identical creases on both sides. A change in the creasing pattern indicates some kind of internal alteration, meaning something is structurally wrong with the hip, back, or leg. In this case I feel sure it is the hip."

Rose reached down and picked up the baby, holding her close. "What are you trying to say, Doctor?" she said, her eyes full of tears.

The doctor put his hand on Rose's shoulder. "I can't say for sure," he said, "so I want her to be examined by an orthopedic surgeon. He will be able to give us a definite diagnosis. It looks like a dislocated hip."

Rose sat down on the chair beside the table, still holding the baby close to her breast. The doctor continued talking, and in a very quiet and kind way, outlined what we might expect. Joann would probably need braces, maybe even a body cast. The treatment would take a long time, and even then the chances of having the problem corrected were not 100 percent. There was a definite possibility she would be a cripple all her life, walking with a limp. She might have one leg shorter than the other, or another kind of abnormality.

"You must not wait," the doctor said. "Take her to an orthopedic surgeon."

We made an appointment with the surgeon for the following Monday, and took Joann home.

That night, back in our apartment, Rose and I sat up talking. Both of us were shattered, and not only from the prospect of having a crippled child. It all seemed so unfair.

"I don't understand," I said to Rose as we sat awkwardly in our tiny living room. "Here we are, trying to serve the Lord, and He's let this happen to us."

Rose was silent, her pretty face tense, her lips trembling a little. I wanted to get up, go across the room, take her in my arms, and comfort her. But I was too disquieted inside myself. I had nothing to give.

"We've been telling other people about our belief in healing," I blurted out, "and now we have a deformed child."

"If God allowed us to have a deformed child," Rose finally said, "then He must expect us to keep her and take care of her."

"I'm not arguing that," I said bitterly. "I love this baby and will do everything possible to see that she is healed. If she's not healed, we'll raise her and love her all our lives. It just doesn't seem fair, though. The world is full of people who don't love God, who don't even know God. A lot of these people hate God, yet they have normal children. Why should we have a deformed child?"

It was an unfair question. I knew Rose didn't have the answer to it any more than I did. I also knew that people who ask questions of God show their lack of faith. I was realizing I didn't have faith at all, at least not the kind that I thought was necessary to see our child healed.

The next morning, as I was dressing for class, Rose sat on the side of the bed. She had been up most of the night with the baby, and her face looked drawn from loss of sleep. "Dick," she spoke with hesitancy. "We've seen the Holy Spirit do so many wonderful things at Miss Kuhlman's services. Don't you think we ought to take Joann and have faith that God will heal her?"

Rose had dropped out of Miss Kuhlman's choir just before the baby was born, and although we had been back to some of the meetings, both in Pittsburgh and in Youngstown, Ohio, shame and embarrassment had prevented us from telling anyone about our baby's condition. Only my parents and Rose's sister knew.

Mulling over Rose's question in my mind, I stood in front of the mirror for a long time, fiddling with the knot on my necktie. Faith? I had just realized that I didn't have any faith at all, at least not the kind needed for Joann's healing. But I remembered something I had heard Miss Kuhlman say over and over: "Do everything you possibly can. Then, when you've reached the end of your resources, let God take over."

We had been to the doctor. The only possible recourse was braces and possible surgery, with no promise of healing. Rose was right. Now was the time to trust God completely.

Friday morning we left the house to take the baby to the Miracle Service at Carnegie Auditorium. Sitting in the car, we bowed our heads in prayer. "Lord Jesus, You have written in Your Word that we have the privilege of coming before You and asking You, in Your mercy, to touch the body of our daughter. But we do not demand it of You, Lord. We don't even make a 'claim' on it, for although it is already given us, we know it is still in Your mercy. We simply ask, Lord Jesus, for You to heal our little girl."

It was such a simple prayer, not the kind I had often envisioned myself praying. In my imagination I would stomp up to the Throne of Grace and throw God's promises back in His face, demanding He keep them. But now, face to face with a problem that was bigger than we were, bigger than medical science, Rose and I realized that the only thing we could fall back on was the mercy of God.

The service was similar to the hundreds we had attended before, only this time we had not come as spectators. We came expecting.

It seemed to be one of those days when little Joann was especially uncomfortable. She whimpered and fussed with pain several times. Not wanting her to disturb the services, we remained at the back of the auditorium, with Rose holding her. Whenever Joann cried out, Rose took her back into the lobby, returning when she calmed down. We had given our seats to someone else and were standing against the back wall of the auditorium as the Miracle Service proceeded.

Joann was wrapped in a blanket, and every so often Rose would lift it and peek under. She believed that when God started to work, she would see something happen.

Near the close of the service, something did happen. Ever since Joann was born, the toes on her right foot had been curled tightly under her foot. Now as we stood against the wall, those tiny little pink toes gradually began to relax, until they looked like the toes on any healthy four-month-old child.

Rose nudged me, her face radiant. "God has started to work," she said. "His presence is on this child. I'm going to the platform." She was determined, and I could see there was no use trying to stop her.

We started down the aisle. I kept expecting one of the ushers to step out and confront us, for they had strict orders to keep anyone from the front unless they had first been interviewed and approved by a personal worker. But there were no ushers around. We kept going right on down the aisle. As we walked, Miss Kuhlman came off the platform and headed in our direction. We met in the center of the auditorium.

"Rose," she said, a look of surprise on her face. "Is there something wrong with the baby?"

Rose tried to speak, choked, and then tried again. "Y-y-yes, Miss Kuhlman. She was born with a dislocated hip."

Miss Kuhlman shook her head in amazement. "Why didn't you tell——" Then she interrupted herself, and turning to the packed room, said, "I want everyone here to stand and begin praying. God is going to heal this precious little child."

Rose pulled the blanket away from Joann and held her toward Miss Kuhlman. All over the room, people were standing, praying with their eyes shut. I was praying, too, but I kept my eyes open. I wanted to see what was happening.

I watched closely. Miss Kuhlman reached out her sensitive fingers and touched Joann's toes ever so gently. She didn't pull. She didn't even close her fingers. She just lightly touched the baby's toes and began to pray. "Wonderful Jesus, touch this precious little baby. . . ."

I saw it! With my own eyes I saw it! That leg, turned so grotesquely to the right, began to straighten. It swung slowly until the toes were pointed straight up, matching the toes on the other foot. It all looked perfectly natural. Yet I knew what I was seeing was impossible. Some exterior force had moved that leg. But Miss Kuhlman was not moving it. Rose, her eyes closed and her face lifted toward heaven, was not moving it. And of course, little Joann was not moving it. Who, then, but God!

I kept my eyes fixed on the leg as it rested in a natural position, and I knew the healing was complete. "Thank You, Lord," I kept repeating over and over under my breath. "Thank You."

Miss Kuhlman finished praying, and everyone sat down. Rose wrapped the baby in her blanket, and we started for the back of the auditorium.

"Did you see it?" I whispered as we reached the back.

"See what?" Rose asked. "I was praying. Weren't you?"

"I was praying, too, but I had my eyes open. Couldn't you feel it?"

"Feel what?" Rose looked at me strangely.

"Joann's leg, her foot. I saw her leg move. It straightened right out. I saw her being healed!" I was so excited I could hardly keep from shouting.

Rose's eyes widened, and joy flashed across her face. "Jesus!" she whispered. "Oh, Jesus, thank You."

We pushed open the swinging door and almost ran out into the lobby. There we pulled back the blanket and looked again at Joann's legs. They were perfect. No longer was one leg pulled up against her stomach as it had been. No longer was the right foot turned out. Both legs were just as straight as could be, both feet turned exactly right.

"Let's go home," I said. "I want to spend the rest of the day praising God."

Not only did we spend the rest of the day praising Him, but most of the night as well. After supper, which the baby took without any problems, we laid her on her stomach in her crib. We stood, holding hands beside the crib, and watched. For the first time in her life, Joann picked up her head from the mattress and looked around. We stayed up until three that morning, watching her. She would sleep, then wake, coo, gurgle, and sleep some more. It was as if she were making up for all the lost time when her life had not been a joy-filled existence.

The next morning we could still see the perfect healing in her legs. I could manipulate both of them with ease. The only time she cried out was when I started to twist her leg in an outward circle as I had been able to do just the day before. Our Joann was perfectly normal. The only difference between her legs was the two creases in the flesh of one leg, compared with the one crease in the flesh on the other—a reminder that something had been structurally wrong.

On Monday we kept our appointment with the orthopedic surgeon. He looked at the child and read the note from our family doctor. "What did your doctor send you over here for?" he asked, as he pulled at Joann's legs.

"He thought her right hip was dislocated," I said.

He examined her even more closely, and shook his head. "I don't understand this. There's nothing wrong with this child. Her left leg turns in just a little—but that's not abnormal. You don't need my services. This baby looks perfect to me."

We were delighted to hear the medical confirmation of her healing. And Joann was eating normally—no more stopping to cry out.

On Friday, just a week after Joann had been healed, we went back to our family doctor. He asked us what had happened and why we were back so soon. We told him the story, omitting nothing.

He never batted an eye, but kept right on examining Joann and making notes. We told him what the other doctor had said. He kept trying to twist her leg, back and forth, round and round—giving her the same examination he had given her just the week before.

Nodding to Rose, he indicated that his examination was finished and that she could dress Joann. Then, sitting down, he tipped his chair back. "Well, children change," he said. Then he added, "But they don't change that fast. That had to be God."

We were ecstatic with joy. The healing was complete, and even the doctor gave God the glory.

Now, years later, I am on the staff of one of the greatest medical centers in the world. In this capacity I see no conflict between medicine and spiritual healing. The doctor doesn't heal. He can give a man medicine, but the medicine doesn't change his organs, it just improves the way they work. All healing is of God. Surgeons can cut out the bad tissue or cells, which sometimes allows the body to heal faster. But no surgeon reaches in and heals. He just sews the body back up after he's done his part. It's God who heals.

God has provided us with a great number of wonderful drugs, surgical skills, orthopedic skills, nursing skills—and the Christian has the additional benefit of being able to look beyond what the doctor can do, to what God can do.

Some of my medical colleagues sincerely deny this. Others, equally sincere, go further and deny the existence of God. But when it comes to facing the fact that some of their "incurable" patients are healed after they turn to God, they are sincerely baffled.

To some, it may seem strange that men of science, dedicated to being intellectually honest, would ignore this entire avenue of healing. But the things of the spirit are not the same as the things of the natural mind. In fact, the natural mind is at enmity with the spiritual mind. Any person, even a skilled scientist, who does not want to face the fact that he is in rebellion against God and needs Jesus Christ, will go to any end to block out God's message of salvation. The same thing is true in recognizing God's power to heal. However, those who sincerely desire to come into a knowledge of all truth will eventually come to Jesus Christ, "in whom," Paul says "are hid all the treasures of wisdom and knowledge" (Colossians 2:3).

It wasn't until recent years, after I joined the staff at Johns Hopkins University as an assistant professor of medicine, that I began to fully appreciate the magnitude of God's grace in healing little Joann. It wasn't my faith, nor

Rose's, that caused it to happen. Neither of us had the kind of faith necessary to "claim" healing. It was all God's mercy—His undeserved favor.

When we went into that meeting we had a reason to expect a miracle. We had seen many others healed, and we of course knew that God loves little children. But even so, we didn't have the faith we felt was necessary to see such a miracle come to pass. Yet we felt we had to give God a chance to touch our child by releasing her to Him. And when we released her, He reached out, took her, and healed her.

Through this miracle, I have learned the difference between faith *in* God, which most of us have, and the faith *of* God (the same faith God has), which is a gift of the Holy Spirit. Faith *in* God allows us to believe that God will do a wonderful thing. But unless we have the faith *of* God, we need to do everything humanly possible first, believing God may want to work through medical science, and leave the rest in His merciful hands.

Many people try to force God to do something, coming into His presence, almost demanding that He act. Occasionally God will honor such demands, not because He has to but because He feels sorry for us. I feel much safer, however, simply depending upon His mercy and grace to supply all my needs.

I had often wondered if many of the healings I had seen weren't psychosomatic. From a basic study of human nature, I knew that some probably were. But a four-month-old baby doesn't know enough to have a psychosomatic healing. What we saw that day in the aisle at Carnegie Auditorium was not a mental process; it was purely physical. And it was instant. There's no medical term to describe it except the word "miracle."

I am constantly asked, "Why imperfection? Deformity? Why does God allow sickness to come to people, especially Christians? Why did imperfection come to Joann?" These are sticky questions, especially for a doctor. I really don't have an answer. However, as far as Joann is concerned, I am absolutely convinced now, although I wasn't then, that

God allowed this particular deformity to come on her that her healing might be a testimony to Him. We felt if God could trust us with a crippled child, then He had an even greater thing He would like to trust us with—the testimony of His healing power.

FIVE

When Heaven Comes Down

GILBERT STRACKBEIN

Gilbert and Arlene Strackbein live in a comfortable house nestled among the pines in Little Rock, Arkansas. Gilbert is a successful salesman with an office supply firm. They have three beautiful girls and are active in the new movement of the Holy Spirit which is sweeping the nation. However, it has not always been that way. This is Gil's story.

Once when I was applying for a sales position the company psychologist asked, "Why do you want this job as a salesman?"

"Well," I replied, "selling is what I know, what I've always done."

"That's hard to believe, Mr. Strackbein," the psychologist frowned. "Normally a salesman has to like people; but according to this psychological test you took, you don't even like yourself."

He was right, of course. I didn't really care whether I liked people or not. As a salesman I was only interested in two things: getting the order and getting out.

I had always withdrawn from people. Reared in a strict German-Lutheran home in south Texas, I didn't even speak English until I went to school. Proud of my heritage, I found great satisfaction in believing that my German mind could out-think anyone else when it came to mechanics, electronics or logic. Over the years I came to believe I could do anything if only I set my mind to it. Even though I made my living as a salesman, I spent my spare time in my workshop, doing things like building computers.

Arlene was 19 when we got married. After we moved to New Orleans she began to have fainting spells and lost a good deal of her energy. But I simply refused to believe that she was sick. Sickness, to me, was a sign of weakness. When our first little girl, Denise, was about three years old, I decided that Arlene needed another child. This would get her mind off her so-called problems, I figured, and give her something constructive to think about.

Arlene's pregnancy wasn't that simple, however. From the beginning there were complications that meant even more medical attention. Her kidneys posed a threatening problem, both to her and the baby. She had horrible leg spasms, and to avoid the risk of miscarriage, the doctor finally put her to bed—for seven months. Irritated over this show of weakness on her part, I withdrew even further, having as little to do with her as possible. Although she was in the first stages of a terrible disease, little did I realize that my own spiritual sickness was even worse.

Arlene had been attending a Methodist church in New Orleans. The ladies of the church, realizing she was having to battle her problem alone, began dropping by to fix our dinner, since the doctor had forbidden Arlene to get out of bed, except for bathroom privileges. If anyone came to visit when I was home, I would answer the front door and then disappear out the back. As much as I detested Arlene's taking to bed, I was even more disgusted that people from the outside were interfering in our lives by trying to help.

The difficult pregnancy was only a beginning. Over the next several years her condition grew worse—weakness, muscle spasms, kidney infections, dizziness, blurred vision. She'd get better, she'd get worse, sometimes having bouts of poor muscle coordination, every one of which seemed to leave her with even less energy. The doctors couldn't put their finger on what was wrong, and I still stubbornly refused to acknowledge that there was anything wrong at all.

One evening I came home to dinner and found the table already prepared. Some of the ladies from the church had dropped by with a full meal, had set the table and left.

Knowing how I felt, Arlene got up to sit at the table with me. She got as far as the kitchen door before she collapsed. She wasn't unconscious, but it was as though all the muscles in her body just ceased to function at the same time.

I was frightened. I wanted to run, but knew I couldn't leave her there helpless, on the floor. I picked her up, hollered for a neighbor to stay with our two young children, and sped to the hospital.

At the emergency room, the nurse who had been working over Arlene began to scream. "Doctor, I've lost her blood pressure."

The doctors rushed to her side. It took emergency treatment to get her heart beating again. It was then I realized my show of strength was all a façade. Faced with a really impossible situation, I had no answers. I hated Arlene for her weakness but I hated myself even more for being unable to cope.

One night I came home late and found Arlene propped up in bed, dozing. Across her chest lay an open book—*I Believe in Miracles* by Kathryn Kuhlman.

Snorting inwardly, I picked it up, opened the front cover and saw a note penned on the flyleaf from Tom and Judy Kent. I knew the Kents: Judy had worked in the same office with Arlene while Tom was studying medicine at Tulane. He was now a practicing physician in California.

Arlene awoke and saw me standing over her. "Tom sent it to me," she smiled, gesturing toward the book. "He said that he and Judy were praying for a miracle of healing for me."

I shook my head and handed the book back. "How can a medical doctor believe in garbage like that?"

"Please, Gil," Arlene said, her eyes filling with tears. "Just because you don't believe in a God of miracles, don't rob me of my faith too. I've got to have something to believe in."

"Believe in yourself," I said. "That's all you have to do to get up out of that bed."

But even though Arlene could *get* up, she couldn't *stay*

up. She tried. She made a gallant effort to keep going, but it
seemed she always wound up in the hospital.

We moved to Little Rock, Arkansas, where I took a job
with an office supply firm. In my spare time I did everything possible to keep from thinking about Arlene's deteriorating physical condition. It bothered me that even though
the doctors couldn't diagnose her problem, every few
months they would have her back in the hospital for more
tests and treatment.

After our third child, Lisa, was born, Arlene began attending a Thursday night service at Christ Church Episcopal. Wanda Russell, her Sunday school teacher at the
Methodist church, came by after supper each Thursday
and drove her to the meetings. I thought it was foolish, but
I knew Arlene needed some time away from the house. So
I didn't object—that is, until one night when she got in
later than usual.

"Arlene, why is it that you want to go to an Episcopal
meeting? We've got a Methodist church near by."

Arlene walked awkwardly to the sofa and sat down.
"That Methodist church doesn't believe in healing," she
said.

"You mean to tell me you've been going to healing services?"

Arlene just nodded.

"No intelligent person believes in that stuff," I said deliberately. "It's all superstition. And I don't want my wife
being seen at one of those quack places."

Arlene struggled to get up, but her legs refused to work
properly. "Please, Gil, I need this. Don't take it away from
me."

"Listen," I said firmly, "I know all about these things.
Back when I was a boy in south Texas, there was a Pentecostal church down the road from us. We used to go down
there after dark and look in the windows. They had healing
services, too, and they shouted in strange languages, rolled
on the floor, screamed, ran around the room and collapsed
across the altar rail moaning like wounded animals. I'm not
going to have my wife involved in that kind of nonsense."

"Oh, Gil," Arlene said, her lips quivering. "It's not like that at all. Reverend Womble says he believes God is going to heal me."

"I refuse to accept this business about God," I said. My temper was beginning to flare. "This healing business is sheer nonsense and I forbid you to ever go again."

Arlene leaned back on the sofa and closed her eyes. Tiny tears streaked their way down her cheeks. "You met my father after Jesus came into his heart. But what I remember about him when I was a tiny child wasn't so pretty; he was an alcoholic. He would go crazy with drink. There wasn't enough food in the house because liquor was more important to him than my mother or me. Mother tried to live with him, but finally she just gave up. We moved across town on my sixth birthday, and in a fit of alcoholic rage, Dad tried to tear down the door and take me away with him. Mother and I huddled together inside the house, crying and praying, until he went away.

"As I grew older I thought the most wonderful thing in the world would be to have a husband who loved God and me both. To me, heaven would be having a Christian family. I thought I had found it all when I found you, Gil. Then you went off to the service, and when you came back, you hated God. I don't know what happened."

I was stung. "You've got everything you need," I spat out. "We live in a nice house in a nice neighborhood. I make a good salary and have never denied you anything, even medical attention. I don't mind if you go to church on Sunday, I don't even object to you leading the children's choir."

"I really don't need you, you know," Arlene said, looking me straight in the face. "When I was little I used to pray for the Lord's angels to protect me and I know they did. You can keep me from attending the healing services, but you cannot take away my relationship with God. He is all that I need."

Shaking with anger I stalked out of the house to my workshop. When I finally went to bed it was past midnight.

Even though Arlene had her face buried in the pillow, I could still hear her muffled sobs. I wanted to reach out, to put my arm around her. But to be tender, to be gentle, to cry—all these were signs of weakness and I had been raised to be strong. I got up the next morning, fixed my own breakfast, and left the house without even saying good-by to the girls. I hated myself for it, but knew no other way.

Even though I was making good money and had received several promotions, inside I was coming apart faster than Arlene seemed to be coming apart physically. I was arranging "business" trips out of the city for several days at a time. Arlene suspected my immorality, but I rationalized my permissiveness by saying that she was not able to meet my needs. Alcohol tranquilized my conscience and it became my constant companion.

Arlene's condition deteriorated after Lisa was born. She had been in and out of the hospital more than twenty times with things like urological flareups, but this was different. Her blood pressure soared to over 200, and her left arm was partially paralyzed—her hand refused to close into a fist. The attending physician called in a neurologist for consultation. There was some talk she might have a brain tumor.

Three days later, standing in the hall outside her hospital room, the doctor leveled with me. "We suspect a brain tumor, Mr. Strackbein. We'd like to do an arteriogram, but Arlene shows an allergic response to every dye we have in Radiology. The test itself might kill her. I don't like it, but we'll just wait to see what else develops."

I swallowed hard and found I could not look him in the face.

"We'll do the best we can and will let you know if we have to operate."

It wasn't a brain tumor. Instead the diagnosis came back that it was a disease of the central nervous system—either myasthenia gravis, multiple sclerosis, or both—and she had had it for years.

They allowed her to come home, but told her to stay in bed as much as possible. One evening while I was watching television in our den she staggered in from the bedroom. Her face was ashen.

"You'd better watch me," she said, "I'm shaking all over."

When I put my hand against her back, I could feel the muscles rippling in spasms under the skin. "Just lie down and relax," I said. "You'll feel better in a little while."

She gave me a look and returned to the bedroom. Fifteen minutes later I heard her get up, go to the bathroom . . . and scream. When I got to her she was sprawled on the floor, unconscious and completely limp. As I started to pick her up I could feel the muscles in her body coiling and recoiling under the skin.

Then the convulsion hit, her back tightened and pulled her head backward. At the same time her body went stiff and her eyes rolled back in her head. Her tongue turned back in her throat and she began to gag.

I managed to get her up off the floor and suddenly she went limp again, a dead weight in my arms. I carried her to the bedroom and called our next-door neighbor, Edna Williamson, to see about the children while I rushed Arlene to St. Vincent's Hospital. By the time I got the phone back on the hook Arlene's unconscious body was convulsing again. The spasm lasted about a minute and then subsided. Moments later it began again.

I had Arlene out in the car by the time Edna arrived. She was admitted to the Constant Care unit of the hospital. Two days later the final report came back. It was definitely multiple sclerosis, with a possibility of myasthenia gravis.

A long time ago I had remarked to Arlene, "One day I'll find something I can't overcome by myself, and when I do, I'll be a better person for it." Now it was upon me. I had always been able to do whatever I set out to do. If I needed more money I could go out and work an additional six hours a day, but simply being strong wouldn't cure Arlene of multiple sclerosis. I had reached my limit.

I brought her home and hired a licensed practical nurse who spent eight hours a day with her. For two years we staggered on, at a cost of $137.50 per week plus a drug bill which was almost as much, plus additional trips to the hospital. Finally I got a call from our insurance company. They felt their obligation was finished; and from now on we would be on our own.

At the same time, I had almost totally withdrawn. Arlene had asked for a divorce and with my typical German logic, I told her I would not allow it. Many nights I wished I could reach out and give Arlene the comfort she so desperately needed. How I wished I could gently put my arms around my children and draw them to me. But I could not. I was strong, stubborn, and the wall I had built around myself was so strong that I could not escape from it either.

As I left my office one afternoon, Dick Cross, who worked across the hall from me, stopped me at the elevator. Dick worked for Investors Diversified Services and said he had been wanting to contact me about investing in mutual funds. I didn't have the heart to tell him that mutual funds were the least of my interests, so I wound up making an appointment for him to come by the house on Monday at 7:00 P.M. I knew Arlene went to physical therapy that evening and figured I'd let him come, hear his sales pitch, and then send him on his way.

When Dick arrived, I quickly explained our situation. He was preparing to leave when Arlene arrived home. After a few brief comments Dick said bluntly, "I guess you know there is no cure for multiple sclerosis."

"I know that," Arlene nodded. "But I believe God can heal me."

"I believe it, too," Dick said.

For the next four hours Arlene and Dick sat and talked about God's power to heal. "The man's out of his mind," I thought. "People just don't talk about things like this, not intelligent people anyway." But Dick was no fool. He was a successful investment broker who happened to believe in the supernatural power of a personal God. He was a guest in my home and even though I wanted to throw him out, I had no choice but to sit and listen.

Arlene asked Dick about his own personal experience and his story was almost more than I could comprehend:

Dick had been very much like me, so wrapped up in his business that he was unaware his home was falling to pieces. Then his little boy, David, was involved in a serious bicycle accident that left him in critical condition, with a blood clot on his brain. A neurosurgeon was called in to examine him and stand by for possible emergency surgery. Following X rays, David went into convulsions and then lapsed into a coma.

"I know you won't understand this," Dick's wife, Virginia, said, "but I've called some of my friends and we're praying. We have turned David over to the Lord."

Dick said he didn't know what she was talking about. Then he remembered that many years before, Virginia had confessed that she had been on the verge of suicide, but she attended the healing services at the Episcopal church and had been spiritually delivered.

Minutes after Virginia's prayer statement the doctor reappeared in the lobby to say that although David had regained consciousness, surgery might still be necessary. However, David's improvement was marked and steady. Within forty-eight hours the crisis was over. He had been healed.

From that time on, Dick Cross was a believer. His faith in God had grown rapidly as he had seen many other persons healed through the same power of prayer.

Had I not personally invited Dick to our house I would have believed this entire conversation had been set up just for my benefit.

Sitting there, listening to Dick and Arlene talk, I began to realize that one of my problems across the years was that I had always been afflicted with logic—I wanted to figure things out scientifically. Dick, on the other hand, operated on a different plateau—the plateau of faith. He just accepted things on faith, as recorded in the scriptures. Something had happened to Dick Cross. He had been like me, but now he was free. He loved people. In fact, he loved people he had never even met before—like us.

While the animated conversation between Dick and Arlene continued, my mind was working in other areas. I was trying to figure out, logically of course, what my options were. I had reached my limit. Either I had to admit there was nothing that could be done and resign myself to Arlene's dying, or to put my trust in the doctors, or admit there was a God who was concerned. I couldn't accept the first, the second had proved to be insufficient, which left me with the third option. What was I to do with it?

Dick Cross was different from most people I knew. He hadn't even mentioned what church he attended. He wasn't trying to get us to join an organization. He just talked about Jesus and the power of the Holy Spirit. By the time he left, I had determined to begin an honest search for the power of God.

I began the next night, after dinner, by reading the Bible. The only Bible I had ever read before was the King James Version. But someone had given Arlene a Living Bible. Long after she had gone on to bed, I was still poring through its pages, trying to check out the things I had heard Dick Cross mention.

In the beginning I was thinking only of Arlene's healing. But the more I read the Bible I realized that it also contained the answer to my own personal needs—the needs I had never discussed with anyone.

Dick and Virginia started coming by the house on regular occasions. Although he was a brand-new Christian, he tried his best to answer all my questions. Finally, he suggested that we go with them to a teaching session to be held at the Central Assembly of God Church.

I backed off. The scenes in that church were still vivid in my memory from childhood; but Arlene wanted to go and I finally agreed. However, I told her that if she passed out on the floor like I had seen others do in that church, I was just going to leave her there. Pride was still on the throne of my life.

The Assembly of God Church was much different than I had expected. The teacher that night made sense. On a blackboard he drew a small circle. He said that represented the life of a Christian. All around us, he said, was the power of Satan. As we grow in Christ our circle enlarges, pushing back the powers of darkness, extending our perimeter and allowing us to conquer the ground Satan has held for such a long time. This ground, he said, contained many wonderful things such as personal communication with God, health for the physical body and cleansing for the soul.

I had always thought that it was our task to sit inside our little circle and "hold the fort." Now I saw that it is Satan who is on the defensive and it is our privilege to go out and possess the land. *Logically,* this made sense. Even the gates of hell could not prevail against the growing, expanding power of that circle.

At the close of the service the minister gave an altar call. Before I knew it, Arlene and Virginia were already on their way to the front. Virginia was supporting Arlene to keep her from falling. I began to feel uncomfortable. Instead of the minister praying for Arlene to be healed, however, he put his hands on her head and prayed that she be filled with the Holy Spirit. I made my way toward the front, but Arlene seemed to be in another world. Virginia was holding her up (I wondered if Arlene had told her what I had said about leaving her on the floor) and out of Arlene's mouth flowed a strange and melodious language. My logic took over again and I refused to accept what I was hearing. I waited, and then helped Arlene back to her seat. Pride kept me from asking her about the experience. God still had some breaking to do before I would be able to hear Him for myself.

Dick and Virginia began bringing us "charismatic" books, that is, they had to do with healing, the baptism in the Holy Spirit, the gifts of the spirit and salvation. One of them was Kathryn Kuhlman's book, *I Believe in Miracles,* which Arlene did not have the heart to admit she had read years before. Because of her poor vision, I now had to read aloud to her. God had a beautiful way of cracking my hard shell.

One night, after Arlene had gone to bed, I was sitting in the den reading the Living Bible. It was the first part of July, about a month after Dick's first visit in our home. The air conditioner was not working that night and the house was hot—as only it can be in Arkansas. But I wasn't aware of the heat, only of the desperation in my heart. Finally I stopped reading and put the book in my lap. "Lord," I said out loud, "I need some help." It was that simple, but it was the first time I had ever prayed for help. Yet from that point on, things began to change.

Two attacks almost put Arlene out of commission for good. The first was a heart block which almost killed her; then a coronary insufficiency put her back in the hospital for the second time in less than a month. And yet, things had already begun to change.

I was visiting Arlene in the hospital on a Sunday afternoon in the middle of August. Dick and Virginia arrived, bringing with them a friend, Leeanne Payne, who had taught literature at Wheaton College, Wheaton, Illinois, and was now working on another graduate degree. I didn't know it at the time, but they had come to lay hands on Arlene and pray for her. Uncertain how I would react to a prayer session in the hospital room, Dick wisely invited me downstairs for a cup of coffee while the women remained with Arlene, "chatting."

We found a table in the coffee shop and almost immediately Dick told me he had just been "baptized in the Holy Spirit." He said it had happened in a dream and then again the next day while he was awake. Ever since, he said, his life had been running over with joy.

I didn't really understand what he was saying. All I could think about was Arlene up there in her hospital room on the fifth floor and the fact that visiting hours would soon be over.

We took the elevator back up. Arlene's door was closed. I paused momentarily before entering. There was a strange quietness. The usual sounds of the hospital, the soft tones of the girls' voices at the nurses' station, the squeak of rubber shoes on the tile floor, the clanking of medicine carts, the loudspeaker's paging doctors and nurses, the sounds of radios and televisions in the other rooms—all were sucked up into a great vacuum of silence. I knew that God was behind that closed door.

I pushed it open. Arlene, dressed in a white hospital gown, was lying on the bed. The heart monitor, with its ominous wires, was attached to her body. Virginia was standing on the left side of the bed, Leeanne on the right. They had laid their hands on Arlene's body and all three of them were praying softly in a language I did not understand.

Instantly, every hair on my body stood straight out. I glanced at my arms and the hairs were like the quills of a porcupine. Fortunately I wore a short hair cut because I felt the hair on my head was standing straight out, too. It was as if I had stepped on a high voltage line, only there was no shock, no pain—just a tremendous current of power surging through my body.

The two women finished praying and I walked them down to the car to meet Dick. I was still much aware of that tingling surge of power inside of me, even after I got home.

My first thought was that I had picked up some kind of strange disease from the hospital. I searched every medical dictionary I could find, hoping to discover what was causing this tingling, hair-standing-up experience. I found nothing. By Wednesday I didn't care, for I realized that during these last days I had been happier than I had ever been in all my life. That night, sitting again in my den reading the Bible, I laid the book aside and spoke out loud, "Lord, is this You trying to tell me something? If it is, you are going to have to make it so I can understand it."

Dick had told me about people who "put God to a test." This was a new experience for me, but I needed to know. "Lord," I said, "You know I had these sores on the back of my neck for two years. If this is You trying to tell me something, would You please heal them?"

I went on to bed and when I awoke the next morning, the first thing I did was to put my hand on the back of my neck. The sores were gone—healed. For the first time in my life, I knew, really knew, that God was real—and that

He cared about me. As I stood in front of the mirror shaving, it also occurred to me that if God could heal sores on the back of my neck, He could also heal my wife. As the full realization dawned on me I almost cut my chin off.

That afternoon, though, as I pulled into the parking lot at the hospital, all the hair on my body returned to its normal position. The tingling feeling was gone too. I was terrified, fearing I had done something to displease God, but the moment I parked the car I had a new sensation, even more pronounced than the first one. It was like a bucket of warm air being dumped on me. There was no lightning, no thunder, and I didn't hear anything with my ears. Yet deep within, in a place where only the Spirit hears, a voice spoke saying, "Arlene is going to be all right."

It was then I knew. There was not a moment of doubt. I *knew* as certainly as if an angel had appeared and sat on the hood of my car, that she was going to be healed.

Although Arlene had been the strong one up to this point, when I arrived in her room I found her in the worst state of depression I had ever seen. The doctor had given his final report. Her abnormal EKG pattern and a coronary insufficiency, were not caused by the multiple sclerosis. They re-opened the strong possibility that she also had myasthenia gravis as well. She was weaker, her vision was worse, and it was impossible for her to stand alone. Yet in the midst of all this, I had a faith that just wouldn't quit. I knew she was going to be healed.

She returned home from the hospital totally bedridden, the sickest she had ever been; her bathroom privileges were limited. Even her friends who were once so optimistic, now seemed depressed. She grew steadily worse.

A month later the phone rang at my office. It was Arlene. "Gil, Kathryn Kuhlman is going to be in St. Louis next Tuesday, I want to go."

Logic took over real quick and I began to list the reasons why it was impossible for her to go to St. Louis. It was 400 miles away. There was no big city between Little Rock and St. Louis in case she needed a hospital. She needed to be close to her specialists here in Little Rock. Suppose we had car trouble and had to stop alongside the road? . . .

When I finished, all I heard on the other end was Arlene's soft sobbing. "Please, Gil, it's my life."

I felt myself slipping back into my shell. Rather than lose my temper I simply said, "We'll talk about it when I get home."

That night, with Arlene in bed and me sitting in a chair beside her, she told me that earlier in the week, Edna Williamson had dropped by. Seeing Arlene's copy of *I Believe in Miracles* Edna said, "You know, I have another of Kathryn Kuhlman's books, *God Can Do It Again*. I'd like to swap with you."

Ashamed to tell her that she could no longer read, Arlene allowed the exchange to be made. The next morning Edna was back. She and Arlene began talking about miracles, and why they didn't occur around Little Rock. Arlene said she thought it helped to have a climate of faith surrounding you. Even Jesus could not perform miracles in his home town because people said, "No, no." Arlene then added that she believed if she could ever get into a service where the people were of one spirit—waiting, expecting, and believing, that God would touch her and heal her.

Then this morning, Virginia Cross walked in and dropped the bombshell. "Kathryn Kuhlman is going to hold a Miracle Service in St. Louis next Tuesday."

Arlene had never been to such a meeting so it never occurred to her how difficult it would be to get in. Even so, she was determined to go. "I just believe that God is telling me to go to St. Louis," she concluded.

"Maybe God has told you to go," I said smartly, "but He hasn't told me to take you."

No sooner had I uttered the words than every hair on my body stood straight up again. I tried to talk but my tongue refused to move. Finally, mouth open, eyes wide, I cleared my throat and in a voice that sounded like it was coming from the far side of the house, said "Okay, we'll go."

Arlene's face was a mixture of joy and amazement. "Oh,

Gil . . ." But I was on my feet, literally staggering out of the room.

I knew better than to argue any more. I was in the presence of *The Lord!* We left the next Monday night after I got home from work, with Arlene stretched out on the back seat of the car. We spent the night at Poplar Bluff, Missouri, and arrived in St. Louis about noon on Tuesday. I knew absolutely nothing about the city so we just traveled the highway right into the center of town. Turning off on the Market Street exit we were suddenly in front of the auditorium. The meeting wasn't supposed to start until 7:00 P.M. but already a large crowd was waiting in front of the closed doors.

I began to fear we had bitten off more than we could chew. But God had gone before us. The Holiday Inn on Market Street gave us their last room. Minutes later, Arlene was resting comfortably and the motel manager had promised to drive us to the auditorium at 4:30 P.M. It was a steaming hot day in St. Louis with the temperature about ninety degrees. I had brought a couple of camp stools but they did little good. Arlene had been in bed since her first heart block in July, and this was September 19. Lately, she hadn't even gotten out of bed to eat her meals but here she was, 400 miles from home, sitting on a camp stool on the sidewalk in the broiling sun. I was afraid she wouldn't make it into the building.

The people, waiting with us, sensed Arlene's condition. Unlike those who shove and curse in front of a football stadium, they took turns fanning Arlene and bringing her iced drinks. The side door where the wheelchairs were lined up opened at 6:00 P.M. I went up to the fellow who was manning the door and begged him to let Arlene in, too. He shook his head. "Sorry, friend, I have strict orders. Only those in wheelchairs go in now." He closed the door, firmly. The old despair and frustration began to well up inside me. Arlene's condition surely warranted a wheelchair, but her fear of becoming too dependent upon one prevented me from getting it. I wanted to run. I couldn't stand the sight of all those suffering people. They were like the sick who must have crowded around the pool of Bethesda. Yet, sick as they were, they were filled with joy and singing and helping one another. I returned to Arlene determined to stick it out with her.

Ten minutes later the front doors opened and we were swept by the moving crowd into the huge auditorium. I had never seen anything like it. Moments later we were seated in the exact center of the immense auditorium. A huge choir was already on the stage, practicing, and the very seats seemed alive with power and expectation. Suddenly the entire congregation was on its feet, singing. Miss Kuhlman, in a soft white dress with full sleeves, was standing center stage. "The Holy Spirit is here," she whispered, so softly I had to strain to hear. As we waited, it happened again—that silence I had experienced in the corridor outside Arlene's hospital room, settled over the huge auditorium. In that mass of people there must have been coughing, scraping of feet, rattling of paper—but I heard none of it. I was enveloped in a soft blanket of silence.

Miss Kuhlman was standing in the middle of the stage, her left hand raised, her finger pointing toward Heaven. Her right hand rested gently on an old, battered Bible on the lectern. And there was silence, like there will surely be in Heaven following the opening of the seventh seal on the Great Book.

Miss Kuhlman was not at all as I had expected her to be. She was warm and friendly, informal. She welcomed people and made them feel at home. Then she turned to the wings and made a sweeping motion as she introduced her concert pianist, Dino.

"Do you know who he is?" Arlene whispered as the handsome, dark-haired young man took his seat at the piano. "Longing to hear some good piano music, I once phoned the Baptist Book Store and they sent me some of Dino's records. All this time I have been listening to his music and didn't even know he was associated with Kathryn Kuhlman."

Miss Kuhlman began to preach, but it was unlike any preaching I had ever heard before. She was talking about

the Holy Spirit as if He were a real person. As I listened I
began to understand that she had not only met Him, she
walked with Him day by day. No wonder He was so real to
her—she knew Him better than she knew any other man in
the world.

Suddenly she stopped, her head cocked as if she were listening. Was she listening to *Him?* I strained to see if I
could hear Him also. Then she raised her arm and pointed
high into the left balcony.

"There is someone up there, right in this section, who
has just been healed of cancer of the liver."

I twisted in my seat and tried to look up in the balcony.
Had the Holy Spirit actually told her that? Does He speak
to people so they can know things like that?

The information of sickness and healing came so fast it
made my head swim. People began streaming down the
aisles, heading for the platform to testify of their healings.
When the first man came to the lectern, Miss Kuhlman
acted like it was the first miracle she had ever seen in her
life. Surely, I thought, this woman has seen hundreds of
thousands of healings, yet she is as excited as if it were the
first time. Is this the secret of her ministry—that she has
never lost the wonder?

Miss Kuhlman talked with the man for a moment and
then reached out to pray for him. "Holy Father . . ." she
began, and the man crumpled to the floor. The same thing
happened to the next person who came forward. And the
next, and the next. I tried to figure it out logically, but it
defied calculation. It was as if God were saying to me,
*There are some things you cannot comprehend, and the
power of My Holy Spirit is one of them.*

As the service progressed, something was happening inside me. I was growing soft. Like a hard, crusty sponge
held under water, I felt myself growing tender and gentle.
My eyes were filling with tears and I began to pray for
other people—complete strangers—in the service. As I
prayed I felt love flowing out. It was a new and magnificent experience.

My prayers shifted to Arlene, who was sitting beside me.

I prayed, asking God to heal her. In all these years of marriage, it was the first time that I had been willing to pray for my wife. I had believed she would be healed; I knew God had been leading us. But never had my heart softened enough to reach out in love and ask the Lord to touch—and heal—her.

Almost instantaneously Arlene leaned toward me. "Do you feel a draft?"

"I feel a breeze," she whispered, "a soft caressing breeze all over my body."

I looked around, but there was no place the breeze could come from. I dismissed it and focused my attention back on the stage when I saw a woman about five seats down from us leaning over several persons trying to talk to Arlene.

"Is the Lord dealing with you?" she said, loud enough that the entire row could hear.

A little embarrassed, Arlene whispered back, "I don't know."

The woman—a complete stranger to us—asked, "What is wrong with you?"

"Tell her I have multiple sclerosis and a heart problem," Arlene whispered to the lady next to her.

The lady was not satisfied. She kept passing messages down the row. "Ask her how she felt when she came in."

"I barely made it," Arlene whispered back.

"Ask her how she feels now," the little woman almost shouted.

I was becoming annoyed with this rude interruption and turned to ask Arlene to be quiet. She was staring at her hands. "The tremors," she whispered with a shaky voice. "They're gone. The swelling is gone. I can see. My eyes are normal."

The little lady was half-standing now, leaning over the others with a great excitement on her face. "You must go forward," she shouted, "and accept your healing."

The next moment Arlene was on her feet, clambering over me, stepping on people's feet, making her way out of the row into the aisle. I could hardly breathe. I, too, knew she had been healed.

I followed her with my eyes as she headed down the aisle toward the front. An usher stopped her momentarily, then motioned her forward. She climbed the steps to the stage like a normal woman. Gone were the spastic movements, gone were the spasms, gone was the staggering. Like the man at the pool of Bethesda, she had waited for an angel to stir the waters so she could get in, only to find she didn't need the pool—all she needed was Jesus. She had been made whole by the touch of His hand.

The stage was crowded with people and the service was coming to a close. It was impossible for Arlene to get to the lectern to testify. It made no difference. As the mighty choir began to sing, Arlene stood on the far side of the stage, leaning against the piano, her face uplifted and her voice blending with the choir as she sang the words to an old hymn.

> Though Satan should buffet, tho' trials should come,
> Let this blest assurance control,
> That Christ has regarded my helpless estate
> And hath shed His own blood for my soul.

The service was over, Miss Kuhlman was walking off the stage, but as she passed Arlene, she turned slightly and reached out in a gesture of prayer. Instantly Arlene collapsed on the floor. Only this time I knew it was not multiple sclerosis, but the power of God.

The auditorium was engulfed in song as the thousands of people began raising their hands and singing over and over, *Alleluia! Alleluia!* I had never seen people raise their hands like this, but before I knew it, my hands were up also, doing the same thing they were doing, praising the Lord.

Arlene finally made her way back to her seat. No one seemed to want to leave. The few times I had been to church there was always a mad dash for the door the minute the preacher said "Amen." But these folks didn't want to leave. They wanted to stay, hug each other and sing.

Perfect strangers came up, put their arms around me and embraced me. Everybody was saying "Praise the Lord" and "hallelujah"!

It was seven and a half blocks back to the motel, and the manager had promised to come for us if we called. Arlene just grinned. "Let's walk," she said. And we did.

Back in the room I reminded her that it was time for the anti-convulsant medicine. Without it she could go into terminal convulsions before the night was over.

"I believe God has really healed me," she said, holding the little bottles in her hand, "and I don't need this medicine."

"That's between you and the Lord, honey," I said. She didn't take the medicine—and she hasn't taken any since.

A week later Arlene literally bounced into her neurologist's office. The week before she had to be almost carried in. He took one look and exclaimed, "Something has happened to you! What was it?"

"I've been healed, doctor," she said. "I went to a Miracle Service in St. Louis. I knew you would have forbidden it, so I went to a higher authority and asked Him."

The doctor nearly bit the end off his pipe, but he had to agree that something wonderful had happened. He checked Arlene's reflexes, her eyes, even had her jump around to check her coordination. He finally returned to his charts shaking his head.

"In my 25 years of medical practice I have seen only three cases which defied medical explanation. I know there are remissions in multiple sclerosis, but this is more. It has to be of God."

They laughed together, joyously. "I don't know what you did or what you are doing," he added, "but whatever it is, just go on doing the same thing. And be sure to say a prayer of thanksgiving every night."

It would seem that Arlene's healing should have been the climax of our lives. But instead, it has been only the beginning; three months later I moved into the full dimension of the Holy Spirit. I attended a small home prayer meeting and the teaching that night came from the Gospel story of

Peter, who at Jesus' command, walked on the water. The teacher said, "We all have two choices. We either stay in our safe boat or we jump over the side and come to Jesus. If you've not done that, now is the time to *jump*."

And *jump* I did. Literally! I leaped from my seat, landing with both feet in the center of the room. "I want it," I said. "I want it now." I was serious.

Somebody pulled a chair into the center of the circle. I sat while the people gathered around and laid hands on me. A soft-spoken, white-haired Baptist pastor began to pray, and in moments my life turned right side up. Unlike those first experiences when the Holy Spirit came *upon* me, causing my hair to stand on end, this time He came *into* me—and the change has been permanent.

The other evening, as our family sat around the dinner table, we went through our customary time of worship. Each of us read a Bible verse, we held hands, and then each in turn, prayed individually. As we finished I looked up to see Arlene with tears on her face.

"A long time ago, Gil," she said softly as the girls listened, "I told you that to me Heaven would be having a Christian family, with the father as the priest in the home. Even if I had not been healed, just to be part of this wonderful family would have made it all worthwhile. Heaven has literally come down."

Arlene's right. Heaven has come down. Each gathering of our family turns into a worship service. Arlene and I are taking turns teaching a Bible class in our Methodist Church, and more and more people are coming. I guess they're just like we were, eager to hear about the power of the Holy Spirit who heals not only sick bodies, but sick husbands as well.

SIX

Speak to the Mountain

LINDA FORRESTER

Linda and John (Woody) Forrester live in Milpitas, California, a residential community on the southeast side of San Francisco Bay at the base of Monument Peak. Woody is a computer programmer for the near-by city of San José. They have two daughters, Teresa and Nanci.

The mountain has always been there. It stands like a solitary monument rising half a mile up out of the San Francisco Bay basin. In the winter it is sometimes snowcapped; in the summer it is partly covered with brown grass. Less than ten miles from our house on the flatlands, it is often obscured by smog or clouds. But it is always there, looming over us.

The natives in the South Bay area seem to take the mountain for granted. Rain erodes it. The sun blisters its bare sides. A few hardy souls climb to its peak. But by and large it is just there, and will always be. Nothing can remove it. It is like disease. Since Adam's sin, disease has been with us. Man has learned to live with it. Some try to hide it in the clouds, pretending it isn't there, teaching there is no disease. Others ignore it, hoping it won't come to their house. Many have tried to conquer it through medicine and research. Nearly all accept it, though, as they accept the mountain that dominates the landscape of life and defies those who would try to cast it into the midst of the sea.

I was one of those who was afraid of disease and tried to

ignore it. People in our family didn't ordinarily get sick. If they did, we always found a shot or a pill that made it go away. Until Nanci became ill. This time, things were different.

Nanci, our fifteen-month-old baby, had been an active child ever since she started walking. In fact, she never walked—she ran. Recently, however, she had begun to act strangely. She had been doing a lot of falling, and each fall resulted in an ugly bruise. The bruises remained until she was covered with them, and looked as if she had been badly beaten.

Then one Monday morning in January, 1970, Nanci woke with a burning fever. I started her on baby aspirin, but by the second day her fever had climbed to 105 degrees and remained there. I called Woody at his office in San José, and he told me to take her to the emergency clinic at Kaiser Hospital in Santa Clara. This was the hospital where Nanci had been born, and we knew several of the doctors and nurses.

A young doctor examined her in the emergency room. He found infection in her ears and throat, prescribed medication, and sent us home. Two days later, her condition unchanged, I took her back to the hospital. Always before, we had been able to overcome illness with medication. This time it seemed to loom over us, insurmountable.

During the week I noticed something else. Nanci had developed a tiny, bright-red blood blister in her groin. The first day it was only the size of a pinhead. Now it had grown to the size of my little fingernail. The doctor looked at it, said it was probably a boil that would eventually come to a head, gave us more medication, and sent us home again.

By Saturday morning, I was near the panic stage. In spite of all the medicine, Nanci was sicker than ever. "We've got to take her back to the hospital," Woody said.

Teresa sat in the back seat and I held Nanci in my arms as we drove toward Santa Clara. Always before, she had been wiggly, squirmy. This morning she lay in my arms unmoving, too weak even to whimper. Her body was burning with fever.

Dr. Feldman examined her briefly with a concerned look. "This medication should have knocked out the fever. I don't like the looks of that sore on her groin, either. Take her upstairs, get a blood count, then come back down and wait here."

Following the lab tests, Dr. Feldman reappeared. I could tell by his face that he was worried. "Nanci has severe anemia," he said. "I want you to put her in the hospital."

I was relieved. I had been afraid they would just give her some more pills and syrup and send us away. Anemia didn't sound too bad, and I was glad they were going to keep her in the hospital. The responsibility of caring for a very sick child by myself was too frightening.

The attending physician on the pediatric floor was Nanci's own doctor who had been with us since she was born, Dr. Cathleen O'Brien. "Nanci is going to get a complete physical this afternoon," she said. "I don't want you here. You can come back tonight about six o'clock and see her then."

We left Teresa with a neighbor and returned to the hospital about dusk. I was shocked when I walked into Nanci's room. She was lying on her back in her crib with tubes running into both arms. Her eyes were closed.

Dr. O'Brien appeared at the door. "Linda, I'd like to see you and Woody in my office. We have some results from the tests."

I felt my heart pounding in my throat as we followed her down the tiled hall. Dr. O'Brien motioned us to seats in her tiny office. My fear almost screamed out as I looked up and saw the tears in her eyes.

"This afternoon while you were gone, Nanci had a bloody nose and then two pure blood bowel movements. We have not pinpointed the problem, but it is one of two things: either a widely diffused cancer tumor that is untreatable—or she has leukemia."

I heard Woody suck his breath in through his teeth. I grabbed his hand and felt him begin to shake. "Oh no," he stammered. "Oh please, no." I wanted to cry, but Woody had already broken down. I knew that one of us had to maintain some kind of strength. I looked up at Dr. O'Brien.

"All the signs point to leukemia," she said. "We're going to do a bone marrow test in just a few minutes, but you can go in and see her first if you wish."

I turned to Woody. "Please call Pastor Langhoff. Ask him if he can come." Odd, how people go along as we had gone along, living our lives as if God didn't exist. Then, face to face with death, we reach out for spiritual help.

I had been raised a Roman Catholic. When I met Woody, after my divorce, we agreed to make a compromise between his evangelical faith and my Catholic faith and join a Lutheran church in Milpitas. We seldom attended services. We knew almost nothing about God. We never read the Bible or prayed. But with death staring us in the face, we called for the only person we knew who was supposed to know God—Pastor Langhoff of the Reformation Lutheran Church.

Pastor Langhoff, an elderly man, had been sick himself. In fact, he got up out of bed to join us at the hospital that evening. He ministered to us as a father would minister to his children, staying with us when the nurse came to take Nanci down the hall for the bone marrow test.

I knew what they were going to do. I had seen the long needle they would insert in her hip socket to suck out some bone marrow. I stood in the room and shuddered as I heard her terrifying screams.

Woody and the Pastor had stepped out in the hall to talk. I was alone in the room when I became aware of a spiritual Presence for the first time in my life, a sense that the Son of God was there. I had never met Jesus Christ. I only knew about Him, and not much at that. But for one moment Jesus Christ was in the room with me.

Half an hour later Dr. O'Brien reappeared. "I'm sorry," she said. "It is definitely leukemia."

I broke down crying, but when I noticed Woody's agony, I grabbed hold of myself again and hung on. I had no one else to cling to. Dr. O'Brien said we could stay as long as we wanted, but I had a horrible feeling that Nanci was going to die that night, and I didn't want to be there when it happened. I wanted to run. But where do you run when the mountain is all around you?

We left the hospital and drove home. The moon was just coming up over Monument Peak, which towers over our house to the east. Nanci's sickness was like that solid mountain. You could shout at it, kick it, dig at it, blast it with dynamite. But there it stood, immovable.

Our neighbor called as soon as we got in. "How's Nanci?" she bubbled cheerfully. "I hope she's all right."

"No!" I screamed into the telephone. "She has leukemia."

There was a long pause on the other end, then a soft voice. "Do you want us to come over?"

"No," I said, getting back in control. "We need to be by ourselves. If you can keep Teresa tonight, we'll see you in the morning."

We spent the night at home, together but alone. We wanted to reach out to each other, but with all the perfunctories stripped away, we discovered that we didn't even know each other. We were two lonely mortals faced with an impossible situation, slowly going down the drain.

I walked through the semidark house, going from room to room, weeping. For long moments I stood in the doorway of Teresa's room, looking at her white poster-bed set against the lavender walls. Was God punishing me because I had been divorced? Teresa was a child of my first marriage. Was God going to take Nanci to punish me? "Why, God? Why?" I wept. "Why have You done this to my little baby? She's so helpless. So defenseless. Why are You so cruel to torture us this way?"

I turned and stepped into Nanci's room. The moon reflected off the top of the mountain into the bright yellow room, now so still, so desolate. The bed was still unmade from that morning. I reached down and picked up a little rubber duck from the floor. I squeezed it, and it whistled. In my mind I could remember the hundreds of times Nanci had squeezed it in the bathtub, giggling as the whistle gurgled and bubbled under the water. I gently placed the rubber duck on the dresser and reached out to the furry pink pig. I touched the little wind-up key in his side, and the music box slowly pinged out a few plaintive notes: "When the bough breaks, the cradle will fall . . . down . . . will . . . come . . . baby . . ."

I screamed out at the walls and staggered into the kitchen. Woody was sitting at the table, staring into the darkness. It was almost three in the morning, and sleep was impossible.

"We've got to have a plan of action," Woody said, his words mechanical and hollow. "We've got to be positive. We can't let our mental attitude affect Nanci. Even if we're coming apart on the inside, we've got to put up a smiling front for her."

How empty, I thought. How phony. Yet we had nothing else. We agreed that this would be our course of action.

The next morning, Sunday, we returned to the hospital. "She's awfully sick," Dr. O'Brien admitted. "But she is small, and that is in her favor. We should be able to get the disease into remission in a short while. Even so, you must not get your hopes up."

"How long?" I asked. The question sounded like a melodramatic line from a Class-B movie.

"If we can get her into immediate remission, she could last as long as two years," Dr. O'Brien said hopefully. "However, children like this usually last about a year in remission and then go downhill very rapidly."

We went in to see Nanci. They were giving her a blood transfusion. A hematologist was on his way down from Stanford to help with the final diagnosis. They told us what to expect. More bone marrow tests, many more blood transfusions.

"How do they die when they die?" I stammered. Even as I asked the question, I realized that I had already turned Nanci into an object in my mind, an impersonal third person who was getting ready to disappear forever.

Dr. O'Brien was very kind. "Usually, when a small child

dies from leukemia, it is from a stroke. There could be some suffering, but she will probably go quickly."

Woody and I had been attending encounter sessions in our community. Our marriage had been rocky, and we had reached out to this particular level of humanism to try to find help. One of the couples in the encounter session heard about Nanci and called. Their little girl had just died from leukemia, and they wanted to come over and share their experiences.

It was horrible, yet we kept saying we needed to know so we could be prepared when death came. They told us all the details: how their child had become bloated from the drugs, how she had lost her hair, how she had suffered extreme agony and finally died. They told us what to expect in our relations with each other and other members of the family. Nothing was ever said that could project hope.

The doctors had slowly controlled Nanci's raging leukemia. By the second week it was in a state of temporary remission, where the drugs would hold it in check until it unleashed its fury in a final, fatal attack. But the blood blister, which they now described as a blood ulcer, had grown until it covered one entire side of Nanci's groin. The doctors said it was a "secondary effect" of the leukemia and contained a germ that could kill her. Ironically, the only medication that could heal it was fatal to most of those who had leukemia.

One night after Teresa had gone to bed, Woody and I sat at the kitchen table. We had cried ourselves out, and finally I said, "Woody, let's try God."

"You mean you want to take her to a faith healer?" he asked disapprovingly.

"Definitely not," I bristled. "Those people are a bunch of charlatans."

Woody was perplexed. "I thought you said you wanted to try God."

"I mean prayer," I said.

"But I don't know how to pray."

"Neither do I," I said. "But we've got to do something."

He nodded. I reached out and took his hand and stumbled through a few words. "God, please let them find something to treat her with."

It was such a faltering beginning—like tossing pebbles at the mountain, hoping it would get up and run away. But it was a beginning, and the next morning when we got to the hospital, Dr. O'Brien was smiling for the first time.

"Good news," she said. "Stanford has come up with a drug to treat the ulcer. It's a minor miracle."

The surgeon at Kaiser opened the blister, and there followed weeks of painful treatment. However, Nanci was improving.

This first encounter with prayer convinced me that there was more power available than I had realized. I began praying every day before I went to see Nanci.

Then something else happened. A neighbor was a fellow room mother in the PTA. One afternoon, after we finished talking about PTA matters, she said, "You know, Linda, God loves you, and He loves Nanci."

That hit me. No one had ever said that about me or Nanci. It was a wonderful new concept. God loved me, as an individual. And God loved Nanci.

"The Bible is full of stories of Jesus healing people," she went on to say. "The church I belong to doesn't necessarily believe that Jesus still heals, but I do. I believe that if God loves you, He is able to heal you, too." Her words were like a candle in a dark room. I groped my way toward it.

Several years before, when I was going through my divorce, I had ordered a Bible from Sears Roebuck. At the time I thought it would be lucky to have a Bible around the house. Now I began to understand that the Bible was far more than a good-luck charm. I went to the drawer in my bedroom, found it, and promised myself that I would read a chapter a day, starting with the book of Luke.

Almost immediately a verse leaped up out of the past and into my conscious mind. I didn't know where it was found, or even if it was in the Bible. But over and over, day after day, it kept ringing in my mind: "Him that cometh to me, I will in no wise cast out."

I increased my prayer time. I visited Nanci at the hospital each morning and then, after lunch, read my chapter and prayed before Teresa got home from school. It became a meaningful spot in my day.

One afternoon my neighbor asked me if I had ever heard of Kathryn Kuhlman. "She believes in miracles," she said.

I looked at her. "Don't tell me you believe in faith healers?" I said sarcastically.

She smiled gently. "Before you pass judgment, why don't you tune in her broadcast over KFAX?"

I trusted her, and the next day got home from the hospital in time to hear the eleven o'clock broadcast. I liked what I heard. Miss Kuhlman was talking about an experience called the "new birth." Although I had no idea what she was talking about, somehow it all rang true. I especially liked her positive, happy nature. Many of my friends were negative. One pastor we had talked to in the hospital even suggested that "death is the finest healing of all." I needed to hear a positive voice, one that would point me to light rather than darkness.

One day, after listening to the half-hour broadcast, I opened my Bible to read my chapter in Luke. It just happened to be the account of the Crucifixion of Jesus Christ. As I read, the startling realization of truth came flooding in on me. *Jesus Christ died for me.* It was *my* sins that put Him on the cross. He died because He loved *me.* I began to weep and sob. "Oh God, I'm sorry You had to die for me."

Yet even as I said it, I felt the most joyful lightness fill my inner being. It was the heady sensation of good wine, but it was in my spirit, not in my stomach. Suddenly I knew what it was. I had been born again. I was sitting on the green sofa in the living room, shouting and laughing and crying all at the same time. "Thank You, God, for saving me. I love You! I've known for years You died for my sins. Now I know You died for *me.*"

In that moment I came alive. I was a new creature. Everything about me changed. At the same time, Nanci's healing became more than a tiny candle flickering in a dark room—it became a huge ball of light, like the sun itself, flooding my being. It *was* possible. God could heal her.

In the days ahead I read on through the book of Luke and into John. At noon one day, after listening to Miss Kuhlman and praying, I picked up the Bible and read from the sixth chapter of John. There it was—that verse: "Him that cometh to me I will in no wise cast out."

Along with it came another revelation, so startling I was sure no one had ever understood it before. In no place in the New Testament was there an account of anyone who came to Jesus for healing and was turned down. He healed them all!

It seemed so impossible. Everyone—the medical experts, my friends who had lost their child—said Nanci was going to die. There was no hope. Yet inside me there was a faith springing forth from the parched desert of my life. It was as tiny as a grain of mustard seed, but it was there. I knew it was just as impossible for me to believe in Nanci's healing as it was for me to speak to the mountain and command it to jump into San Francisco Bay. Yet, didn't the Bible say that all things were possible with God? I clung to that.

I made a decision to trust Him, even if I didn't understand it and it didn't make sense. God would have to give her new blood, new marrow for her bones. But I decided to trust in His word, regardless of what anyone might say.

"Father," I prayed, "You have promised that him who comes to You, You will in no wise cast out. I'm coming to You with this need. I believe You will be true to Your word." It was just that simple. Now all I had to do was wait.

After five weeks the doctors allowed us to take Nanci home. "She's not well," they warned us. "And she's not going to get well. If you're super-lucky, she could live another year and a half. But after that the leukemia will overpower the drugs."

Nanci's first days out of the hospital were grim. Two days after we brought her home she developed bleeding ulcers on her lips. These quickly spread to the inside of her mouth, gums, and down her throat. The doctors diagnosed it as scarlet fever, complicated by the drugs we were giving her, which could cause similar symptoms. The hand-size ulcer in Nanci's groin was draining, but it had to be cleaned three times a day with hydrogen peroxide. Following the cleaning we had to tie her on her back in the playpen, spread-eagled, and hold a light bulb over the open ulcer to dry it out.

A visiting nurse came twice a week to help, and things gradually became a little better. After six weeks Nanci was able to move around a little by herself, but she was still a sick little girl.

It was hard on Woody. He couldn't help but notice the big change in me, and he didn't understand it. "Honey, you've got to watch it," he warned. "You can't afford to get all psyched up like this. When Nanci dies it's really going to tear you up."

"You don't understand," I told him. "For the first time I can accept her death—if it happens. I know that God is with me, and with her. Even more, though, I believe God is going to heal her."

"I wish I could believe that," Woody said, his eyes filling with tears. "I wish I could."

One afternoon my neighbor phoned to tell me that Miss Kuhlman was coming to Los Angeles for a Miracle Service. She gave me a phone number to call for information.

The woman in charge of making reservations told us the special round-trip plane to Los Angeles would cost seventy dollars. We didn't have the money then, but she said she would put our name on the list for June, the following month, in case we could make it.

Janet, a teen-age neighbor, had been Nanci's baby-sitter since she was a tiny infant. A group of teenagers, called Young Life, met at Janet's home on Tuesday nights. When they learned we were going to take Nanci to the Kathryn Kuhlman service, they wanted to back us in prayer.

The next Tuesday night I took Nanci down to Janet's, where more than 100 kids had gathered for the Bible study. They agreed that on the Sunday we were to go to Los Angeles, they would meet at Janet's house to fast and pray. They, too, believed God was going to heal her.

The week before we were to leave, I drove up to Fre-
mont to a Bible bookstore. A friend had mentioned several
books she wanted me to read, including two books by
Kathryn Kuhlman: *I Believe in Miracles* and *God Can Do
It Again.* While in the store, I browsed through a tray of
plastic bookmarks for one to mark my Bible. I kept coming
back to a particular one and finally purchased it, not notic-
ing the Scripture verse printed on the back.

On the way home, driving south on the Nimitz Freeway,
I was suddenly overcome with hopelessness. What kind of
fool was I? Everyone said Nanci was "incurable," yet here
I was, buying books, skimping on money to buy airline
tickets, planning to take her all the way to Los Angeles to
attend a Miracle Service conducted by a woman I had
never seen. I began to cry.

Turning off the freeway onto Dixon Landing Road, I
looked up. There was the mountain, looming above me. It
was more than I could stand. I pulled off the road, crying.

When my weeping finally subsided, I reached down on
the seat beside me, groping for a Kleenex. In the process
my ring became entangled with the cord on the little book-
mark. I glanced at the Scripture verse that was written on
the plastic. I could hardly believe my eyes: *If ye have faith
as a grain of mustard seed, ye shall say unto this mountain,
Remove hence to yonder place; and it shall remove; and
nothing shall be impossible unto you* (Matthew 17:20).

I looked up at the mountain and felt myself smiling
through the tears. "Get out of my way, mountain. Nanci is
going to be healed."

I could hardly comprehend the vastness of the crowd at
the Shrine Auditorium. We were directed to seats on the
main floor. It was warm when we arrived, and I took off
Nanci's shoes, asking Woody to hold them. Nanci had been
fretful on the plane. She hadn't gotten her nap and was
squirming and wiggly as we took our seats. Woody, too,
was uneasy.

"This is all right for you," he said, "but I just don't think
I can sit through four hours of church."

The meeting started, and the tremendous choir began to sing. Then Miss Kuhlman introduced Dino. I love music and I was fascinated by this handsome young Greek who stroked the keyboard of the concert grand piano like an angel stroking a harp.

But Nanci wasn't interested. She squirmed and wiggled. During the hushed moments when Dino was caressing the keys with his feather touch, Nancy began to cry. Immediately, I was aware of an usher standing in the aisle, leaning over the people between us. "Ma'am, you'll have to take the baby out. She's disturbing other people."

"Take her out?" I thought indignantly. "We've been saving our money for two months to make this trip, and now they're telling me to get out."

I looked at Woody. He nodded. "Why not walk her around?" he whispered. "Then come back."

I felt my temper rising, but I bit my lips and stumbled out over the people between us and the aisle. Torn between embarrassment and anger, I walked to the lobby.

Nearly two years old, Nanci was heavy for me to carry, but I walked back and forth with her in my arms until finally she calmed down. Then I returned to my seat. In minutes she started to fuss again. The usher reappeared. This time he wasn't too friendly. "Ma'am," he said in a stern voice, "many of these people have come from great distances at great sacrifice to attend this meeting. You'll have to take the child out."

Well, I had come from a great distance also. I started to argue, but the usher gave me a curt gesture with his thumb as if to say, "Out, lady!" I didn't want to cause a scene, so I picked Nancy up, stumbled over knees and feet, and headed back toward the lobby again. I was furious.

"This is some Christian meeting," I mumbled to a man standing at the door. "You can't even attend a healing service with a sick child without getting thrown out. Some meeting!"

I walked the lobby carrying Nanci. Woody still had her shoes, and I didn't want to put her down on the dirty floor. I sat on the steps. I went to the ladies' room. I paced back and forth. The more I paced, the madder I got, and the more Nanci squirmed and cried. It just didn't seem right. We had saved up our money. I was the one who wanted to see Kathryn Kuhlman. Yet there was Woody, who hadn't even wanted to come, sitting comfortably in the meeting while I was out here.

I finally sat back down on the steps. "Well, God," I fumed, "if You're going to do it, You'll have to do it some other day, because You can't even see us out here in the lobby." I gave up.

I could tell from the activity in the auditorium that the healing part of the service had probably started. Just then a middle-aged lady walked through the lobby. She was radiant with joy. "What do you need?" she asked.

I nodded at Nanci, who was twisting and wiggling in my arms. "She has leukemia," I said. "And we can't get in the meeting because she fusses and disturbs people."

The woman just beamed. "Dear Jesus, we claim this child's healing." Then she began to thank God. "Thank You, Lord, for healing this child. I praise You for making her well. I give You all the glory."

Oh, boy, I thought, this place is loaded with nuts today. But I could not escape the woman's love and joy. She actually had the faith to believe that Nanci was healed. Slowly my bitterness and resentment began to drain away, and as she stood there, her hands in the air praising God, my own mustard seed of faith began to return.

"You know, there's a lot of activity going on inside," she said. "Why don't you come over here and stand in this doorway? That way you can see, and if the baby begins to fuss, you can go back into the lobby."

I could hardly believe what I saw. There was a long line of people coming up both sides of the platform. All were testifying that they had been healed.

Nanci, who had been struggling and straining in my arms, grew quiet. She was saying over and over, "Hallelujah!"

Hallelujah? Where had she picked up that word? We certainly didn't use it around the house. I had not heard anyone at the meeting use it. Nanci's vocabulary had been limited to words such as "Mommy," "Daddy," "hot," and "no."

"I'm going back to my seat," I told the woman next to me. My back was aching from holding Nanci, and I was tired of being pushed around by every mountain that came my way. Again I crawled over knees and feet and finally collapsed beside Woody.

Minutes later, Nanci was asleep in my lap. I listened as Miss Kuhlman kept calling out the healings that were occurring throughout the auditorium.

"A hip. Someone is being healed of a serious hip condition.

"Someone in the balcony is being healed of a back problem.

"A heart condition . . .

"Leukemia . . ."

Leukemia! The various distractions had almost made me forget about the prime reason for our being in the service.

"Leukemia. Someone is being healed this instant of leukemia," Miss Kuhlman repeated.

Then I knew. It was Nanci. I began to cry.

I didn't want to cry. I had promised myself I would remain very unemotional, even if Nanci was healed. But I couldn't help crying. I looked over at Woody. He was looking straight ahead, but the tears were just pouring from under his glasses.

Suddenly, without warning, Nanci kicked me in the stomach. Hard. Her head was in the crook of my left elbow and her body was pressed against mine. I reached out and grabbed her feet so they wouldn't kick me again, but then I felt it a second time. This time I noticed her feet were motionless. The kick had come from within her body. It was a tremendous thump from deep within her that I had felt against my stomach.

I looked at her face, usually so pale. It was red, flushed, and covered with beads of perspiration. Something was going on deep inside her body. At the same time, I felt a gentle warmth and tingling going through me. I could not contain myself any longer: "Oh, thank You, Jesus. Thank You."

On the way back to the airport, all we could do was cry. Woody warned me not to get excited. "If she is healed, time will prove it," he said wisely. I knew he was right, but there was no way to turn off my tears of joy.

The following Tuesday we went back to Dr. O'Brien for a regular checkup. I told her everything. She listened patiently, and then I noticed tears beginning to well in her eyes. "What's the matter?" I asked.

"Well," she said hesitantly, "the place you are describing —where the kick came from—is the location of her spleen. It is one of the vital organs involved in her disease."

"Do you think she's been healed?" I asked.

"Oh," she said, reaching out and touching my arm, "I *want* to believe it with all my heart."

"Why don't you then?" I asked.

"Because I have never seen it happen," she said. "It's so hard to believe something when you've never seen it happen before. You can understand that, can't you?"

Of course I could. But now I had eyes to see with that I had not had before. Standing to leave, I said, "Nevertheless, it has happened. Just because you've never seen a mountain move doesn't mean it won't."

Dr. O'Brien patted Nanci on the shoulder. "There is no test to prove it now. Only time will show whether the healing is real or not."

Time *has* proved it. Day after day, Nanci's color improved. Her appetite and vitality returned. We cut way back on her drugs. Every test over the last four years has come up negative. There is no trace of the disease left in her body.

As wonderful as Nanci's healing has been, the healing in our home and in our lives has been even more miraculous. Talk about mountains that needed to be moved! The situation in our home was like a whole range of mountains— jagged, rocky ones. Yet since Nanci's healing, Woody has accepted Jesus Christ as his personal Saviour and both of us have received the Baptism in the Holy Spirit. Our home, once headed for divorce, has come into divine order.

A mountain range of miracles! And it all started with faith as tiny as a grain of mustard seed.

SEVEN.

Is This a Protestant Bus?

MARGUERITE BERGERON

I could not stop the flow of tears as I looked at the magnificent petit point handed me by this woman from Canada. Each stitch in the needlework was an act of love, for it came from fingers that had once been bent and twisted by arthritis.

Mrs. Bergeron, a resident of Ottawa, Canada, was a sixty-eight-year-old Roman Catholic who had never been inside a Protestant church. For twenty-two years she had been a victim of crippling arthritis, so severe she could scarcely stand for ten minutes at a time. Her husband, disabled from a heart condition, is the proud possessor of a rare medal given him by the Canadian Prime Minister upon his retirement after fifty-one years of service with the postal department. They have five children and twenty-three grandchildren.

The phone was ringing in our small apartment in a suburb of Ottawa. "Dear Mary, Mother of God," I prayed. "Don't let it stop ringing before I get there."

I pushed myself up out of the rocking chair and put my hand against the wall to steady myself, painfully inching my way toward the telephone table. Every step brought shooting pains into my knees and hips. For twenty-two years I had been crippled with arthritis, and this winter had been the worst ever. I had not been able to get outside the house. The intense Canadian cold stiffened my joints so I could hardly walk. Even the simple matter of crossing my living room to answer the phone was almost more than I could manage.

I gripped my rosary and finally reached the phone. My son Guy, who lived in Brockville, Ontario, said, "Mamma, do you know Roma Moss?"

I knew Mr. Moss well. He was badly crippled, just like me. Surgeons had fused several of his spinal disks. His back wouldn't bend, so he couldn't sit down. "What's wrong?" I asked Guy, fearing the worst and even saying it out loud. "Is Mr. Moss dead?"

It's strange, now that I think back on it. I never considered that any news would be good. I was always expecting bad news. After years of hearing my doctor tell me, "You'll never get better, only worse," I believed that all sick people automatically got worse and worse until they died.

"No, Mamma," Guy said excitedly. "Mr. Moss isn't dead. He's been healed! He can walk! He can bend! He's not even crippled anymore!"

"How's that?" I asked gruffly. Instead of rejoicing, I felt threatened. Why should he be healed when the rest of us had to live on in our misery?

"He went to Pittsburgh, Mamma," Guy bubbled over the phone, "to a Kathryn Kuhlman service. While he was there, he was healed. Why don't you go to Pittsburgh, too? Maybe you can be healed."

I had heard of Kathryn Kuhlman and had even seen her program on television, but I always figured healing was for someone else, not me. "Oh, I'm too sick to even walk out of the house," I said. "How would I ever get all the way down to Pittsburgh?"

Guy told me about a chartered bus that made the trip from Brockville to Pittsburgh every week. "Let me call and make reservations for you," Guy begged.

I didn't feel good. Just standing beside the phone talking to Guy made me weak. My body had been twisted and swollen by the arthritis for such a long time.

I could remember several years before, when we played a little game at a birthday party for one of my grandchildren. They had blindfolded a little boy and let him go around the room feeling the people's hands and guessing whose they were. He identified me first of all because my knuckles were horribly swollen and my fingers bent in like claws.

What was all this talk about healing? Did Guy think he knew more than the doctors who said my case was hopeless? I shook my head in despair. "No, Guy, don't make any reservations now," I sighed. "I'll talk to your father and let you know something tomorrow night."

I hung up and crept laboriously back to my rocker. For a long time I sat in the dimly lighted room, crying because I was old, and the pain was so bad. I tried to think back to when my body was young and agile, and beautiful. I could remember when Paul and I first fell in love. We were so proper, he with his French Catholic background and I with my Scotch Catholic ancestry. One night he had shyly reached out and touched the back of my hand, slowly intertwining his fingers with mine. He loved to touch my hands, softly, tenderly, reaching my heart.

Now I couldn't bear to have Paul touch my hands. The pain was too great. I was old and gnarled, like a weathered oak high on a craggy mountain crest. I could not remember the time when I had not lived in pain. The pain made it almost impossible for anyone to reach my heart.

That night I spoke to Paul about Guy's call. Since his retirement from the post office Paul had developed fluid around his heart. That affected his legs, so he was partially crippled also. But Paul encouraged me to go to Pittsburgh, even saying he wanted to go with me. "We can't lose anything," he said.

"But it's six hundred miles," I argued. "I don't know if I can stand all that riding and bouncing."

Paul nodded. He was so understanding. Yet something in him kept pushing me. I finally agreed to go, and the next day I called Guy.

"Your father will go with me," I said. "But before you make any reservations, I want to see Mr. Moss. I want to see with my own eyes if he is really healed."

Guy was elated and said he would arrange for me to talk to Mr. Moss, who lived close-by.

The next day as I listened to Mr. Moss, I could hardly believe my ears. It was the most fantastic story I had ever heard. A Mrs. Maudie Phillips had arranged for him to ride the bus from Brockville to Pittsburgh. There he had attended a Kathryn Kuhlman service held in the First Presbyterian Church, and he had been healed. To prove it, he stood up in the middle of the room, bent over, and touched the floor. He ran, stomped his feet, and twisted his back in all directions to show that his bones and joints were as good as new.

To me, the most incredible part of it was that he had been healed in a Protestant church. I had been Roman Catholic all my life. In Canada, during my childhood, relations between Catholics and Protestants were so tense that they sometimes threatened to go to war against one another. Ever since I was a little girl, I had been taught that entering a Protestant church could mean losing my salvation, and I had held my breath whenever I even passed a Protestant church.

In all my sixty-eight years, I had never been inside one of those places. Now Mr. Moss was telling me he had been healed in a Presbyterian church. The thought was almost more than I could stand.

"Dear Mary, can this be so? Does God love Protestants, too?" I shuddered to think of it. Yet there was no denying what had happened to Mr. Moss. Once he had been obviously crippled; now he was perfectly healthy. I swallowed hard, gritted my teeth, and nodded to my husband. We would go.

Guy made reservations. The bus would leave on Thursday morning.

"Should we tell the priest?" Paul asked.

"Oh, no," I objected vigorously. "It is bad enough for *God* to know we are going into a Protestant church without the priest finding out, too."

It weighed heavily on my mind. What would happen

when our Catholic friends learned we had done this thing? Still, I was convinced we should go.

On Thursday morning Paul arose early. But when I tried to get up, I screamed out in pain. Usually my arthritis hurt in one place or the other. That morning, however, I was in intense pain all over my body. Every joint was on fire. All I could do was lie in bed and cry.

Paul came out of the bathroom and stood beside the bed, helpless. When I had pain in my foot or knee, I could sometimes rub it to ease it. But that morning any movement, any touch, caused streaks of liquid fire to run through me. Never had the pain been so agonizing. The tears wet the pillow under my head, and I couldn't even wipe them away because my hands hurt so much. My fingers were hooked tightly around the wads of Kleenex I had put in my hands the night before, trying to keep them from drawing up into tight fists. No amount of prying could open them. I wanted to die.

"I can't go," I sobbed to Paul. "God doesn't want me to go in that church. This is His judgment on me for even thinking about it."

"That is not so, Mamma," Paul said, almost sternly. "God wants you healed. He would not do a thing like this to you. You must get up."

"I can't go. I can't walk. I can't even get out of bed. I can't do anything. It hurts me even to live."

"You must get up, Mamma," Paul pleaded. "God doesn't want you to lie here and die. Try. Please try."

Moving each joint was like breaking ice in a stream. Every movement cracked something loose. The pain was unbearable, but I worked my joints back and forth until I finally managed to swing my legs off the side of the bed. With Paul's help, I got to my feet. We labored to pry my fingers open.

"Now get your dress on, Mamma," Paul said. "We shouldn't be late for the bus."

Dressing was awfully hard—and pulling on my girdle was impossible. I began to cry again.

"Keep trying, Mamma," Paul said. "Keep trying. This may be your last chance to be healed."

"Do you think I would go without my girdle?" I wept. "It would be indecent."

But Paul kept on pleading with me, and I finally got ready to go—without my girdle. We made our way out to the car and drove to the place where we were to meet the bus.

At the parking lot Guy's wife introduced us to Mrs. Maudie Phillips, Miss Kuhlman's representative in Ottawa. She was warm, friendly, and outgoing, and extended her hand toward me. I jerked back. "I'm sorry," I said, "but I cannot shake hands with anybody. If anyone touches me, I faint with the pain."

She smiled, and I felt she understood. That helped. Yet the fear of mingling with Protestants was settling on me again.

I turned to Paul. "I should have gone to church first. I should have confessed this great sin to the priest. Then I wouldn't feel so bad."

Guy overheard me. "Mamma," he said, "even if I have to carry you in my arms, you're going to get on that bus."

I gave in, and Mrs. Phillips and the bus driver very gently helped me aboard. Every step, every touch caused me to cry out, but at last I was in my seat beside Paul. Ahead of us lay a six-hundred-mile trip.

As the bus got under way, Mrs. Phillips was up and down the aisle, talking, answering questions, and ministering to the people, like a shepherd tending sheep. Each time she passed my seat, I stopped her. I had so many questions.

Many of the people on the bus had made the trip before. In just a little while they began to sing. I had never heard such singing. The bus was like a church rolling across the countryside, but it was a different kind of church from any I had ever attended. I was worried and grabbed Mrs. Phillips as she passed.

"Is this a Protestant bus?" I whispered.

"No," she laughed. "This is a Jesus bus. Usually we have some Catholic priests along. They even lead us in singing."

"Catholic priests on a Protestant bus?" I asked. "How can it be?"

Mrs. Phillips grinned. "The bus doesn't care whether you're Protestant or Catholic. Jesus doesn't care, either."

"But we're going to a Protestant church in Pittsburgh," I objected. "How will they pray? How should *I* pray? May I pray like I do in my church?"

Mrs. Phillips was so gentle, so patient, so understanding. After six or seven such questionings, she knelt down beside me. "Mrs. Bergeron," she said, "do you believe there is only one God for us all?"

I could feel my eyes filling with tears. I did not want to dishonor my faith, my church, my priests. They had all meant so much to me. But how could I explain it to this kind woman who had so much love shining out from her? "Oh, yes," I said. "I believe in one God for us all. I pray to Mary, but I love God. I know that only God can heal me."

"Then just trust in Him," she said. "God loves you, but He can't do much for you when you keep asking so many questions. Why not lean back in your seat and let the Holy Spirit minister to you?"

I began to relax a little, although I wasn't sure who the Holy Spirit was. After crossing the border into the United States, I even drifted off to sleep.

I don't know how long I dozed. I was still half asleep when I happened to look down at my feet. Somehow, during my nap, I had put one ankle on top of the other as it rested on the footrest. It couldn't be! It had been years since I had been able to cross my legs. I blinked my eyes and looked again. My ankles were crossed. And even more remarkable—there was no pain. "What is happening?" I blurted out.

Paul looked over at me. He had the strangest expression on his face. I was too excited to notice that something was happening to him also. "What did you say?" he stammered.

Then I noticed my hands. My fingers, which had been so bent and gnarled, were straightening out. The pain was gone from them, too. "What's happening?" I said again.

"What's wrong, Mamma?" Paul asked again.

"Listen," I whispered. "But don't tell anybody. They will think I am imagining something."

"Imagining what?" Paul said.

"Look at my feet," I whispered. "See, my ankles are crossed—and there is no pain. And look at my fingers. My hands don't hurt anymore, and my fingers are getting straight—just like a little girl's. I am being healed even before I get to Pittsburgh! I am being healed on this Protestant bus!"

Paul pulled off his glasses. His eyes were filled with tears. At first I thought he was crying about me, but then I sensed there was something else, too. "What's the matter with you?" I asked.

"Something is happening to *me*," he said, the words tumbling over each other. "While you were sleeping, I dozed off. When I woke up, I felt a warm feeling, like a heat wave, going through my chest and down into my legs. It was so strong that for a minute I couldn't see. I was blind. Then you woke up. My sight has come back. And I think I'm being healed."

Just then the bus pulled off the freeway into a refreshment area. Mrs. Phillips came back to our seats. "We are going to stop and have a cup of coffee," she said. "Let me help you to your feet."

"I don't need any help," I said, laughing with joy and not caring who heard me. "I can walk! I can get up and down those steps all by myself!"

I rose to my feet and walked down the aisle, with my husband right behind me. Down the steps into the parking lot. All the people crowded around me. "Mrs. Bergeron," they said, "what has happened to you?"

"I don't know what has happened," I said, feeling the happiness just bubbling out of me. "But I haven't felt so well for twenty-two years."

We spent Thursday night in a hotel in Pittsburgh. Just the month before I had gone to my doctor, begging him to give me something for the pain. "Look at my knees," I had told him. "Look at my fingers. They hurt so bad I cannot sleep at night."

He had been gentle yet firm. "Mrs. Bergeron, there is nothing we can do. My own mother died from this same condition. We doctors can do nothing but give you pills to help relieve the pain." So he had given me pills. Pills to take in the morning, pills to take at mealtime, pills to take at night. And each time I swallowed a pill, I was swallowing eleven cents.

That night in Pittsburgh I left my pills in my suitcase. I didn't take a single one, and the minute I put my head on my pillow, I was asleep. Never had I slept so soundly. For more than twenty years I had been able to sleep only on my stomach or back, but that night I slept on my side, curled up like a little girl.

I was wide awake at four o'clock. The hotel room was still dark as I slipped out of bed, feeling younger and healthier than I had in years. I could hardly wait to get to the Miracle Service—even if it was in a Protestant church.

The night before, Mrs. Phillips had told me she felt I had been healed on the bus when I said, "I love God and know that only He can heal me." She quoted a verse of Scripture: "And they overcame him by the blood of the Lamb, and by the word of their testimony" (Revelation 12:11). But it didn't matter when it happened. All I knew was that, like Mr. Moss, I was not the same person I had been. And neither was Paul. His heart pains were gone, and he felt brand-new. We were well.

We had been told that often people had to wait for hours outside the church before the doors opened. I had been afraid my legs would not hold me if I had to stand for that long, and so I had brought along a stool to sit on. As it turned out, I didn't need it. For three and a half hours I stood outside the First Presbyterian Church in downtown Pittsburgh, wishing I could find someone to give that stool to. It had been years since I could stand for longer than ten minutes; now I was standing for hours, enjoying every moment, holding the stool on my arm.

The doors finally opened and the people surged in. Miss

Kuhlman came to the platform and the service got under way with glorious music. In just a few minutes she stopped the singing and said, "I understand there is a lady here from Ottawa who was healed on the bus."

She was talking about me. Paul and I accepted her invitation to come to the platform. I forgot I was in a Protestant church. I even forgot I was standing in front of 2,500 people. I sensed Miss Kuhlman's special love for all people, like myself, and before I knew it, I was responding to her suggestion and stomping my feet, clapping my hands, and bending over to touch the floor—in front of everybody.

Since I was the first person to come to the platform, I didn't know what sometimes happens when Miss Kuhlman prays for people. She reached out and put her hand on my shoulder, and suddenly I felt like I was falling down. "Oh, no," I thought. "What is a big woman like me doing, falling down in front of all these people?"

But I could not stop myself. It was as if the heavens opened up and God Himself reached out and touched me. I was glad there was a strong man to catch me before I crashed onto the floor, or I think I would have gone all the way through that Protestant platform and into the basement. He put me down easy.

I climbed back to my feet, amazed that there was no pain in my body. "Thank you," I said to Miss Kuhlman, choking it out between the tears. "Thank you very much."

"Don't thank me," she laughed. "I had nothing to do with it. I don't even know you. You were healed even before you arrived here. I have no power. Only God has the power. Thank Him."

I returned to my seat and began to thank Him. The people were singing, as they had on the bus. Only this time it didn't make any difference that most of them were Protestants. I wanted to sing, too. Since I didn't know the words to the songs, I listened to the woman beside me and began to sing the words after her. I knew it sounded terrible, because I was always one phrase behind everyone else, but I couldn't help that—and it didn't matter! I was so happy. When the people around me raised their arms to praise

God, I raised mine, too. For the first time in twenty-two years I could raise my arms, and now it was in worship. So I kept on singing—one sentence late—raised my arms, cried, and praised God for my healing.

It was two o'clock in the morning when we arrived back in Brockville. Guy was at the door of his home when we pulled into his driveway. "Mamma, are you all right?" he asked, as I stepped out of the car that had brought us from the bus stop.

All his friends who were waiting at his home crowded around. "Don't ask her, just look at her!" they shouted to Guy. "Look at her! She's healed! God healed her!" I was dancing around the living room in the middle of the night. "Oh, Mamma!" Guy said, gathering me in his arms. He was crying, the people were crying. But not me. I was dancing up and down.

As soon as I got home, even though it was almost three o'clock, I called my daughter Jeanne. "I'm healed!" I shouted over the phone. "I'm healed!"

"Mother?" she replied in a sleepy voice. "What are you saying?"

"I don't have arthritis anymore," I laughed. "Call everyone. Tell everybody. I am no longer sick."

It was five o'clock when I finally got to bed. I had been up for twenty-four hours, but even so, I felt full of youth and strength. And so did Paul. The very next day he went to the golf course with Guy and walked five holes with him. Oh my! God had been so good to us.

Sunday afternoon, one of our other sons, Pierre, and his wife and three children came to Guy's to see if I was really healed. Pierre's face was wreathed in a huge smile as he walked around me, looking at me closely from every angle. "Mamma, you *are* healed. Now you will live to be an old lady unless a truck runs over you. And even then, I would be more afraid for the truck than for you."

One of my granddaughters, little Michele, piped up, "Mamma, when you were in Pittsburgh I went to Catholic school, put my hands up, and said, 'Jesus Christ, cure my grandma,' and He did."

My seven-year-old grandson chimed in. "Now, Mamma, you won't have to walk like a penguin anymore."

God was doing something else. Not only had He healed my body, but He was working on my attitudes as well. Like many people who live with pain, I had become crabby, hard to get along with. I didn't realize it until I heard my daughter-in-law talking to Jeanne on the phone. "There's been another miracle, too," she said. "Not only is Mamma healed from arthritis, but she's not nagging anymore. Something wonderful has happened down deep inside her."

The next Sunday morning I made all my family walk with me to the Sacred Heart Church. When I got there I told the priest, "Father, God has healed me of arthritis."

I wanted him to really understand about it, so the next Sunday I took all the priests a copy of Miss Kuhlman's books.

Two weeks later I went to see my doctor. As I walked in the office the nurse exclaimed, "Why, Mrs. Bergeron, what has happened to you? You look so good."

Minutes later the doctor came into the waiting room. "Hey, Doctor," I said, "I have no more arthritis. Look at my hands. Look at my knees. Look! I'm walking."

He stood in the middle of the room, watching as I walked around it. Then he took my hands in his and examined my fingers and wrists. "I know what you are thinking," I laughed. "You are thinking, Well, Mrs. Bergeron has no more arthritis, but instead she has a good case of being crazy."

He laughed and motioned me back into his office. "No, I don't think you're crazy," he said seriously. "Your condition was hopeless, incurable. Now you're well. I don't understand it."

I reached in my purse and pulled out one of Miss Kuhlman's books. "Read this, Doctor," I said. "And you will send all your patients to Pittsburgh. Then you will have to go out and find another job."

He laughed again, took the book and put his arm around

my shoulder. "That would make me the happiest man in all the world," he said, "just to see all my patients as well as you are."

The following month Paul and I were once again on board the bus as it left for Pittsburgh. This time there were seventeen members of our family and some other friends who went along. A young Catholic priest was on board, and all the way to Pittsburgh we sang choruses and praised God.

"Are you working for Miss Kuhlman?" one woman asked me.

"No," I answered, "I'm working for God."

Always before, when I wanted to ask God for something, I was afraid. So, instead of going to Jesus, I went to Mary, the Mother of God, to ask her to intercede for me. Now I understand that God loves me so much that I no longer have to be afraid of Him. When I pray, I say, "God, it's me, Mrs. Bergeron." And He always stops whatever He's doing and listens. That's the way God is.

EIGHT

Healing Is Only the Beginning

DOROTHY DAY OTIS

My guests on my weekly television program, I Believe in Miracles, *have included medical doctors and bartenders, famous educators and little children, fashion models and housewives. All have been touched by Jesus in a special way and testify of changed lives.*

However, few guests thrill me as much as the professional stage and TV performers who put all their acting ability aside and through genuine tears of thanksgiving, share with the world what Jesus has done for them.

Such was the case with Dorothy and Don Otis when they appeared on my program in the CBS studio in Los Angeles. Dorothy Day Otis heads one of Hollywood's most successful talent agencies. She represents top artists in the field of television, motion pictures, and the theater. Don operates a flourishing advertising agency. Both are well-known and highly respected in the Hollywood performing arts community. "For years Don and I have appeared on television," said Dorothy, "but the only meaningful show we ever did was the Kathryn Kuhlman program." That's because they did this one totally for Jesus' sake.

I thought it was natural to feel bad. I had never felt really well, and for years I was aware that my health had been deteriorating. I tired easily and had constant backaches, which I tried to ignore. But I could not ignore my stomach, which reacted violently to almost everything I ate. I lived on large amounts of cottage cheese, custards, and Jell-O, and hated even to look at regular food.

When the pain became unbearable, I went to doctors. Several internists looked at me, all diagnosing my plight as "severe stomach condition," a malady that seems to be the constant companion of so many caught in the Hollywood whirl. The doctors prescribed pills, which I took faithfully, but I didn't get well.

For years I dragged around with a backache, a stiff neck, no energy or appetite, spending most of each weekend in bed. Sometimes I wondered out loud if my stomach trouble and general ill health were connected with my backaches, my peculiar walk, and the fact that my shoes wore out unevenly. But the doctors just looked at me and shook their heads—and sent me marching down to the drugstore for more pills.

I had majored in drama in college, and afterward went on to a career in fashion and television. For two years I lived in San Francisco, conducting my own interview and cooking program on TV and being hostess for a Sunday afternoon movie. Later I moved to Los Angeles, where I continued my work in modeling and appearing on TV.

I rose each morning at 5:30 A.M. in order to be on time in the makeup department and at the hairdresser. All day long I was in front of the lights, on camera, or working with people. Late at night I would literally collapse into bed. With my strenuous schedule, I didn't think it unusual that I was in almost constant pain and felt utterly exhausted all the time. After all, everyone else around me seemed to feel the same way.

Six months after I arrived in Los Angeles, I met Don Otis. His background was similar to mine—radio and television performer, disk jockey, program director, and now owner of his own advertising agency.

I had gone to Don's office to be interviewed for a television commercial. After I left he turned to a co-worker and said impulsively, "That's the girl I'm going to marry."

"Oh, really?" his friend asked. "What's her name?"

Don didn't know and had to go to an outer office to find

out from a secretary. Returning, he grinned. "Her name is Dorothy Day, and I'm still going to marry her."

One year later I was sick—as usual—but we were married. Don had to make all the arrangements, including getting permission to use the beautiful Mission Inn in Riverside for our wedding ceremony.

At the time I was a Presbyterian who went to church only occasionally. Don was a Methodist who never went to church. "Nominal Christians" was the phrase I used to describe us. Don, who is more frank, looks back and says we were "Rotten Christians."

Despite my poor health and our total lack of spirituality, we were both highly successful in our chosen careers. Don's advertising agency was thriving, and I was appearing constantly on television. Then, just as I thought I was learning to live with my poor health, Don's health began to break.

He had smoked heavily since he was fifteen, and suddenly after all those years his breathing became affected. He could take only short breaths, and bit by bit was forced to curtail all his physical activities. He couldn't even climb the steep incline behind our beautiful hillside home.

A physical checkup disclosed a dreaded condition—emphysema. There was no cure. Don was so discouraged, he didn't even consider stopping smoking. He figured he had it now, so stopping smoking wouldn't make any difference.

In 1966 Harold Chiles, a top Hollywood agent, offered me a job representing children for dramatic roles and television commercials. He and Don both felt my years on television qualified me for the job. It meant advancing into an entirely new field in my profession, and I was fascinated by it all. When Mr. Chiles died, I bought the agency from his estate, and suddenly I was in business, heading up one of Hollywood's most successful talent agencies.

Then my own health broke. At five feet, nine inches, my normal weight had been 130 pounds. But I began losing. I turned away from all food, even cottage cheese, and my weight rapidly slipped to 110 pounds. I looked like a skeleton and once again began to make the rounds of the doc-

tors' offices. None of them could help me. I forced myself
to go to work, even though I felt terrible. Only my love for
my job kept me going.

A close friend of ours had been attending the Kathryn
Kuhlman services. She urged Don and me to go also, feeling certain that if we did, we would be healed. The idea of
God didn't interest me much, but I did buy Miss Kuhlman's books and read them. Don read them, too. They
were extremely interesting and even brought tears to my
eyes. But when the weekends that Miss Kuhlman was to be
in town approached, I found it easier to collapse in bed
than to attend the services.

"One of these days we'll make it to the Shrine Auditorium," I kept telling my enthusiastic friend. But it took us
three years to keep that promise.

Don and I attended our first Miracle Service in January,
1971. Even now I find it difficult to describe my feelings as
I waited outside the Shrine Auditorium for the doors to
open. Several thousand people were milling about the
doors, but they weren't strangers, simply friends we had
not met before. It was like a great family reunion. There
was such love for each other, such compassion for those
who were sick. All were talking and sharing in the joy as
they looked forward to what was about to happen. Even
before the doors opened, Don and I knew that God was
there.

We returned the next month. I sat in the auditorium,
crying over the healings and praying for the sick people all
around me. For the first time in my life I felt the presence
of a loving God who cared enough to touch people in their
misery and make them whole.

But _I_ wasn't being made whole. My backaches became
more intense. And even worse, my neck became so stiff I
could not turn my head without turning my entire upper
body. I looked and walked like one of those Egyptian
mummies in the old horror movies.

In March, 1971, I went to see an orthopedic chiropractor, Dr. Larry Hirsch. He made a preliminary examination
and then suggested spinal X rays.

When I returned to his office several days later, he held up my X ray. "Look at this," he told me. Even to my inexperienced eye, it was obvious that my spine did not go up the center of my back. Dr. Hirsch diagnosed the large calcium deposits in every vertebra as a growing arthritic condition. As if that wasn't enough, my pelvic bone was askew, causing my right leg to be one inch shorter than the left.

This explained some of my problems—why my shoes wore out unevenly, why my neck was stiff, and why my lower back hurt all the time. Dr. Hirsch also said my stomach trouble could be caused by pressure on the nerves.

I recalled that while I was attending the University of Iowa, I had fallen hard on the ice one day. The campus nurse had taped my lower back, but the pain had continued for a long time afterward. Dr. Hirsch said this could have been the beginning of my problems.

"You should be in bed," he said. "Most people with similar conditions can't even move around."

He measured my legs and inserted a lift in my right shoe. "If there's not decided improvement within a week," he said, "you should see a specialist."

That was Friday. I left the office discouraged, promising to come back on Monday for another examination.

On Sunday Don and I drove into Los Angeles to attend the Miracle Service at the Shrine Auditorium. After standing at the door for more than two hours, we hurried to get seats. Between Don's wheezing and my shuffling gait, we had to settle for seats in the top balcony, five rows from the back. "One nice thing about being up this high," Don said breathlessly, "at least we're closer to heaven."

Early in the service I began telling God everything that was the matter with me, as if He didn't know. Off and on during Miss Kuhlman's sermon I lapsed into prayer. Then I heard Miss Kuhlman say, "Someone in the balcony has been healed of a stomach ailment. You haven't eaten in a long time."

I felt my breath beginning to come in short, rapid gasps, as if I were hyperventilating. "Someone is also being healed of a back condition," Miss Kuhlman added.

My rapid breathing increased until I had no control over it. I was gasping for air, and at the same time I began to sob uncontrollably. I knew I was making a scene, but I couldn't help myself. Yet in the midst of it all, a great warmth settled over me, like a blanket on a cold day.

My violent sobbing startled Don. He tried to help, but I couldn't speak. I couldn't tell him what was wrong. He handed me his handkerchief, and when I turned to take it, he almost shouted, "You turned your head! Look at me, Dorothy! You turned your head!"

It was true. Without my realizing it, my neck had become limber, loose. Still breathing heavily and sobbing, I began to turn my head back and forth, then nodded it vigorously up and down. All the pain was gone. I staggered out into the aisle and toward a personal worker.

"I've been healed," I sobbed.

The woman looked at me very calmly. "How do you know?"

I was almost hysterical, shaking my head and gasping for breath. "I can twist my neck," I choked out. "And my stomach has been healed, too."

"Your stomach?" she said. "How can you tell if your stomach has been healed?"

I didn't know. I hadn't even thought of it. The words just came blubbering out. "I just *know*," I insisted. "If I can move my head, I know God has healed my stomach, too."

The woman grinned, convinced. She took my arm and helped me down the stairs to the main floor. There was a long line of people on the stage, waiting to testify about their healings. I stood in line, still sobbing.

"Where is Don?" I suddenly wondered. I glanced out into that sea of faces, trying to spot him. Then I saw him, coming down the aisle on the arm of a helper. He, too, was sobbing. Seeing me, he began to laugh at the same time. We met in each other's arms.

"I've been healed, too, Dorothy," he said. "This warm feeling came over me as you left. I began to cry. Then I realized I could breathe normally. Look!" he said. "For the first time in eight years I don't have to take tiny little breaths." He was laughing and crying at the same time—but with normal breaths.

Just then Miss Kuhlman called Don and me forward. Something had happened deep inside Don. Not just in his lungs, but in his soul. I could tell it as he stood at the microphone, breathing deeply, joy written all over his face. Miss Kuhlman kept trying to ask him questions, but he could only say, "Look! I can breathe!"

Realizing she wasn't going to get much information from either of us in our hysterical state, she put her hands on us and began to pray. I felt Don reach for my hand, and the next thing I knew, both of us were lying on the floor. I didn't hear anything. There was no definite sensation, just a marvelous warmth and peace that settled over us. I vaguely remember hearing Miss Kuhlman say, "This is only the beginning. Yours lives will be completely changed from this moment on."

Oh, how right she was!

I realize, as I look back at that moment, that God's touch did much more than heal my body. Yet because the physical healing was so sensational, it took time before I realized the much deeper, inner change that had taken place at the same time.

By the time we reached home that night, all the pain was gone from my lower back. The first thing I did was take the lift out of my shoe. Don was so elated about his "new" lungs that he went out and climbed the steep hill behind our house. He hadn't been able to do that for a long time. Then we went out and had a big steak dinner. It was the first steak I had eaten in years.

The next morning I kept my appointment with Dr. Hirsch. He took one look at me and said, "What's happened?"

I didn't know Dr. Hirsch very well and was hesitant to say much. "I want *you* to tell *me*," I said.

It was easy for him to tell that my stomach muscles were relaxed, but it was when he examined my spine that he really knew something had happened. "This is *not* the same spine that I examined on Friday," he said.

"Do you have a minute, Doctor?" I asked, encouraged to tell him all about it. He nodded, and I launched into a long story about the Kathryn Kuhlman meeting the day before.

"If there are any changes, Dorothy," he said, "the X rays will reveal them."

He took a series of pictures then and told me to come back in a couple of days. That evening, however, I remembered I had forgotten to tell him I had taken the lift out of my shoe. I called him at his home.

"Oh, no," he argued. "Put it back. You will undo any good that has happened. Even if God has healed your stomach, your right leg will always be shorter than the left one." But wearing the lift made me feel unbalanced. I *knew* that both legs were now the same length.

Two days later I returned to his office. Don went with me. The first thing Dr. Hirsch did was measure my legs. Then he measured them again. He had a funny look on his face when he said, "They're the same length."
— I began to cry. "I know it," I said. "I just wanted you to know it, too."

Dr. Hirsch had not had time to examine the X rays, so all three of us looked at them together. The doctor was dumbfounded. My spine was perfectly straight. The "L" turn in my tail bone was gone. All the calcium deposits had disappeared. My neck was in perfect alignment with my spine and skull. Most amazing of all, my pelvic bone had made a noticeable turn and was in the correct position.

Dr. Hirsch exclaimed, "If such a thing were possible, I'd say you had a complete back transplant."

Dr. Hirsch gave me the two sets of X rays, taken eight days apart. I keep them in my office and show them to everyone. They are more precious to me than a Picasso.

Don was less concerned about proof of his healing. The simple fact he could breathe was enough for him. In fact, he immediately went out and joined the Beverly Hills Health Club and began working out for hours at a time. He also stopped smoking, just to thank the Lord. Don was different inside.

Nine months later he did go back to his doctor. After a

complete physical, the doctor began telling Don what good shape he was in. Don thought he was hedging, and asked outright, "Look, Doctor, what about my emphysema?"

The doctor cleared his throat. "Medically, Don, there is no cure for emphysema. Even a one percent improvement would be classified as an arrestment."

"Well, do I have a one percent improvement—or what?"

"There's *nothing* wrong with your lungs," the doctor said. "That's all I can say."

The greatest miracle, however, goes far deeper than spine or lungs. Miss Kuhlman was right. When the Holy Spirit entered our lives, everything changed. We have joined a dynamic, Bible-teaching church in Burbank. Don joined the Full Gospel Business Men's Fellowship, and both of us often share our testimony before large groups. We know Jesus is alive, not only because He healed our bodies but because He changed our outlook as well. Even though we're busier than ever before in our professions, we both feel we are missionaries, witnessing for the Lord Jesus Christ about the tremendous experience of being born again—and being filled with the Holy Spirit.

My business associates and clients call my office the "happy office." I know it's not just because of the bright yellow wallpaper, but because the Holy Spirit fills that office with His joy, guiding me in my work. I pray for my clients and see things happening, in their professions and in their lives, things that only God can bring about. It's wonderful.

Yet the most wonderful part is this: We know this is only the beginning of what God has in store for us:

> . . . *Eye hath not seen, nor ear heard, neither have*
> *entered into the heart of man, the things which*
> *God hath prepared for them that love him.*
> *But, God hath revealed them unto us by his Spirit.*
> *(I Corinthians 2:9-10).*

14 April 1972

TO WHOM IT MAY CONCERN:

Mrs. Dorothy Otis presented herself in this office with multiple spinal complaints on March 3, 1971, at which time we took full spine X-rays (radiographic views from the top of the head to the tail bone). These X-rays showed a double scoliosis with a 1″ shortening of the right leg, with nerve impingement to the entire intestinal tract.

Mrs. Otis was then treated. Progress was slow. Five days later she visited the Kathryn Kuhlman Miracle Service. The following day she was re-examined and it appeared as though a new spine and pelvis had replaced the existing one, and the leg was corrected to its proper length. Also the intestinal tract had entirely relaxed and returned to a normal functioning.

We X-rayed Mrs. Otis again that same week and confirmed that the curvature had completely eliminated itself. The spine is now straight, and there are no stress areas.

In my past twenty years of practice, I have never encountered this occurrence without treatments of long duration. There has been a miraculous change in structure.

Respectfully submitted,

Dr Larry Hirsch

Dr. Larry Hirsch
Chiropractic Orthopedist

NINE

The God-Shaped Vacuum

ELAINE SAINT-GERMAINE

Eliza Elaine Saint-Germaine, whose Hollywood stage name was Elaine Edwards, was once proclaimed one of the brightest young stars in the TV and motion-picture industry. However, like so many caught in the maddening whirl of wealth and fame, she inadvertently looked to Satan for happiness, rather than to Jesus Christ.

Saint Augustine once said that inside every person is a God-shaped vacuum. A young drug addict described it as a "hole of loneliness" deep in the soul of every creature. You can try to fill that hole, that vacuum, with all kinds of perverted love, but it is made for the love of Jesus. Nothing else really fits.

Looking back to my childhood, I believe my parents were trying to be godly. They were always in church, and I cut my teeth on the pew of a Southern Baptist church in Dearborn, Michigan. But it was all a Sunday kind of religion. My parents had no personal source of power to help them translate the principles they learned at church into their lives—or their home. Daddy had a drinking problem, and Mother was always negative. I grew up equating God with unhappiness.

There was very little physical affection displayed in our home, and my heart was screaming to be filled with love. Denied it at home, I sought it elsewhere, and at the age of fifteen I married a sailor and went with him to California.

After my young husband was shipped overseas, I discovered I was pregnant. Unwilling to settle down and raise children at the age of fifteen, I caught a bus back to Michigan and had an abortion.

Returning to San Francisco, I met another man, a handsome Lieutenant Commander in the Navy who was stationed aboard a submarine. Still desperately searching for love, I let myself get swept off my feet—and married him, even though I already had a husband.

World War II was still going on, and before long my number-two husband was ordered to sea. Shortly afterward, my number-one husband returned. I met him, telling him I wanted a divorce. He was deeply wounded, but seeing I had made up my mind, he agreed.

It was almost a year before my second husband returned from his overseas tour. I met him in New York, and on our first night together, decided to confess the entire truth in hopes we could start clean. Instead of hearing my confession and loving me through it, however, he rejected me. Horribly distraught, he had our marriage annulled.

Still desperate for love, I followed him to Washington, D.C., to plead with him to return. He refused to see me. In Washington I met a man ten years my elder. There followed another whirlwind romance, and six months later I was married for the third time.

At the age of seventeen I had already lived a lifetime. I had committed bigamy, had an abortion, been divorced twice, and was now married again.

My third husband was interested in acting. I had worked as a model and offered to help support us if he wanted to go to school. We moved to Los Angeles where he enrolled at the Pasadena Playhouse.

He was a natural actor and was signed as the star of a highly successful TV series. Our marriage was in trouble immediately, for he began touring the nation doing personal appearances. Again, I needed love—and acceptance. With him gone much of the time, I was beside myself with loneliness, and this time I tried to find satisfaction in a career. I, too, enrolled at the Pasadena Playhouse.

As with my husband, acting came naturally to me. Finishing my course at the Playhouse, I went into legitimate theater. Stardom was mine from the very beginning. I thought I had finally found the one thing that would bring fulfillment and fill that empty hole in my inner being.

For awhile everything fell into place. In 1954 I was cast in the starring role of *Bernadine* for the West Coast premiere. On opening night I played before two thousand people who had packed into the beautiful playhouse. I was a smashing success. When I came out on stage, the people couldn't take their eyes off me. Patterson Greene, the renowned critic, reviewed the play and said it was unbelievable.

I fit the part of Bernadine perfectly. But like me, Bernadine was an illusion. She didn't exist. Standing on stage, listening to the roar of the crowds as they shouted and applauded my performance, I felt detached, unreal. Yet it was satisfying, and I drank in all the applause, accolades, praise, and acceptance my fans could give. I basked in it, soaking it up. To me, it was the epitome of fulfillment to be loved and admired by fans from all over the nation.

Soon I moved into another state of illusion. I signed with Edward Small and began to star in films. He told me he was grooming me to be the biggest name in Hollywood. I starred in films for Allied Artists, and in some TV specials. I played roles on *Playhouse 90* and *The Millionaire*, and co-starred with Chuck Conners in some of his first shows. It was nothing for me to work on the film set all day and then fly off somewhere for a stage show that night. I was riding the crest of an exhilarating wave of success.

But waves eventually become foam and bubbles—and always return to the sea. I was still empty. One October morning I left the house early. Ed and I had acquired a beautiful mansion in LaCrescenta in the foothills. Driving my Cadillac to the studio in Hollywood, I began to muse, What is this for? Why am I doing all this? These philosophical questions were coming out of the deep emptiness of my life. I had everything—fame, wealth, a beautiful home, a handsome husband famous in his own right. Yet I was

miserable. A line from Robert Burns's *Tam O'Shanter*
slipped through my mind.

> *But pleasures are like poppies spread,*
> *You seize the flower, its bloom is shed;*
> *Or like the snow falls in the river,*
> *A moment white, then melts forever.*

I had surrounded myself with all the pleasures my senses
could appreciate. I had made a business of seeking happiness. Driving to the studio, I drew a line under it all, added
it up, and came up with zero. I remembered a verse from
my childhood Sunday school days: "All is vanity, a striving
after the wind." From that day on I began to search for
spiritual truths. However, I did not know that there are two
different sources of spiritual energy and power. And in my
ignorance, I became channeled in the direction of darkness.

I began by joining a prayer group that met weekly in a
home near ours. But nothing ever happened there. It was as
powerless as my childhood religion had been. Like me, the
people were all searching, but none had found anything.
We spent the evenings intellectualizing about prayer. When
we finally got down to praying, it wasn't real, and there
were never any answers. It was all empty, meaningless.

I shifted to Religious Science, and from that I moved
into a study group that was examining Eastern religions.
Southern California is filled with empty people who are
turning to everything that offers hope. A vacuum, even a
God-shaped one, attracts anything that is not tied down—
especially evil spirits.

Ed was gone for days at a time, and I went into a deep
depression. I didn't even want to get out of bed. I was losing interest in my career and found myself bumbling even
when I did show up on the set.

"Something is wrong," I told my psychiatrist in September, 1959. "My career no longer offers me happiness.
My marriage is not fulfilling. I feel guilty for having all the
things that should make me happy, and remaining so miserable."

She heard me out and then told me about a new method of drug psychoanalysis that had been developed by Dr. Sidney Cohen at UCLA. Taken under controlled situations, a controversial new drug was supposed to rapidly accelerate the process of analysis: Five sessions with the drug was equivalent to an entire psychoanalysis, which usually took years. I readily agreed to the program, which involved taking the drug once a week. The name of the drug was lysergic acid diethylamide—LSD.

I had just finished co-starring with Agnes Moorehead and Vincent Price in an Agatha Christie film called *The Bat*. Although I didn't believe in evil spirits at the time, I now realize that my part in *The Bat* simply set me up for the LSD trips I was about to take.

On September 19, I entered a private rest home in Culver City as an outpatient. My psychiatrist, excited about the entire venture, assured me the drug would expand my mind, deepen my awareness, and be the answer to all my problems. She said that she would be in and out of my room, taking notes and asking questions, while I was under the drug's influence.

Naturally, I believed her. But it was all a tragic, horrible mistake. Instead of freedom, I found myself in a bondage far worse than I had ever known before. Instead of five sessions on LSD, I had sixty-five sessions—one a week for a year and a half. The only way to come down off the LSD was to take other drugs, or to drink liquor. I took mescaline, which is another hallucinogen, and I began going to pieces.

Soon we "graduated" from single trips on LSD to group therapy. Under the supervision of the UCLA psychiatrists, about a dozen of us gathered early on a Saturday morning and spent the day—and late into the night—on an LSD trip. We psychoanalyzed each other, taking out our rage on each other and infecting one another with our own individual problems. In a short time I had picked up the symptoms of all the others in the group—much to the seeming delight of the psychiatrists, who were convinced that we were finally encountering reality.

During one of these LSD trips I relived a traumatic automobile accident I had been in at the age of three. All the fear and terror came sweeping back. My psychiatrist was beside herself with joy: "Oh, you're getting to the last piece in the puzzle of your problem. You're finally getting your life straightened out."

But instead of straightening out, my life was being wound into a knot of confusion that could not be untangled. During a year and a half of sheer terror the drugs unleashed every evil and demonic power that had ever taken residence in my mind. My brain never stopped running in high gear, and each day the effects of the drug returned in horrible flashbacks. I started gobbling all kinds of narcotics to try to pull me down from the LSD "highs." It wasn't long before I was in the grip of an addiction that was to last for twelve long years.

On the film set, I was scarcely able to function—flying into unexplained temper tantrums, refusing to take orders, and showing up so drugged that I couldn't even read my lines. "Elaine," Edward Small said, "you could be one of the greatest actresses on the screen, but you're ruining yourself. Snap out of it."

I was unable to control myself. Outside forces, far more powerful than my own will, had moved in. I was no longer my own.

In 1961, I was to co-star with Mickey Rooney in *The Seven Little Foys* for a TV series. I could barely drag myself around the set and finally bombed out completely. I knew that my days as an actress were numbered.

My final experience with acting had weird supernatural overtones. One of my former directors called me from Albuquerque, New Mexico. "Elaine, we've got a problem," she said. "We're only two days away from the opening performance of *Dulcie*, and Jean Cagney, who's playing the lead, is sick. Can you take over?"

"No problem," I said. "I can handle it. I'll fly in tonight."

After I hung up I began to wonder why I had agreed. I had never done comedy. I was a slow studier in acting, and it usually took me weeks to learn a part. Dulcie is the whole show, and I hadn't even read the part. This was ridiculous.

I had an LSD session slated for that afternoon and went on to the rest home for the treatment. When I took the drug, I had a vision. I saw a tremendous shaft of light, and in the middle of it stood a man, beckoning me to step out of the shadows and join him. I was scared, but it never occurred to me that the light could be anything but good. As I stepped out of the shadows into the shaft of light, I felt a great surge of power and energy. It was as if I could do anything, as if I were almost God Himself.

I left the rest home still feeling the effects of this great new energy. I stopped by the director's Los Angeles office, picked up a copy of *Dulcie,* and read it through on the plane to Albuquerque. I knew I had mastered it.

I was met at the airport and driven to the theater for a rehearsal. The director was pacing the floor, having some second thoughts. "You'll never get it done, Elaine," she said. "It's impossible. You're to be on stage for the full two and a half hours." But I had a superhuman confidence. We started with the rehearsal.

"You're not writing down your blocking," the director said. The blocking includes all the stage movement, and in a play like this would usually take at least three weeks to learn.

"I don't need to write it down," I smiled mysteriously. I had never felt such tremendous energy and power in all my life.

That night I went home and worked on my lines for about two hours. The next day, at dress rehearsal, I had my lines perfected.

It was the biggest show ever to be staged in Albuquerque. The critics went wild. "She's like a light when she comes out on stage," one of them wrote. "She actually picks up the rest of the cast and carries them along."

The play ran for two weeks and drew the largest crowds in local history. During this time I did things I had never dreamed I could do, such as lecturing to drama classes at

the University of New Mexico. I seemed to float along in
the power of this tremendous energy—never dreaming it
could be from Satan.

My husband flew out for the closing-night performance,
and after the show, all hell broke loose. He ripped into me.
I had never seen so much wrath and rage come from one
human being. Even though I suspected he was envious of
my success, I was not able to withstand the onslaught of his
attack. I wilted under it, and by the time we got back to
Los Angeles, whatever power I had was gone. The energy
had disappeared. I felt like Cinderella at the stroke of midnight as I moved back into the depths of depression. The
darkness settled in again, so thick this time I could not
break out. I knew I would never act again.

I went back to LSD. Drugs in the morning, drugs at
noon, drugs at night. Down, down, down.

My husband's producer enticed him back to New York
to take a leading role in a TV soap opera. He became involved not only with the program but with his leading lady.
Our marriage of nineteen years was doomed. He got a divorce and married his leading lady. I remained in California, broken in spirit and emotionally destitute.

I started visiting a psychologist who was experimenting
with the occult. He believed he could activate certain ener-
gies from the "outside" that would form protective "trian-
gles of light" around me. He called them vortexes of energy that would come into my body and open my mind to
higher levels of knowledge. It was all associated with the
Shakti, the female energy of the Hindu god Siva.

I attended twice-a-week sessions in a desperate effort to
find truth for my shattered life. Instead, I kept sinking into
darkness. This led to astrology classes, spiritism, and alpha
brain-wave courses. It still hadn't occurred to me that energy and power could come from other than good sources.

In our group therapy session my psychologist led us to
call on certain "ascended masters," spirits who would come
and impart knowledge. I was especially urged to call on
one known as "The Tibetan," who could empower me with
great wisdom. By this time I was so involved with the oc-

cult that it seemed I would never unsnarl the tangled web of my life.

The old search for love kept coming to the surface. I became involved with a divorced actor/director and lived with him for almost two years. This man abused me and on several occasions tried to kill me. It was a nightmare. In a reckless effort to break his bondage, I moved out in the middle of the night. Two weeks later he found me and almost killed me before I consented to move back with him.

Months later, when he became deathly ill, I managed to escape and moved into an old apartment on Havenhurst off Sunset Boulevard. It was the same apartment Carole Lombard had lived in before she was killed. John Barrymore had lived across the hall. My occult friends were wild about the place, saying they could sense all kinds of spirits living there. They urged me to make contact with them, but I was afraid and withdrew into my world of drugs and loneliness.

One of my friends was a famous Jewish astrologer and a personal friend of the newspaper columnist from Toronto, Canada, who had set up the Bishop Pike séances. This columnist had interviewed Kathryn Kuhlman, and my Jewish friend let me read the accounts of Miss Kuhlman's ministry. I was excited. For the first time I felt a tinge of hope. Could it be that in spite of the swirling world of demons and darkness, there burned a true light, untainted by the powers of the underworld? I was fascinated by the hope and began attending Miss Kuhlman's monthly meetings at the Shrine Auditorium in Los Angeles.

On several occasions I heard Miss Kuhlman speak out against the very things I had been involved in—the occult, astrology, spiritism. She seemed to know what she was talking about. Unlike my psychiatrists, psychologists, and psychoanalysts, she spoke with authority. Instead of asking questions, she gave answers. And when she prayed she got results. I determined I would go about setting myself free from my bondages.

I began to pray for healing, asking God to take away my need for drugs. And I decided to exorcise my apartment, to cleanse it of all evil spirits. I knew nothing of the mechanics of exorcism, so I asked some of my spiritist friends about it. "I want to do it the Bible way," I said.

They had all kinds of suggestions, and one of them was to burn frankincense and myrrh (certainly that was in the Bible). This seemed like a good idea to chase off the evil spirits, and I decided to lace the mixture with something called "dragon's blood powder" to make it more potent.

One night I filled the apartment with incense and walked through it quoting the Ninety-first Psalm for good luck and to bolster my courage. Then I lit the frankincense and myrrh tablets, put the burning pellets in a flat dish shaped like a pie pan, sprinkled on the "dragon's blood," and set the dish on the floor near my bed.

The minute I turned my back, I heard a thump and smelled a different kind of smoke. Whirling around, I saw that the dish was turned upside-down on the floor. The underside of my bed was on fire!

I raced into the bathroom, got a glass of water, and ran back to the bed. Kneeling beside it, I lifted the box springs with my left hand to throw the water on the fire.

Suddenly I felt some superhuman force smash the mattress and springs downward, pinning my hand between the burning springs and the bed railing. At the same moment the fire literally exploded from the bed.

I tried to pull my hand loose. It was stuck. I was pinned against the burning bed. Flames raced through the room, igniting the curtains and walls. "God help me!" I screamed. Then I gave a final jerk, yanked my hand free, and stumbled out of the room into the hall.

By the time the Fire Department arrived the apartment was totally destroyed. After the embers cooled, I went back in. The bedroom was charcoal, like the inside of a crematorium. I had lost everything—except my life.

In February, 1972, I returned to the Shrine Auditorium for another Miracle Service. Since my brush with death, I could hardly wait to get back and be in the presence of the Holy Spirit. That Sunday afternoon, sitting about halfway back on the main floor, I began to pray for others around me. Suddenly I was aware of the darkness in which so many walked. How many others—thousands, millions—must be stumbling along as I was, trying to snatch themselves loose from the clutches of the Evil One?

As I prayed, I became aware of a Presence around me and over me. I knew at once who He was. I had never met Him before, but we needed no introduction. I had been searching for Him all my life, and suddenly He was there. Jesus was there.

I felt a great warmth go through my body, and I began to weep. Sometimes I brought people with me to the services, but this Sunday I had come by myself. I was grateful not to have to explain what was happening to me. Jesus was there, engulfing me with His love. And in that moment I knew I was loved with a love far greater than any man could ever give. I was being held in the arms of the Father Himself. It was as though there had been a vacancy in my heart all those years, with a sign on it that said, "Reserved for Jesus Christ." Now He had come, and all my love needs were met.

I knew I would never need drugs again. It was just like that—definite, absolute. I was healed.

After the service dismissed I made my way through the crowd. I could hardly wait to be alone. Always before I had needed people around me, great mobs of admiring people. Now I wanted—needed—no one else. Just being with Him was enough.

I ate a quiet dinner in a small restaurant off the main thoroughfares and then drove to my tiny, one-room apartment. I went first to the bathroom and emptied the contents of the bottles and boxes in the medicine chest into the toilet. Never again would I be a slave to drugs. Then I pulled my roll-away bed out and opened it up. It was so natural to kneel down beside it, to pray and thank Him for what He had done.

That night, for the first time in nine years, I slept peacefully. No drugs, no bad dreams, no insomnia. I realized the meaning of the verse: "I will both lay me down in peace and sleep; for thou, Lord, only makest me dwell in safety" (Psalm 4:8).

All my troubles didn't end with that one experience. There have still been discouraging and lonely times. Most of my old "friends" have drifted away, and I am having to form new friendships with Believers. There are still times of distress and temptation, but now I know I am not alone. I am loved. And I am learning to let Him fight my battles for me.

Sometimes at night, after I have turned the lights out, I am aware of evil forces around me. I no longer go through rites of exorcism, nor do I even speak to the spirits. I simply pray, "Jesus, I need Your help. They're back. Will You come and make them go away?"

He always answers my prayer.

TEN

Skeptic Under a Fur Hat

Jo Gummelt

The wife of a former senior Southern Baptist pastor in Washington, D.C., Mrs. Jo Gummelt was recognized as one of the top Congressional aides on Capitol Hill. A native of Mobile, Alabama, she graduated from Baylor University and then moved to Fort Worth, Texas, where her husband, Walter, was a graduate student at Southwestern Baptist Theological Seminary. Since 1958 the Gummelts have lived in District Heights, Maryland, where Walter has served in many high-ranking denominational positions.

Like most Southern Baptists, I believed the Bible was the inspired record of God's revelation to mankind. I thanked God for the way He had spoken to the prophets and the apostles. I believed that when Jesus touched people they were healed. I believed that following His ascension to heaven those 120 believers in the upper room at the time of Pentecost, and many others in the Early Church, received the power of the Holy Spirit. I believed these same men and women spoke in tongues, performed miracles, laid hands on the sick and saw them recover. But for some reason I failed to understand that God could pour out His Spirit on me, today, in the same fashion.

It's not that I didn't want to receive His Spirit, feel His power, even manifest the gifts of the Spirit. I did. In fact, I had been leading a ladies' group in our church in a study of the Holy Spirit. It's just that I thought Pentecost was some-

145

thing in the long ago. I had to die, almost, before I could receive God's truth of life today.

Back in 1949, after I graduated from high school in Mobile, Alabama, my father brought me to Washington, D.C., for a graduation present. Dad had been sick most of my life, but he saved up enough money for two Greyhound bus tickets and a visit to my older brother, who had a job in the library of the Supreme Court.

My brother knew Truman Ward, the majority clerk in the House of Representatives. Mr. Ward offered me a job as a typing clerk, and at sixteen I became the youngest steno on Capitol Hill. Three days later, the late Senator Spessard Holland of Florida offered me $3,000 a year to be one of his secretaries. That was more than Daddy had ever made back in Mobile, and I knew I was in Washington to stay.

Marriage held no appeal for me as I buried myself in the excitement of Washington politics, soon graduating to a higher-paying job with another congressman. My drive for efficiency and perfection made me an ideal aide—and I loved it. Three hours of sleep a night, plus a fifteen-minute nap at lunch following a fifteen-cent hotdog, were all I needed. But already I was developing life and work patterns that would almost destroy me before I was forty years old.

During those first years in Washington I came in contact with a group of young people from the Metropolitan Baptist Church who were different. I could tell from their joy and their constant witness that they had something I didn't have. They had victory. These Washington young people stimulated me to a new thirst—to be like Jesus, to give my life totally to Him in full-time service. The "fullest time" service I could think of was becoming a missionary doctor. Maybe it was Dad's constant sickness; maybe it was reading about Jesus laying hands on the sick and healing them—whatever it was, I wanted to see people healed, and medical missions was the only healing outlet I knew about.

I enrolled at Baylor University in Waco, Texas. My employer, the late Representative Prince Preston of Georgia, helped me financially, and told me that when I ran short of money, I could come back to Washington for a semester, and my job would always be waiting. I took advantage of his offer, and alternating between Waco and Washington, finally graduated in six years.

It was while I was at Baylor that I met Walter Gummelt, a handsome, wavy-haired blond with an athletic build. Walter graduated ahead of me and went on to Fort Worth where he enrolled at Southwestern Baptist Theological Seminary. We were married immediately after my graduation. My ambition of becoming a medical missionary had been replaced with an even greater ambition—that of being a pastor's wife. Following Walter's graduation from seminary, we returned to Washington. I went back to work and Walter accepted the call as pastor of the Parkway Baptist Church, a new congregation in District Heights, Maryland.

Immediately I was back in my old life-style, working unbelievably long hours, eating poorly, and doing every task with precision perfection. I was able to maintain my health for the first several years. But then, gradually, the pressures of being a pastor's wife, coupled with the incredible pressures of working in Congress, began to take their toll. I began to lose weight. Some mornings I would awake more exhausted than when I had gone to bed. I had several miscarriages before I was finally able to carry a baby to fullterm pregnancy. I worked right up until little Gordon was born, and then after a brief layoff, I was back on the job—addicted to work.

When my boss failed in his bid for reelection, Walter suggested this was a sign from God for me to quit working. However, before I had time to consider his advice, I was offered one of the top political plums. A congressman from Texas asked me to become his administrative assistant—the top aide in a congressman's office.

The job demanded a perfectionist, and I had developed the reputation on Capitol Hill of being just that—driving, efficient, loyal. I accepted the position and drove myself unmercifully managing his office, directing all the personnel,

writing speeches, and staying to do legislative research long
after the office closed. Night after night I dragged home
after dark, and sitting on the piano bench in the front room
with papers spread out before me, worked until the early
hours of the morning.

My weight continued to drop. I had three more miscarriages and developed three bleeding ulcers—a congressional trademark and the inevitable consequence of inner-
office conflicts and harassment from jealous male subordi-
nates who wanted my job. I was working seventy hours a
week, getting less than four hours sleep a night, and still
trying to take my place in the church beside Walter.

Then the headaches started again. The migraines would
begin with a low, dull pain in the back and on one side of
my head. Within an hour the pain was like fire roaring
through my brain. It was like having my skull in a giant
vise, squeezed so tightly I thought my head would explode.
With the pain came nausea, wave after wave of it, as my
body convulsed in agony.

The doctor said I had a "classic migraine personality,"
and put me on drugs. I began taking massive doses of Dar-
von Compound. It's nonaddictive, I was told, but I soon realized I was psychologically hooked. I increased the dosage
as the migraines became more severe—and more frequent.
Then, as in some nightmarish comedy, my hair started falling out. I blamed it on the miscarriages and the fact I was
getting older, but the prospect of being bald was something
less than funny. I bought a wig.

One windy spring day I left work early. Our offices were
in the Sam Rayburn Building, and as I walked out the front
door, I saw the circular drive lined with the big black lim-
ousines of Cabinet members. Each had a chauffeur standing beside the fender. I knew there was a special committee
hearing being conducted and thought little about it—until I
stepped off the curb. The wind lifted my wig and sent it
bouncing across the open circle in full view of all those uniformed men.

I screamed for help, but no one moved. Guards and
chauffeurs all stood with open mouths and watched as my

wig bounded over the grass and came to an ignominious stop in the middle of a tulip bed. Then they began roaring with laughter, and I could just picture congressmen from all over the building rushing to their windows as I scampered after my wig, slapped it back on my head, and marched down the driveway to the parking lot. To the men it was hilarious, but I wanted to cry. Why did I have to wear a wig? Why couldn't I be normal? I sat in my car in the parking lot and wept.

Several months later, groggy and weak, I crawled out of bed one morning and stumbled into the kitchen to fix Walter's breakfast. Standing at the stove, I began to cry, tears splashing on the hot burners and sending up little puffs of steam. I don't have a home anymore, I thought. Walter doesn't have a wife, because I'm married to my job. Yet he never complains. He's like the Rock of Gibraltar, while I'm coming apart at the seams. I dreaded the thought of facing another day in that congressional office.

I felt Walter's arm slip around my waist from behind, felt his face against the side of my neck, and smelled the faint aroma of his shaving lotion. How long had it been since I had stood and watched him shave? I used to have time for that, back when we were struggling along in the seminary.

I remembered those early years of our marriage. Our little duplex apartment on Stanley Street near Seminary Hill, the commuting to Wichita Falls where Walter preached on the weekends. We didn't have any money, but we could walk the deserted streets of downtown Fort Worth late at night and look in the windows. Sometimes, for an evening's entertainment, I'd go with him to the campus and sit beside him in the library while he pored over the Bible commentaries, preparing for a test. Or maybe we'd just walk around in the rotunda, looking at the pictures of the past presidents of the seminary, and holding hands. Now I had no time for things like that, no time just to sit and look at him. No time to walk the streets, hold hands, window-shop. No time to splash shaving lotion on his freshly razored face and giggle as we rubbed noses. The tears kept rolling down my face and onto the hot stove.

"It's not worth it, Jo," Walter said gently. He was always gentle, kind. "Give it up. We don't need the extra money. Give it up before it kills you."

He was right, but it was too late. I went to the doctor, and he just shook his head. Bleeding ulcers, migraine headaches! He put me on permanent total disability. "Get lots of rest," he cautioned, "or something drastic could happen." He didn't know it, and neither did I, but something drastic already had happened. I had begun to die.

Walter thought it would be good to take our camping trailer and drive up into the Allegheny Mountains for a week's vacation. I didn't feel like camping. Gordon was six years old and a bundle of energy. Yet I went along, determined to make the best of it.

Leaving the trailer in a campground in the Allegheny State Park in lower New York, we drove up to the Canadian border to visit Niagara Falls. It was a tiring day, walking the concrete paths, climbing the steps, riding the boat to the base of the roaring falls. On the way back to the trailer, with Gordon asleep in the back seat, I began to feel sick with a different kind of sickness than I had ever had before. I felt tremendous pressure on both sides of my lower back, like the water of the Niagara River building up behind a dam. When I tried to move around in the seat, the pain grew worse. The road we were riding on was under repair, and every bump sent spasms of agony through my body. Then, slowly, I became aware of something else—a spreading paralysis moving across my back. I gasped and gripped Walter's arm, my fingers digging into his flesh.

"What is it, Jo?" he said, alarmed. "You're white as a sheet."

"I don't know," I choked out. "But I'm scared. I'm losing all sensation in my back." This wasn't a simple ulcer or headache. The pain throbbed through my back and into my stomach. Wave after wave of nausea caused me to gag. For the first time in my life, I knew what it was like to feel the fingers of death.

By the time we reached the trailer it was dark. I collapsed on the bed while Walter took Gordon and went to find out about a hospital. He returned, saying the nearest one was miles away. I bit my lips. "Maybe if I rest I'll feel better." Walter was concerned but submitted to my insistence to wait until morning. But as the night wore on, I got worse. I felt like my body was falling to pieces inside.

Early in the morning I pulled myself out of bed to use the bathroom. I passed something out of my system, and when I did, the pain seemed to ease. I stumbled back to bed, and just as the sun rose above the trees, I dozed off.

It was midmorning when I awoke. The camper was empty, but I could hear Walter and Gordon outside. When I started to raise up, I discovered I was lying in a puddle of blood.

Walter insisted on rushing me to a hospital, but once again, as I calmed him down, I was able to persuade him otherwise. "Just take me home. If I can just get into my own bed I'll be all right."

But I wasn't all right, and Walter rushed me to a specialist in internal medicine.

The minute I described my symptoms, I saw the look of alarm on the doctor's face. "You just don't ignore this kind of bleeding, Mrs. Gummelt," he said. After taking Xrays, his voice was stern. "I want you in Doctors' Hospital tonight."

I could tell something was terribly wrong. "What is it?" I asked.

"We'll know more in a few days. But right now it looks like you're literally passing parts of your kidney."

The diagnosis: a form of renal papillary necrosis, a rare and very severe kidney disease that results in the deterioration of the inner kidney. The urologist described it by saying my kidneys were like two rotten sponges, waiting for any subtle bacteria to come through my system to attack them and cause additional deterioration. Almost half of each kidney was already gone, breaking off and passing from my system. I was dying.

Walter sent a letter to the congregation, asking them to

pray for me. Although praying for the sick—praying in faith and with authority—was foreign to most of the people in our church, there was a group of our women who realized that God had prepared them for this time and this place—to pray for my healing.

About a year before, some of the young housewives in the church had come to me, begging me to teach them. They wanted a deeper walk with the Lord, but didn't know how to find it. They seemed to sense that despite my frayed nerves and sick body, I could point them in the right direction.

Many years before, while I was a student at Baylor, something had happened to me. One afternoon, walking across 8th Street in Waco, I was hit with the overpowering realization that the Holy Spirit lived within me. Tears welled up in my eyes, and I could hardly find the sidewalk on the other side of the street. "How thrilling, yet how awesome," I gasped. "I take Him every place I go!"

In that moment the Holy Spirit had become a person to me, hearing all my words, knowing all my thoughts, seeing all my actions. For weeks I walked around the Baylor campus oblivious to problems, immersed in the Holy Spirit, in love with the Lord. I started tithing not only my money, but my time in Bible study and prayer. At the end of the period I was spending something like five hours a day in communion with the Lord. But it hadn't stayed with me. It was an affair rather than a love relationship. Yet, even though my infatuation with the Holy Spirit faded, my knowledge of His power remained.

Therefore, when these young ladies came to me, seeking a deeper walk with the Lord, it was natural that I should begin to teach them what the Bible had to say about the Holy Spirit. I knew I was a novice. I suspected that even though I was speaking all the right words, I really didn't understand what I was saying.

"Pentecost is not in the past tense," I had said.

"If the Bible is true, then," the ladies asked, "why can't we take it literally? Why can't we expect miracles and healings today?"

As Baptists, we believed the Bible to be the inspired Word of God, and asking such questions brought on frustrations. I wanted to be intellectually honest, but because I had never seen a miracle, never really seen a physical demonstration of God's power, I had trouble believing.

We dug deeper into the Word, trying to find our answers. Somehow, we knew, this deeper walk with God was tied into the doctrine of the Holy Spirit. But what we needed and yearned for was a demonstration of God's power, not just talks about it. That demonstration was to come on Saturday morning, the week after I had been admitted to the hospital.

It was my thirty-seventh birthday. The women in the study group had come to the hospital to visit me. As they stood around the bed, I could tell something was different.

"How are you feeling?" Pat Vandeventer asked. Pat's husband was in the Navy, and they had joined our church not because they were dyed-in-the-wool Baptists but because the Lord had told them to join. Very few people joined Parkway Baptist Church because God told them to, but Pat Vandeventer had.

I was weak, very weak, and under heavy sedation, but I managed a faint smile and said, "A little better. I'm not hemorrhaging as much."

"Praise the Lord!" Pat said softly and winked across the bed at one of the other women. This one, in turn, smiled and nodded at another. Everyone was nodding and smiling, like they knew something I didn't know. And indeed they did—only I didn't find it out for several weeks.

Then, one afternoon while I was alone in my hospital room, Pat came in and told me what had happened that Saturday morning. "When we received the Pastor's letter," she said, "all of us in the prayer group knew it meant you were dying. We also knew that if all the things we had been studying in the prayer group were real, now was the time to find out. Either God heals or He doesn't. It was as simple as that."

"That sounds like you were going to put God to a test," I said.

"No, not that," Pat answered, pulling her chair closer to the bed. "We just decided to meet together and trust Him for your healing. If anything, God was putting *us* to a test —to see if we believed what He said in His Word. The entire group, all eight of us, got up together on that Saturday morning for a sunrise prayer meeting on a little knoll in the municipal park."

I waited quietly while Pat paused. Her eyes began to glisten with moisture. "It was a very sacred and precious time for each of us. As we waited for God, each one of us, in a personal way, received a demonstration of God's power. We all knew you were going to be healed, miraculously."

"I don't understand," I interrupted. "I know I'm better, but that's just because I'm here in the hospital and they're pumping me full of drugs. But the doctor says my kidneys are gone."

"We know that," Pat said, that silly grin reappearing on her face. "But we also know that God has demonstrated His power, the power we've been reading about in the Bible. We know you are going to be healed."

"You say He demonstrated His power? How?"

Pat stood and walked to the window. She talked softly, as if she were reliving those moments at dawn in the park. "Each one of us felt Him at the same time, yet in different ways. I was sitting on the bench, my head in my hands, and it seemed as if my heart would break. We had all come to love you with a love far deeper than any of us had ever before experienced. Now it seemed as if we were going to lose you. We started out by praying for you, but then, just as it began to get light, we all choked up. We couldn't pray any longer, and just sat, weeping silently. Then, deep within my heart, there came a blanket of peace, like new snow that falls and covers the dull, gray landscape with pure white. And I knew, Jo. I knew God *had* healed you. There were no fireworks, no earthquakes, just a deep inner assurance that you were already healed . . . and in God's time you would know it." Pat turned from the window, facing me. "I looked up, and all the other girls were smiling through their tears. At the same moment, they, too, had received the same message. We left the park knowing, and we've not doubted since."

"But I'm not healed," I argued.

"Oh, yes, you are," Pat said firmly, her eyes sparkling with determination and faith. "We know the doctors have told Pastor Gummelt your illness is incurable, but remember, our God is a God of the impossible."

I knew I was deathly sick. But *incurable?* I forgot everything else Pat had said as that one word kept ringing through my mind.

Many, many specialists were called in over the next several weeks. I had the first positively diagnosed case of this particular form of the kidney disease in the Washington area. From one of the urologists I learned that a study had been made of 125 persons in Sweden who had the same condition as mine and similar symptoms. But he hedged when I asked him the results of the study. All I could assume was that all 125 had died. The only encouragement the doctors gave was the hope they could stabilize my kidneys and perhaps stop the deterioration. I knew it was beyond medical power to heal me.

Finally I was dismissed from the hospital and told to spend twelve to fourteen hours a day in bed. The warning wasn't necessary. I was completely drained. Always before I had been able to reach down inside, someplace, and pull out a little more strength or energy to complete a job. But this time, when I reached down inside, I found only emptiness.

The second morning home I waited until Walter had gone to work. Then I got up to open the bedroom window. It took all my energy just to cross the room, and tugging on the window was the same exertion as running two miles through the city. I fell back into bed, panting from exhaustion, the window unopened. I could feel my swollen kidneys bulging through my back.

My reserve strength, that little extra something that keeps a person from dying when he reaches the end of his rope, was gone. "Just one tiny bacterium," the doctor had said, "picked up from impure water, and you could be dead in a short time."

There were other pressures building at the same time. The doctor had told me that I could return to church as soon as I felt like it, but no more than once a week. Before I went in the hospital my weight was down to almost 100 pounds. But when I was released, my body began to retain fluids, and I was swollen, puffy. I didn't want anyone to see me like that.

During the next year I was in and out of the hospital. There were constant visits to the doctor's office for cultures and tests. As my body built up immunity to one drug, he would shift to another—and with it came all the tests to see if the new drug itself might kill me. It seemed I was in the doctor's office all the time, X ray after X ray. To combat the internal infections that were always springing up, I was constantly being treated with new antibiotics. Our drug bill climbed.

Preparing for death is a terrifying psychological experience. My entire life-style was changing. I knew I was dying, and it was very difficult having to adjust to the fact while I was still alive. My family doctor suggested a psychiatrist. "Maybe he can give you some help with these migraines," he said. I hoped so, praying only that I could just lie down in peace and get on with the business of dying.

I wasn't able to function as a wife or a mother. I wasn't able to do any housework. I could hear Gordon coming in after school and hear him creep down the hall past my room to keep from disturbing me. I remembered how it was when I was a child and Dad was always sick and all the children had to creep around the house for fear of waking him up. Now here it was again. I felt horribly guilty. That's all my son will ever remember about his mother, I thought. Sick in bed behind a closed door. Is this horrible thing to be passed from generation to generation?

Then things began to happen. It began with a letter from my younger sister who, having heard my disease was terminal, suggested I read Kathryn Kuhlman's book, *I Believe in Miracles*. Two days later, lying in bed listening to a local radio station, I heard an announcement concerning a convention of the Full Gospel Business Men's Fellowship International to be held at the Washington Hilton. The announcement meant nothing until I heard the name Kathryn Kuhlman. She was to speak at an afternoon meeting. Odd that I should hear that name twice in one week.

God wasn't through yet. The next afternoon Pat Vandeventer came by. "Jo, let's go to the Full Gospel Business Men's Convention. Kathryn Kuhlman is going to speak Thursday afternoon."

Three times in one week couldn't be just a coincidence. Still I resisted. "Sorry, Pat, I can't buy this woman-preacher stuff," I said.

"I thought you were broadminded," Pat chided, her eyes twinkling. "You're not broad, you're just Baptist."

She was hitting me where it hurt, and I knew she was right. I was judging this woman on the basis that I had never seen her name in print in any of our Southern Baptist Convention literature. I read it all, and never, not once, had I ever heard of a Kathryn Kuhlman. I doubted if she was even of the Lord, since Southern Baptists didn't seem to recognize her.

I looked at Pat. "Okay, you're on. My heart is just as hungry as yours for the deep things of the Spirit. And if we can learn something about God from somebody other than a Southern Baptist, I'm ready."

Pat picked me up Wednesday evening and we drove across town to the Washington Hilton for the opening-night meeting of the Full Gospel Business Men's Convention. In my life I had been to many, many Baptist meetings, all the way from local associational meetings to the huge annual Southern Baptist Conventions. But this was unlike any meeting I had ever attended. The keynote was joy, joy and freedom. More than 3,000 people were seated in the lush ballroom, and every one of them seemed to be exploding with joy. I had never seen so many smiling faces.

I was suspicious immediately. People didn't smile like that at the Baptist meetings I had attended. In fact, they didn't even smile like that at our church.

I had brought my tape recorder so I could capture what the speaker had to say, but it was hopeless. The man in the seat next to me was so happy he kept talking at the same time the speaker was talking. Every other sentence that came from the pulpit he answered by his shout of, "Praise the Lord," or "Thank You, Jesus."

I had heard a few "Amens" back at Baylor or at the chapel services at Southwestern Seminary, but never anything like this. I was irritated. Why doesn't he shut up? I moaned inside.

I left the meeting confused. Could all this be real? Were these people genuinely happy, or were they just psychologically unbalanced? As for me, I felt a migraine headache coming on and asked Pat to drive faster.

The migraine was with me when I woke up the next morning. The psychiatrist had prescribed a series of drugs, one pill every thirty minutes for three hours. The drugs made me horribly sick to my stomach, but they did ease the pain in my head. Always before, by the time I had taken the fifth pill the pain would be easing, but I'd be in bed from sickness caused by the drugs. I knew that Pat would have to go to the Kathryn Kuhlman meeting alone.

But this time it was different. Strangely, the head pain went away, and my body, if anything, seemed stronger. I was going to be able to get to the Miracle Service after all.

Walter was president of the D.C. Baptist Pastors' Conference that year. They were having a luncheon meeting, and just before noon Walter called to check on my condition. I told him Pat and I were going to attend the Kathryn Kuhlman meeting.

Walter was chuckling. "Several of the local Baptist pastors are planning to attend," he said. "Most of them are curious and will probably have their coats pulled up around their faces in hopes no one will recognize them." I didn't have the heart to tell him that I had just taken down my big fur hat, the one that pulled down over my ears, and planned to wear it so no one would recognize me, either.

I was in a daze all afternoon. We arrived at the hotel one and a half hours late—but found a parking place right in

front, not realizing that every parking lot and space within
a four-block radius was filled.

We wedged ourselves into the overpacked ballroom,
hoping to find seats near the back where we could sit and
observe. We thought we would have to remain standing at
the door when suddenly two ladies near the front got up
and left their seats. We were seated almost before we knew
it. I kept my fur hat pulled down as far as it would go,
barely able to peek out beneath the brim.

Miss Kuhlman was speaking. There was such a dynamic
hush in the room I could almost hear my own heart beating. Her voice was soft, so very soft, almost indistin-
guishable at times. I had to strain to hear every word. She
wasn't saying anything new or different. Everything she
said I had heard Walter say a hundred times from the pulpit of Parkway Baptist Church. But there was a different
spirit about this place, about her. People had come expecting, and she was speaking with authority. Although deeply
moved, I was still skeptical.

There was a little blind girl behind me, and I began to
pray for her. "Lord, please touch that little girl." I felt the
tears crowding through my closed eyelids. Suddenly we
were all standing as Miss Kuhlman began to sing:

> Lord, I receive,
> Lord, I receive.
> All things are possible;
> Lord, I receive.

"Lift your arms," she said softly. "Lift your arms and receive the Holy Spirit."

"Lift my arms?" Suddenly I was a very proper Southen
Baptist pastor's wife again. What if someone saw me? One
of Walter's pastor friends? One of our church members?
But I couldn't help myself. My hands were already at half-
mast, and it was as if they were tied with puppet string. Up,
up—I couldn't control them. I felt as if my body was being
stretched and that I was going to be pulled up on tiptoes.
Never had I stretched so far, reached so high. When my

hands were all the way up, I felt my palms turn upward
and at the same time my head dropped. I never felt such
humility in all my life. I totally forgot myself, who I was,
where I was, and knew only that God was literally touching
me with a physical touch. It felt like warm water pouring
over me from my head to my feet.

Then I heard a voice, coming down the aisle. "Oh God,
the glory on this one." It was Miss Kuhlman. I didn't even
know she had left the platform.

She touched my wrist ever so lightly. I felt a weight-
lessness, and it seemed I had floated off into space and was
gliding around the ceiling in the arms of Jesus. A man behind me kept saying, "Let me help you up."

I ignored him, wondering what he was doing up there on
the ceiling with me. I just wanted to stay where I was, but
he wouldn't go away. His voice kept ringing in my ears.
"Let me help you up. Let me help you up."

What do you mean, "up"? I thought. I'm already as high
as I can get, up here on the ceiling.

Finally I opened my eyes. I was flat on my back in the
aisle, my hands stretched upward, my lips saying over and
over again, "Praise the Lord! Praise the Lord!" I didn't
care who saw or heard me.

On the way home, Pat and I relived every moment of the
meeting. It never occurred to me I might have been healed.
I hadn't gone for that, anyway. All I knew was I had been
touched by God and that something inside me, deep inside,
was different.

"Let's not tell our husbands," Pat said. "I don't believe
they'll understand." I agreed. But I knew that in God's time
Walter would be ready to hear—and understand.

God's time came one week later. Walter had gotten up
early to attend a pastors' breakfast meeting to help plan a
city-wide revival with Dr. Paul Rader, a Baptist evangelist.
Dr. George Schuler, who had written *Overshadowed,* was
to be there. Walter, as president of the Pastors' Conference, was the moderator.

I slept late that Saturday morning and was awakened by
the ringing of the phone. When Walter came home I was

sitting on the side of the bed talking. I glanced up as he came into the bedroom. He paused and then walked out again. But he kept coming back, in and out, and finally he interrupted saying, "When you get off the phone I've got something to tell you."

Walter never interrupted, and I realized he needed to talk—quickly. I immediately cut off the phone conversation and almost beat him into the kitchen. We sat at the breakfast table and I waited, expectantly. "I need to share something with you," he said. "Something wonderful that happened this morning."

He tried to talk, but I saw him welling up inside. I had never seen him like that before. Walter was solid, stable, very dependable; he seldom showed any emotion. But now, every time he opened his mouth to talk, his eyes filled with tears. He finally reached over, took my hand, and just sat there, looking out the kitchen window, waiting for his emotions to subside. Finally he was able to speak, haltingly, with long pauses between phrases as he fought to keep his voice under control.

"The room was filled with pastors," he said softly, "and the chairman of the revival planning committee was speaking. Then this tall, white-haired man, Dr. Schuler, walked into the room. His hair was like a coarse mane, surrounding his head like a halo. But there was something else surrounding him, too—an aura, a glow. Every pastor in that room stopped talking the moment he entered. There was dead silence. We knew, every one of us knew, that the Holy Spirit had come in with that man. I finally spoke up and said, 'Why don't we all kneel and pray?'

"Immediately, every man in the room dropped to his knees. I don't know what happened. All I know is there was something in the very air of the room that commanded our worship. Never have I felt the presence of God so overpowering."

Walter finished talking, obviously still shaken from the experience. Then it was my turn. As gently as I could, I told him what had happened to me just one week before. He sat listening, solemn and silent. I talked on, telling him how the ladies had prayed, about the meeting, and finally of my experience at the Washington Hilton when Kathryn Kuhlman had touched my wrist.

He just sat there and nodded, like he knew all about it. I could see that God had prepared him that morning by visiting those ministers with this shattering experience, so that no matter what I said, Walter was ready to receive it as from the Lord.

"Were you healed?" he asked.

"I don't know," I grinned. "I haven't thought much about it. All I know is the depression has been lifted. That horrible cloud I lived under is gone. The need to be perfect is gone. The inability to accept myself as imperfect in soul as well as body, all this is gone. I am free."

"But how are you feeling physically?" Walter probed.

"Wonderful," I said. "I've stopped taking all my drugs and antibiotics. For the first time in years I have new strength and energy."

"I believe you've been healed," Walter said, his eyes filling up with tears again. "I think you need to go back to the doctor and have him check you out to make sure."

The next week I was back in the doctor's office. There were more X rays and examinations.

Two days later I took my seat across from his desk. "What's happened to you, Mrs. Gummelt?" he asked.

"I was hoping you'd ask," I smiled. And I told him, in detail, exactly what had happened.

For a long time he sat staring at the wall where his medical certificates hung. Finally he picked up the manila folder on his desk. "I'm closing the book on your case," he said. "You're completely healed. There is no evidence of any kidney problem at all, only scar tissue from past damage. If you ever have any more problems with your kidneys, it will be a totally new case."

I wanted to dance with joy, and later I did. No more drugs, no more swelling, no more bleeding, no more weakness! Now I could live a normal, healthy life as a wife and mother. I knew how Lazarus must have felt when he walked out into the sunshine, blinking. My life had been restored. To God be the glory!

Within three months my weight climbed from 97 pounds to 157 pounds. For the first time in my life I had to go on a diet.

Something else happened. By accepting the Holy Spirit into my life, I was able to accept myself also, the way I was. My tension was replaced with ease. The migraine headaches disappeared. Not only had my body been restored, but my mind had been renewed. Hallelujah!

Six months later I was able to go back to work. It was a new Jo Gummelt who walked into the Sam Rayburn Building on Capitol Hill. I had promised the Lord that if He let me go back to work, I would give Him most of what I made. I went to work for a congressman from Kentucky, willing to be "just a secretary," free from the compulsion to be at the top, to be perfect. Within a short period all the girls in our office had accepted Jesus as Saviour, and half of them had been baptized in the Holy Spirit. Never had I been so aware of the power of the Holy Spirit to witness for Jesus.

About the time I started back to work, Walter, Gordon, and I took a little vacation trip together. The first night out, I went into the bathroom of our motel room to wash my hair. Walter and Gordon sat in the bedroom watching TV. As I ran my hands through the shampoo in my hair, I noticed something different in the texture of my hair. I looked up from the wash basin, brushed the soap out of my eyes, and sure enough, all around the edge of my face was thick, new growth. I was growing new hair. The wig could go back into the closet.

People began coming to me for counsel. Before, I was always to weak to help them. Now I was able to share out of personal experience with a God who demonstrates His love and power. I began spending long hours on my knees in prayer, with the Bible lying open before me. I literally wore indentions in the carpet as the Lord taught me on my knees and gave me a meaningful new prayer language. In the spring, about a year after I had been healed, I had a slight urinary infection. I knew that when God heals, He heals for good. But the old fear came roaring back, and I ran to my doctor.

He examined me, then stood with his hands on his hips, looking at me rather sternly. "You have a minor bladder infection," he said. "I told you when you were here last time that if you ever had any more kidney problems it wouldn't be the same disease. You've been healed."

I left the doctor's office, rebuked but grateful. Washington never seemed so beautiful. The cherry trees around the reflecting basin were in full bloom. The grass on the mall was lush green, and even the tulips were blooming at the Sam Rayburn Building again. The white dome of the Capitol sparkled against the backdrop of azure blue sky. People were hurrying to their jobs. Horns were blowing and traffic was thick. It was the same as it had been for years. But *I* was different. Pentecost had come to me!

ELEVEN

Once I Was Dying . . .

KEITH PURDUE

For the last several years Keith Purdue has traveled with the pianist, Roger Williams, as the drummer in his band. A native of Albuquerque, New Mexico, he studied music at the New England Conservatory under the expert tympanist for the Boston Symphony Orchestra. He now makes his home in a Los Angeles suburb.

I had just finished a full season as tympanist with the Mobile (Alabama) Symphony Orchestra, and in the fall of 1968 I moved to an apartment on Hollywood Boulevard in Hollywood, California. However, before signing the contract that would eventually place me as the drummer with Roger Williams' band, I decided to have a few warts removed.

I opened the yellow pages of the phone book and picked out the first dermatologist listed, a Dr. Samuel Ayres. His office was on Wilshire Boulevard, just around the park.

The warts seemed to be common varieties and I didn't expect any trouble. While in the doctor's office I casually mentioned a mole on the inside of my right arm, between the wrist and elbow, which had recently become red and inflamed. Dr. Ayres took one look at it and said, "That has got to come out."

Dr. Ayres did a rather thorough excision of the area, taking a very large sample of tissue. He explained this was a customary precaution—in case the mole was malignant. I was to come back in a week, after they had studied the biopsy.

When I returned he ushered me into his private office and asked me to have a seat. "Mr. Purdue, it seems we have a problem. I sent the tissue sample to the three leading pathologists in Southern California. Their biopsy report shows every cell to be malignant."

"Wow!" I whistled. "Now what happens?"

"I recommend immediate surgery and want to refer you to Dr. Lewis Guiss, a highly qualified surgeon at the University of Southern California and at St. Vincent's Hospital. He will be able to offer an expert opinion as to how we should proceed."

It was hard to comprehend. I had always pictured myself as a carefree young bachelor, traveling all over the nation, playing in various bands and symphony orchestras. Now it looked like all that might change—even come to an end.

Dr. Guiss called the condition "black cancer," the most serious form, which spreads through the lymph nodes. He hoped the malignancy was still confined to my arm, but stated it could have already spread throughout my body, especially up into my chest and neck. Immediate surgery was necessary.

"Is there a chance my arm will atrophy when you cut the muscles?" I asked. A professional drummer without the full, sensitive use of his arm is like a bird with only one wing.

"Well," Dr. Guiss said, "we're using a new method in which we don't cut the muscles themselves. We just cut the skin, pull the muscles out of the way, and excise the lymph nodes. I don't think you'll have to worry about losing the use of your arm."

Somehow I didn't feel he was as optimistic about it as he should be. Before I left the office I asked him twice more, and he finally confessed that although they could save my arm, he was fearful that the cancer had already spread throughout my body. He gave me a 70 percent chance of survival—if it hadn't spread too far.

I agreed to immediate surgery, but before the hospital

would admit me, I needed a three-hundred-dollar deposit. I didn't have it. I called my mother in Albuquerque and asked for the money. At first she thought I was kidding when I told her about the cancer. Then she realized I wouldn't joke about a thing like that. "I'm coming out to California," she said.

"No, Mom," I argued. "There's no need for you to come out. It would be too hard on you. Just stay where you are and send me the money."

The money arrived, but a week before I was to go to the hospital, Mom arrived, too.

I didn't have a television in my bachelor apartment. I have to spend five to six hours a day practicing the drums, and that doesn't leave much time to watch the tube. Not knowing how long I would be in the hospital, and not wanting Mother to be trapped alone in my apartment without some entertainment, I went down the street to a motel and asked for a quiet room with a TV. Mom's not much of a TV fan, but I knew she liked to watch the basketball games. They would help her pass the time while I was in the hospital.

Mother told me later she was disappointed I didn't let her stay in my apartment, but it all turned out to be God's plan.

The Sunday before I was to be admitted, Mom woke up about seven o'clock and went to the restaurant across the street for some breakfast. Finding the restaurant closed, she went back to her room and turned on her television. Just as the set warmed up, even before the picture appeared, she heard the words "cancer operation." It startled her, scaring her a bit. She had heard enough about cancer lately without it coming over the TV, too. She reached up and turned off the set.

Then she had second thoughts. "I wonder just what that was all about?" she mused, and turned the set back on. She saw Kathryn Kuhlman interviewing a little girl who had been healed of leukemia. Mom listened, intrigued. She was getting ready to write down Miss Kuhlman's Pittsburgh address, intending to write to ask her to pray for me, when the announcer said, "To those of you in the Los Angeles viewing area, Miss Kuhlman will be appearing at the Shrine Auditorium this afternoon."

That afternoon I took Mom for a drive. "Have you ever heard of Kathryn Kuhlman?" she asked.

"No, who is she?"

"Well, I think she's some kind of faith healer," she answered.

Since then I've found out that Miss Kuhlman is no faith healer. In fact, she abhors the use of the term, emphasizing always that she herself has no power to heal anyone. But my mother's term "faith healer" set off some negative reactions in me. My folks had been Baptists for a number of years, and then we joined a Presbyterian church. As far as I was concerned, anything that sounded like "divine healing" smacked of Elmer Gantry, frauds who preyed on ignorant minds, and radio "healers" who hollered into microphones. Actually, I was pretty much disenchanted with the whole area of religion. It seemed like everybody was hanging up a bunch of negative rules, trying to legislate Christianity. I wanted no part of it and rather prided myself on successfully playing the role of the intellectual agnostic. If there was a God, it would be up to Him to prove Himself to me. I wasn't out searching for Him.

However, as Mom and I talked about Miss Kuhlman, something began to grow inside me, like a tiny blade of grass that pokes through the black asphalt of a parking lot. I recognized it as hope—a ray of hope. Maybe, just maybe, there was something to all this. Maybe I could be healed.

"Miss Kuhlman is at the Shrine Auditorium this afternoon," Mom said. "Would you like to go and see her?"

"Sure, why not," I said. "After all, I don't have anything to lose."

We arrived at the auditorium about three o'clock. When we drove into the parking lot the attendant said, "I'll take your money and let you park, but you're not going to get in." He pointed to the front of the auditorium. "See that crowd? The service started more than an hour ago, and some of them have been waiting since dawn and still couldn't get in."

"Well, we've come this far, we might as well make a final try," I said. We paid our money and parked the car.

We walked to the front of the building and began wedging our way through the mass of people. "It won't do any good," a man said. "I just tried the door, and it's locked. They lock the doors from the inside after the auditorium is full. The only way you can get a seat now is for somebody to leave early. Then they let people in one at a time."

We thanked him but continued to edge our way through the crowd until we got to the door. I pulled the handle, and the door opened. Mom and I quickly squeezed through, and it closed behind us. I heard the lock fall into place.

It didn't occur to me at the time that the opening door was the second miracle of the day, the first being when Mom just *happened* to turn on the TV that morning.

We walked through the lobby and stood in one of the tunnels leading into the huge auditorium. Even though the room was packed with people, almost eight thousand of them, it was filled with a reverent hush. An usher stepped up to us and whispered, "If you'll wait just a minute, I'll get you a couple of seats together."

I nodded my head and he moved off, almost tiptoeing so as to keep from disturbing the atmosphere of worship. Looking back, I see this was the third miracle; for even if there was a spare seat in that jam-packed auditorium, there couldn't be two of them together. But a few minutes later we sat down side by side underneath the balcony on the middle left side. Perfect seats!

There was a peace in the auditorium. Yet as I sat quietly, listening to Miss Kuhlman conclude her remarks, I also felt tension. It was the same tension I had felt in the Midwest on hot summer afternoons just before an electrical storm— the feeling of charged air, the impression of molecules dancing through the atmosphere ready to come together in one surging frenzy that will suddenly explode with power.

Miss Kuhlman was walking back and forth across the stage. She wasn't screaming or yelling, as I had thought she would be. She wasn't even preaching, just talking. She said, "I don't want anyone to come up here on the stage until you have been healed."

Amazing, I thought to myself. I had pictured her slapping people on the forehead, vibrating and shaking, screaming commands for the Lord to heal some poor wretch. It wasn't that way, but people started coming forward, testifying that they had been healed while they were sitting in their seats.

Many of them fell to the floor as Miss Kuhlman prayed for them. I surmised they had been bought off prior to the service—surely nobody in his right mind would fall flat on his back like that. Suddenly, in the midst of all this, something happened to me. I did the one thing I had bragged I would never do: I lost control.

I'm not an emotional person. I'm very cynical, skeptical, but I was also desperate. Cynicism, skepticism, and desperation don't make good partners. So I began to cry.

Something else happened. I discovered I couldn't move my arms or legs. More surprising still, it didn't bother me to sit there paralyzed. In fact, it was altogether a very wonderful feeling. Mom later told me that Miss Kuhlman said someone was being healed of cancer, but I didn't hear it. As a matter of fact, I didn't hear much of anything during this time. When the wonderful feeling passed, a new feeling, a conviction, took its place—a deep conviction that I no longer had cancer.

I had not said a word to Mom, but she knew something had happened to me. She turned and whispered, "Do you want to go up on the stage?"

I did not want to go up on stage. Yet before I knew it, I was on my feet, Mom beside me.

An usher approached us. "Have you been healed?" he asked.

Mom answered, certainty ringing in her voice. "Yes, he's been healed of cancer."

There was no outward indication of my healing—just a deep, inner feeling. The type of cancer I had didn't cause pain, at least not in the early stage it was at that time. Since there was no pain to take away, I really couldn't prove that I had been healed. But I had this deep, inner feeling of wholeness.

The usher looked at me and asked the question again. "Have you been healed?"

I realized I was lurching as I walked, and my words were slurred. "Yes, I think so," I managed to choke out.

Then I was on stage. Miss Kuhlman was coming toward me. "Oh, how wonderful," she said—and reached out to pray. The next thing I knew, I was flat on my back, looking up at the high ceiling of the Shrine Auditorium. My hands were stretched above my head. I saw they were gnarled, twisted, and curled up.

My first thought was, "Oh, my God! I'm paralyzed! I've traded my cancer for some kind of horrible paralysis." Then there was an electric tingling all through the upper part of my body, and I thought I was having a heart attack. But it felt good, and finally I quit worrying and just lay there, in perfect peace. Eventually, someone helped me to my feet. Mom and I made our way back to our seats and then out of the auditorium. Several minutes after leaving the building, I was able to open my hands and move my arms with ease.

As we drove back to my apartment, Mom remarked about how much younger I looked. I told her I felt sort of happy, like being a little kid again. It was almost like being born all over.

"Do you want to go ahead with the operation?" she asked.

"I might as well," I said. But inside I knew it wasn't really necessary. Not anymore.

I entered the hospital Thursday. My operation was scheduled for 7:30 the next morning. They prepared me for surgery, painted me with a lot of red goop, put some glucose in my left arm, and gave me some kind of anesthetic. The next thing I knew, I was hearing a nurse say, "You're in the recovery room now."

Then I was back in my own room. Mom was there. Dad was there, too, in from Albuquerque. I looked down at my arm and saw it was bandaged in a splint. I kept wondering if it was paralyzed.

Several days later the doctor came in to remove the splint and stitches. "Well, we have a good report," he said. "The biopsy was totally negative. We found no malignancy whatsoever."

I wasn't surprised, but needed to question him. "I thought the first biopsy showed total malignancy."

He shrugged. "It did, but when we got in there, everything was fine. I don't think you're going to have any trouble at all."

The formerly malignant cells had become benign—the bad had become good. It was an outer manifestation of something else that had happened in the far deeper areas of my life. I had been willing to believe if I could just be shown. I had been shown, in no uncertain terms.

There are still many things about God which I do not understand. But I do recognize Him as God—a God of love and power.

Recently I read a story in the Bible about a blind man who was touched by Jesus and received his sight. Later, when questioned by the religionists of the day about who Jesus was, he answered with what I feel is one of the most profound statements in the Gospels. He said simply, "Who He is, I'm not sure. But one thing I am sure of. I used to be blind; now I can see."

So don't come to me asking me to give you theological answers. I don't have any. All I know is that one day I had the kind of cancer that kills you in a hurry, and the next day I had none. Once I was dying, now I am alive. Of that I am sure.

TWELVE

Living Temporarily

MARVEL LUTON

Married for thirty-five years, the Lutons live near the Mexican border in Chula Vista, California. Their two married children live close-by. Marvel owned and operated a small beauty salon, and her husband Clarence worked as a Monotype operator for the San Diego Union Tribune. Although raised a Methodist, Mrs. Luton joined her husband in the Lutheran church soon after they were married. Since moving from Michigan to California eight years ago, they have both been active in their local Missouri Synod Lutheran church, and Clarence has served as president of the congregation.

It was dusk, with the burnt-orange remnant of a June sunset fading out over the Pacific Ocean as I parked my car in front of our house and walked up the sidewalk. I was exhausted after a heavy day of work in my beauty salon. Strange, I thought, that although Clarence's car was in the driveway, there were no lights turned on in the house.

I opened the door and walked into the semidark living room. On the far side I could hear the parakeets chirping from their cages on the organ bench near the window. Clarence was lying on the sofa. At first I thought he was asleep, but then I heard him moaning softly. I hurried across the room to kneel beside him. "What's wrong?" I asked.

"I'm sick," he said. He struggled to sit up, but his head fell back on the cushioned arm of the sofa. "I've vomited until there's nothing left but dry heaves. My insides feel like they're on fire."

I put my hand on his forehead. He was burning up with fever. "When did it start?"

"On the way home from work." He moaned and twisted on the sofa, his face creased with pain. "Some of us in the shop went out for lunch today. All I had was a hamburger and a glass of milk, but the hamburger tasted funny. I didn't think much about it until I got sick. I think I've got some kind of food poisoning."

"I'd better get you to the hospital," I said, heading for the telephone.

Dr. Elliot, our family doctor, met us at the emergency room of the Paradise Valley Hospital in National City. Tests showed toxic poison in Clarence's bloodstream and kidneys. He was put on the critical list, where he remained for five days. Gradually his strength returned, but even so, it was almost four months before he was strong enough to go back to work. "We came mighty close to losing him," the doctor said.

Although Clarence said he felt fine and was able to return to his job at the newspaper, I could tell that he never did get back to normal.

Ten months later, in April, my mother telephoned me. She had been concerned about the arthritis in my hands. "Marvel, some friends have been telling me about a woman who holds Miracle Services in Los Angeles. I understand that God often heals people at those meetings. One is scheduled this Sunday at the Shrine Auditorium. Would you like to go? Maybe God will heal your arthritis."

Clarence and I had been arguing over some petty matter and I was looking for an excuse to get out of the house. Not telling Clarence where I was going, I drove with my mother to Los Angeles, enjoyed the service, and returned home that evening. Later that night, standing at the kitchen sink, I noticed something different about my hands. The swelling was gone—and so was the pain. Clarence was sitting at the table drinking a glass of milk. "Clarence, look at my hands!" I exclaimed.

He came over to the sink. "Say, the swelling is all gone. Did you find a new doctor?"

Instead of answering his question, I asked, "Do you believe in miracles?"

"Well, sure," he said. "But what's that got to do with this?"

I told him where I had been and what had obviously happened. He was interested enough to go with me the next month to the meeting in the Shrine. In July our pastor and his wife also attended. He was enthusiastic about the meeting, even suggesting that we should start having healing services in our Lutheran church. Clarence and I were a little skeptical about that. I enjoyed the services in Los Angeles, and I was grateful for my healing, but I had some misgivings about changing our methods in the Lutheran church. However, our pastor remained excited. "In fact," he said, "I want the anointing of the Holy Spirit myself."

Almost a year to the day from his first sickness, Clarence took me out to eat in a small Chinese restaurant on the San Diego Bay. We both worked hard all the time, and such a treat was rare. We enjoyed the food and the atmosphere of leisure. About two o'clock the next morning, however, Clarence woke me as he stumbled to the bathroom, violently ill. By the time he got back to bed it was obvious that this was not just a routine upset stomach. He was desperately sick, with extreme pain, fever, and a bloated stomach. Suspecting more food poisoning, I called the doctor immediately.

He sent us to the emergency room of the hospital, where they took a blood sample for testing. This time, however, Clarence's test didn't show any poison in his system, and the nurse called our doctor to give him their report. He came immediately, and since the hospital was full, gave Clarence a shot for pain and told me to take him home, but to have him back at his office promptly at 9:30 A.M.

Clarence looked at the nurses, then at me, shaking his head. "Something's wrong inside me," he said. "Can't I stay here?"

"I'm sorry, Mr. Luton," one of the nurses said. "But

there are no beds available, and you can't remain here in the emergency room. That pain shot will take effect in a few minutes and you'll feel okay. Let your wife take you home."

He agreed, reluctantly. There was no sleep for either of us the rest of the night.

Mike, our son who lives close-by, agreed to take Clarence to the doctor's office at 9:30 A.M. I left for work a couple of hours earlier. Since my beauty salon was right next door to the doctor's office, I expected to hear from Clarence as soon as he finished his examination. But I heard nothing. After lunch I called the office and talked with the nurse.

"Mr. Lutton was extremely bloated when he came in this morning," she said, "and his skin was jaundiced. Dr. Elliot took him right into one of the examining rooms and put him on IV. About noon he put him in the hospital."

Because the Paradise Valley Hospital was full, Clarence was a patient in Bay General Hospital in Chula Vista. His problem: pancreatitis, infection of the pancreas. The bloating slowly subsided, and in about two weeks most of the yellow color was gone from his eyes and skin, so he was allowed to come home.

Very weak, hardly able to get out of bed, he continued to lose weight. In less than a month he dropped from 209 to 162 pounds. During this time the severe pain returned, along with more bloating. I took him back to the doctor.

X rays revealed a large mass in the area of the pancreas. So once again Clarence went back into the hospital, this time for exploratory surgery.

Our pastor was with me when Clarence came out of surgery. He had talked to Clarence just moments before he went into the operating room. Clarence had talked about dying and had told him that he was ready to go. Why would Clarence talk about dying? After the pastor left, I began wondering if he knew something he was not telling me.

It was eight o'clock that night before the surgeon telephoned me. "Your husband survived the surgery," he assured me. "But I can't tell you much more. His pancreas is one solid tumor."

"Couldn't you remove it?" I asked, realizing I knew very little about surgery.

"No," he answered. "We were afraid to touch it—even for a biopsy—for fear he would bleed to death on the operating table. However, we are analyzing the drainage from a large abscess and should be able to tell in a short time if the tumor is malignant or benign."

"Please, Doctor," I said, feeling a tightness around my mouth. "I need to hear you say it in words I can understand."

There was a long pause on the other end of the line. "We've left some drainage tubes in your husband's side," the doctor said slowly. "But the best I can tell you, Mrs. Luton, is that he is living temporarily. That's all."

That night I sat alone by Clarence's bed. Besides the two tubes coming from his side and disappearing under the bed into some kind of suction machine, there was a tube in his mouth that went down his throat, another in his nose, and a third in one arm.

It was a long, lonely night. I sat, thinking of the ups and downs of our many years together. My grandfather had been a Methodist minister, and my roots were deep. But Clarence's mother felt that if you weren't a Lutheran you had no chance of making it to heaven. I felt resentment when Clarence's mother pressured me into leaving my Methodist church and joining him in the Lutheran church. But to please Clarence, to keep peace in the family, and just in case my mother-in-law was right about heaven, I joined the Lutheran church. That was thirty-five years ago, back in Michigan. Since then, most of my bitterness toward his mother had faded, and it seemed we were finally settling down to face our remaining years in contentment here in California. But now this.

I looked at Clarence lying so motionless, both arms strapped to the rails of the bed so he couldn't thrash and pull out the tubes. There was constant whirring and hissing of the oxygen and the pump under the bed, and strange odors.

Clarence moved his head slightly, opened his eyes, and saw me beside him. He nodded and smiled in recognition before drifting back to sleep. I sat looking at one of his hands. The tip of his thumb was missing, cut off in an industrial accident many years before. I remembered how I had fussed at him then, telling him that God was trying to say something to him and he was too stubborn to listen. Now I wished I hadn't said such a thing.

It seemed like our life together had been a constant battle, filled with arguments and misunderstandings. Now all our differences faded into oblivion. All I knew was that I loved him and didn't see how I could live without him. "Dear God, please don't let him die." I buried my face in my hands so the nurses, constantly coming and going, wouldn't see me crying.

Outside the room I could hear the chatter and laughter of nurses going off duty. How could they just walk out of this house of sickness and death and forget about those who just moments before depended on them for life? I wanted to cry out, "How dare you be happy? Don't you know my husband is hovering between life and death?"

The elevator door slipped shut on their laughter. Now only the soft hiss of the oxygen, the whir of the suction machine, and the thumping of my own heart remained as I sat alone, waiting.

There was a soft knock at the door. One of the nurses from the earlier shift entered silently and closed the door behind her.

"I thought you had gone home," I said, glancing at my watch. "It's past eleven."

"I got as far as the parking lot and God told me to come back," she said gently.

"God?"

"I won't try to explain now," she smiled sweetly. "But would you mind if I prayed with your husband before I left?"

"Why no, I don't mind," I said, standing up. But inwardly I wondered. It was strange. I had never heard of nurses praying for patients before, and certainly not when they were off duty. Yet this one had turned around and deliberately come back.

She reached out and gently put her hand on Clarence's shoulder. "Lord Jesus," she said softly, "my friend is so sick. Only You can help him. Please touch his body and heal it, for Your glory. Amen."

She looked at me, and her face was wet. Smiling faintly, she was out the door. I heard the soft squeak-squeak of her rubber shoes against the polished tile as she walked down the long corridor.

I moved over to Clarence's bed and noticed a tear, glistening on the stainless steel bar of the bed rail. I started to wipe it away, but decided to let it stay. I want it to remain there forever, I thought, a reminder of that sweet young girl who cared enough to return.

I stayed with Clarence until three in the morning, and then returned the next morning with Mike and our daughter, Janet, who lived up in Lakewood. Dr. Elliot met us outside Clarence's room at ten o'clock. He told us essentially the same thing the surgeon had said over the phone the night before. "Clarence is very, very ill. He can't possibly live because of the tumor in his pancreas."

"Is the tumor malignant?" Mike asked.

"We don't know. We can't tell at this time, since we couldn't do a biopsy. However, that is immaterial at this stage, because a benign tumor can kill, too, if it attacks a vital organ. And it looks like this is one of those cases."

"How long will he live?" Mike asked.

"We're trying to keep him alive day by day. That's all we can promise you," the doctor said.

Two days later I received a phone call from an old friend, Mary Turpin. Mary used to work in a doctor's office, and I had often fixed her hair at the beauty salon.

"Marvel," she said, "I know this sounds strange, but I wonder if you could meet me up at the hospital. I want to see Clarence."

It was late evening and I knew visiting hours were already over, yet I sensed a note of urgency in Mary's voice, so I agreed to meet her. Mary was in the hall outside Clarence's door when I arrived. She was a middle-aged woman with a soft, gentle face, carrying a large Bible in her hand.

"God told me to call you," she said. "He told me to come up here and read a passage of scripture to Clarence, and then pray for him to be healed."

God had told her to call? This was something new to me. Although I had been active in church affairs all my life, I had met very few people—except for some pastors and missionaries—who claimed to have heard from God. Yet here in this hospital I had talked to two of them.

Mary read from one of the Psalms and then gently laid her hand on Clarence's arm and prayed for him. Clarence was still drugged, but when Mary finished he opened his eyes and said, "That's nice. The pastor has been in twice today. The last time he gave me Communion. I don't mind dying. I'm ready to go."

"I'm not here to prepare you for death," Mary said softly. "I'm here to pray that God will restore your life."

"That's nice, too," Clarence said, his lips cracked and his voice barely audible because of the tubes. "A little Catholic nurse came in a few minutes ago and took my blood pressure. Then she prayed for me. Sure are a lot of people praying for me."

And the number of people praying continued to grow. A week later, when I came in to see Clarence, he told me that one of the nurses had just left. "She belongs to an Assembly of God Church," he said. "She comes in here several times a day and prays for me. This morning she told me she had a dream about me last night. She said she woke up at 2:30 A.M. and prayed for me. She uses a special 'prayer language' at times like this, and she said she prayed nearly all the rest of the night."

"At 2:30 in the morning?" I shook my head, wondering why she prayed then instead of in the daytime when it would be more convenient.

"Yeah," Clarence said. "And I woke up at 2:30, too. I

thought I was dying, the pains were so bad. But in an hour or so they went away, and I feel a little better this morning."

Even so, I could tell that Clarence's condition was deteriorating. The stitches in his incision were not healing, and the drainage from the tubes in his side was continuous. The opening around the drain had not healed either, and often the fluid would ooze out around the tubes. The drainage was so strong, like corrosive alkaline, that it had to be wiped off his skin immediately or it would eat into it. The dressings were expensive and had to be changed several times an hour. And the odor . . . The doctors said it was normal in cases like this, and that was why they kept him in a room by himself. No other patient could tolerate the horrible smell.

On occasions his fever would skyrocket and the nurses would have to work furiously, bathing him in alcohol and packing his body with ice to get the fever down. It was the same nurses who kept coming in to pray. Catholic, Assembly of God, Church of God, white and black—they would slip into his room, hold his hand, and say, "Mr. Luton, may I pray for you?"

Despite the nurses' prayers, Clarence had been in the hospital for eighteen days, his condition getting steadily worse. He began to suffer from what the doctors called hospitalitis, extreme depression caused by the fear of facing death in the hospital.

"He'd be better off at home," Dr. Shaw said. "We've done all we can for him here. He will be happier in familiar surroundings."

Mary Turpin agreed to come as a practical nurse, caring for him during the day while I was at work. We rented one of the suction pumps to attach to the tubes in his side, stocked up on an enormous quantity of surgical dressings, and brought him home in an ambulance. The doctor told me to watch Clarence's vital signs and to let him know if there was any change in his condition.

The incisions remained open, draining. The pump was sucking off about half a gallon of liquid a day, and there was still a lot of drainage around the tubes. The entire house reeked with the odor.

Three weeks after Clarence came home, the tubes stopped draining and his fever shot up. I called the doctor.

"Listen to me carefully," he said. "This is going to be difficult, but you can do it. You take both of those tubes and gently pull them out of his side eight inches, then tape them back to his body."

I followed his instructions, and the tubes began draining again. But sometime during the night, the tubes came out the rest of the way, and when we awoke, the opening in his side was draining freely without the tubes. It was a horrible, foul-smelling, heavy liquid, containing lumps of what looked like decomposed flesh. I took him back to the hospital, where they gave him another shot. It was obvious the doctors held no hope for him whatsoever. Even though they carefully stayed away from the word, we knew he had cancer and could not live much longer.

I was taking him back to the hospital a couple of times a week for outpatient treatment. When I complained to the doctor about the drainage, he scolded me. "Mrs. Luton, you are going to have to accept the fact that your husband is going to have upsets like this."

One evening the phone rang at the house. It was a salesman wanting to know if I was interested in buying a cemetery lot. For a moment I thought the call was a prank, but then I knew it was real. I said yes, I was interested, but preferred that the salesman come by my shop after work rather than to our home.

Three days later I picked out two lots in Glen Abbey Cemetery. I also picked out caskets and arranged for the type of funeral. Then I signed a contract and made a deposit. There was nothing else to do but take care of Clarence while I could—and pray. I didn't know it at the time, but often God's answers to our prayers come in seemingly natural ways.

In November, shortly before Thanksgiving, my mother called. "Have you considered taking Clarence back to the

Shrine?" she asked. I confessed I had thought about it but hadn't done anything. She insisted that I take him.

Early Sunday morning, just four days before Thanksgiving, I got Clarence ready for the trip, surrounding him with pillows for the two-hour drive to Los Angeles, since the slightest bump or jar sent pain through his body. My mother went with us, and we arrived at the auditorium, located just a block off the Harbor Freeway, about 10:30 A.M.

We helped Clarence into a wheelchair and took him around to the side door where the other wheelchair patients were lined up. After a little while someone opened the door and let us in. We found seats in the wheelchair section about six seats from the aisle.

Clarence kept complaining of extreme pain, no doubt aggravated by the long drive. When the service started and Miss Kuhlman came on stage, neither of us was able to pay much attention. Clarence was constantly twisting in his seat, trying to get comfortable, occasionally letting out an involuntary groan. In the midst of this activity, I heard Miss Kuhlman say, "Cancer."

I looked up. She was pointing down into the wheelchair section. "Stand up and claim your healing," she said.

I looked at Clarence. He was staring intently at Miss Kuhlman, but made no move and continued to sit in his chair.

Miss Kuhlman seemed insistent. "Please stand up and receive your healing."

Then we noticed a woman, obviously a personal worker, walking back and forth, up and down the aisle near our section. "What's she looking for?" Clarence whispered.

Before I could answer, she came back to our row, and leaning all the way over the other five seats, looked at me and asked, "What is the matter with you?"

"Nothing," I said. "I brought my husband to be healed."

"Can you walk?" she asked Clarence.

"Well, if I have some help," he said.

"Then come out here in the aisle, sir," she said.

Clarence looked at me questioningly. "Go ahead," I whispered. "They'll help you stand up."

Slowly he rose to his feet. The people sitting between us and the aisle helped him out, their hands supporting him as he shuffled past them.

"What's the matter with you?" the woman worker asked.

"Oh, a lot of things," Clarence answered. "I had an operation on my pancreas."

"Do you have cancer?" she said.

Clarence shook his head, but the personal worker was looking at me. I nodded my head up and down vigorously.

"Come with me," the personal worker said, and walked beside Clarence, half supporting him, as they made their way toward the back of the auditorium.

Minutes later I saw Clarence and another woman coming down the aisle toward the platform. Already I could see something had happened to him. He was no longer dragging his feet; his head was up and his step confident.

"What's this?" Miss Kuhlman asked, as the woman brought him to the platform.

"Miss Kuhlman, this is the man who was healed of cancer in the wheelchair section."

"Were you in pain when you arrived here?" she asked, her face vibrant.

"Yes ma'am, I sure was," Clarence answered, beaming with joy.

"But you aren't now, are you?"

"No ma'am, I'm sure not."

"When did it go away?"

"It left just when you pointed down there and said, 'Somebody has just been healed of cancer.' Only I didn't know I had cancer. But my wife knew, and I guess God knew, too."

"I guess He did," Miss Kuhlman laughed. She was just like a small child who had discovered a favorite toy under the Christmas tree. Then she reached out to Clarence and prayed for him. Moments later, he staggered backward and fell to the floor. I had seen people falling in Kathryn Kuhlman's services before and had wondered what caused them to fall. This time I knew it was the power of God.

When Clarence returned to his seat, I asked him, "Have you been healed?"

"I believe I have," he said, still moving his legs and pushing on his stomach with his hands.

I was certain he had been healed. I could tell it by the new color in his face, and the new strength and vitality in his movements. He was a completely different man.

After the service he pushed his wheelchair to one side and walked to the car. "I feel like a new man," he said. "In fact, you women drivers scared me on the way up here. I think I will drive home." Because it had been almost six months since he had driven a car, we all protested. But he was determined, and got behind the wheel.

If we scared him driving north to Los Angeles, he almost frightened us to death driving back to San Diego.

"Why are you driving so fast?" I asked.

"I want to get back home in time for the evening service at church," he said. "I want to walk in there and tell all those people who have been praying for me that Jesus has healed me." And that's exactly what he did.

Four days later, Clarence sat down to the first solid meal he had eaten since June. It was Thanksgiving Day, the most meaningful one of our lives.

The following week Clarence went back to the doctor. After a thorough examination Dr. Elliot simply shook his head. "It's a medical miracle!" he said. "There is no other explanation."

We waited a month, and then Clarence returned to the surgeon for another physical examination. The surgeon said, "Mr. Luton, I can't find anything wrong with you."

Well, they could call it a medical miracle if they wanted to. But it's far more than that to us. It's God's miracle. The medical people said he was dying. Only God could take him off the temporary status and give him life.

THIRTEEN

Face to Face With a Miracle

LORRAINE GAUGUIN, REPORTER

After an article of mine about Kathryn Kuhlman was published, she wrote a letter inviting me to a Miracle Service at the Shrine Auditorium in Los Angeles. "Together we will continue to be amazed at *what God hath wrought,*" she said.

So when I attended the Shrine service, the word was out that I was a writer. "Interview us," begged some of the kids in the balcony who had just returned from Expo '72. They wanted to tell the world about their commitment to Christ. "The news media don't seem to care," one of the kids lamented. "If we were smoking dope and causing riots, they'd make a movie about us."

"It's a sad commentary on life today," I agreed.

"But things are changing," a middle-aged man sitting in the next row joined in. "Recently I accepted Jesus Christ as my Saviour, and now people listen to me who never used to listen. People *are* beginning to listen."

It's true. People are listening, tuning in. Christian books are selling as they have never sold before. Sales are up 25 to 40 percent. Kathryn Kuhlman's services fill a fathomless void in today's pressurized, chaotic world. People are searching for somewhere to go with their deep, unrequited longings. They know something is wrong but can't put their finger on it. Many are shattered spiritually and physically, with fragmented marriages and degraded self-images. They have lost their personal integrity. Time is running out, and they crowd into the Shrine Auditorium to hear about Jesus, mercy, the forgiveness of sins, and *hope.*

187

The place was jammed. The young and the old (no generation gap here), black and white (not one reference to politics or racism)—seven thousand happy people overflowing with joy. The air was charged with emotion and reverence. I could feel it. Everyone who could stand rose to his feet as the mighty choir boomed and Kathryn Kuhlman entered. They sang *How Great Thou Art,* seven thousand pairs of arms stretching heavenward. I could see the gladness on their faces, as pain was momentarily thrust aside.

Each Miracle Service offers something different to everyone present: Some receive miraculous healings, others invite Jesus into their hearts. Rare is the person who walks away empty without having been touched in some particular way. The special blessing for me, at this service, was meeting a living miracle—Judy Lewis, whom Miss Kuhlman introduced on stage.

Judy had attended the service the preceding month in a wheelchair. She had been brought from Houston by her employer, Raymond McDermott, and a Houston police captain, John LeVrier.

"Judy wasn't healed during the service," Miss Kuhlman told the audience. "But following the service, these two men pushed her backstage. While they were praying, with their backs to Judy, she rose from the wheelchair and not only walked, but ran." Miss Kuhlman laughed. "You folks had all gone home. We had our own Miracle Service backstage, right there in my dressing room."

My curiosity was aroused. I had heard of the lame walking, but only during Jesus' days on earth. Was it still happening? Was Jesus still healing people, even those confined to wheelchairs? If only I could meet Judy Lewis in person, I thought. If only I could come face to face with a miracle. Then I would know for sure.

The following morning one of Miss Kuhlman's aides telephoned me. I could hardly believe my ears. Sensing I was somewhat of a skeptic, Miss Kuhlman wanted me to meet and interview Judy Lewis. Of course I wanted to meet Judy!

It was a sweltering, humid August day as I drove from

the San Fernando Valley over the hills to the Century Plaza Hotel. I telephoned from the lobby and Judy answered. Yes, she and Mr. McDermott were expecting me. I saw her from a distance—a tall, thin, angular woman in her mid-forties, limping briskly down the hall. She was wearing a bright yellow pants suit, and her long red hair was held back by barrettes. As she approached she whacked her hip. "This hardware holds me back some, but I'm coming," she said jokingly in an accent that was pure Houston, Texas.

We made ourselves comfortable in the living room of the hotel suite as she introduced me to Raymond McDermott, a successful middle-aged attorney from Houston.

"I still walk with a slight limp-because of the steel rods and pins in my hip and thigh," she said. "But you should have seen me a month ago. I couldn't walk at all."

The healing had occurred just thirty days before, and Judy was still all but overcome by the fact that she could walk again. All the agonizing pain and embarrassment her injuries caused were gone for good. She whipped color snapshots of herself from her handbag: in a wheelchair a month ago in front of the Century Plaza Hotel on her way to the Shrine Auditorium, in her wheelchair in Miss Kuhlman's dressing room before the Miracle Service began. Then she joyfully pointed to the color snaps that were taken immediately after her healing. She was doing exercises on the hotel veranda!

"Girl, I guess everybody at the hotel thought I was crazy. But I was so excited I didn't care. I kept going up to total strangers and telling them that a miracle had happened to me—*to me!*"

During our conversation Mr. McDermott sat quietly in his chair, smiling. I asked him if he had really believed Judy would ever walk again. "Oh yes," he declared quickly. "Absolutely. I knew it would happen. Because of this girl's faith, I made my own surrender to Christ."

Judy was still chattering, pointing to the snapshots, whacking her hip and exclaiming, "There's no more pain.

A few weeks ago I couldn't touch this thigh. The pain was unendurable. But look! No pain!"

Eventually she simmered down and related the whole story—her years of pain and misery, the nightmare her life had become.

It all began early one May morning in 1952. It was 7:15 as she bowed her head in prayer over the steering wheel of her brand-new car. A lifelong Baptist, she began each day in prayer before going to work as a secretary in downtown Houston. She especially thanked God for the love of her mother and her husband Lester, to whom she had been happily married for ten years.

Traffic was heavy that morning as she stopped for a red light. Glancing in the rearview mirror, she saw a six-wheel truck, loaded with chickens, bearing down on her with tremendous speed. It was too late for her to move out of the way. There was a sickening *crunch,* then darkness. The truck, traveling at more than sixty miles an hour, had totally demolished her car, ramming it into the auto in front and starting a chain reaction that involved five vehicles. Judy was thrown to the floor of her demolished car, seriously injured and unconscious. A nurse in the crowd kept bystanders from moving her until the ambulance arrived.

Two weeks later Judy awakened, slowly and painfully, in a sterile hospital room. Her neck and both legs were in traction. Vaguely she heard a voice she didn't recognize: "I'm afraid she will never walk again."

She couldn't believe what she was hearing. She was twenty-eight years old and had never been sick a day in her life. What had happened to her? Why couldn't she move? She just couldn't be finished at twenty-eight. She began struggling on the bed, and suddenly she felt a cool sensation on her brow and a voice—which to this day she insists was the voice of Jesus—comforting her: "Judy, it will be all right."

"Only the strength of that promise kept me going," she told me, as she remembered the agonies that followed. Her injuries were listed as four ruptured discs (lumbar and cervical), severe neck injury, and severe damage to the central nervous system.

For two years she was in and out of the hospital. Eventually she walked, but in extreme pain and always dragging her left leg. With her job gone and her health deteriorating, she was forced to stay at home. Her life began to center around the three most important things: her mother; her husband Lester, who had stuck with her throughout the entire nightmare; and her Bible.

There were other aspects to Judy's life that had not been there before—the constant rounds of hospitals and doctors' offices. She was allergic to pain-killing medication and sleeping pills, so she suffered without relief and tossed with insomnia. Often she prowled the house at night like some ghostly, haunted specter, dragging one leg, hanging onto chairs and the walls while trying not to awaken her husband. With each step her ruptured discs caused her to grimace in extreme pain.

Judy tried to adjust to her changed pattern of living. The Bible became very precious to her as she called on God for daily strength. At least she had her mother and her husband.

Then, in September, 1960, while Lester was installing a central heating and air-conditioning system in a house, he came in contact with a high-voltage wire. He screamed for someone to cut off the power, but before anyone could get to the switch, he was electrocuted.

Then, before the day was over, Judy received a call from the hospital where her mother was a cancer patient. "Come now," the doctor said. "Your mother is dying."

Judy was adamant. She would not accept the doctor's judgment. Instead, she went to the hospital and brought her mother home to live with her. For the next three years she nursed her tenderly, feeding her through a tube in her stomach.

At the time of Lester's death, Raymond L. McDermott, a noted Houston attorney, had taken charge of Judy's legal affairs. He specialized in personal injury litigation and had helped the Lewis family earlier with claims arising from

Judy's accident. But now there was more disappointment. What Judy thought was a $50,000 life insurance policy proved to cover only health and hospitalization. With her mother to care for, and no income, Judy felt as if the earth had been snatched from under her.

She knew she had to go back to work. But where? Who would hire a woman in constant pain who could not walk normally but dragged her left leg? Ray McDermott said he would hire her.

Being a legal secretary required special study, but Mr. McDermott said she could learn. He encouraged her to take the job.

Judy began work at once. Every night she carted home heavy law books and legal forms to study. Still caring for her mother, she spent her sleepless nights studying legal documents until she became a proficient legal secretary.

Judy's Christian faith never wavered, and when she discovered that despite Mr. McDermott's kindness and generosity, he was not a Christian, she began to pray for him to accept Christ. The McDermotts were happily married with six children, all of whom were churchgoers. Judy developed an obsession to see them born again. Before that prayer was answered, however, more tragedy befell Judy.

Judy's life at home seemed to revolve around her bed. After her mother died she spent most of her time there, reading, listening to the radio, and talking on the telephone. It was the only place she could find any degree of release from her pain. Late one May night Judy dragged herself from the bed to go to the bathroom. Her clock radio read 1:15. She took one more step, felt the cord of the electric blanket across her foot, and then with a violent jerk was hurled to the floor.

Her next sensation was excruciating pain. When she tried to move, she couldn't. She didn't know how long she had been unconscious, but her mind gripped with terror as the word "paralyzed" flashed back and forth. She kept awakening and lapsing back into unconsciousness. There was no one to hear, even if she screamed. Finding that her right arm and hand could move a little, she grasped the bedspread and used it to pull herself toward the bed and the phone, little by little. Each time she pulled, she fell into a black, mind-searing coma. She glanced at the clock radio just as she reached the phone. It was 6:30. She knocked the phone from the table and dialed the operator for help. Then she passed out again.

At the hospital the doctors discovered extensive injuries. X rays revealed a broken hip, three fractures of the pelvis, and further damage to the spine. Part of one of the broken discs had fallen into the spinal canal, blocking and pinching some nerves, severing others. Through surgery, her bones were set with stainless steel rods, plates, and pins. As she recovered, however, she found the slightest touch or pressure on her hip or thigh caused painful muscle spasms. She was paralyzed from the waist down. The doctors gave her no hope of ever getting out of a wheelchair or being free from pain.

Judy was away from her job four and a half months, and finally returned to the law offices in a wheelchair. Her left leg would often go into violent spasms, and it would take several people to hold it down. She was embarrassed by her loss of control over her bladder, and frequently had to be aided to the ladies' room by the other woman who worked in the office.

It seemed aeons, far back in another world, since she had felt that cool hand on her brow and heard those comforting words, "Judy, it will be all right." Had she really heard them? Was there really going to be a time when Jesus would make things all right? Could that possibly mean healing? There was no answer to her questions. Instead, she got constantly worse.

Judy tried to resign from her job, but Mr. McDermott refused to consider it. Each morning he picked her up, and together they drove to work. In the evenings he dropped her off at her door. Then it was sheer torture until the next morning. Often Judy pulled herself, fully clothed, onto the bed, exhausted and filled with despair.

The only solid food she ate was at the office. At home

she lived on Coca Cola, and her weight dropped alarmingly. Her situation seemed utterly hopeless. However, Judy believed with all her heart that *nothing* was impossible with God and, further, that all things worked together for good to those who loved God. She was trusting *Him* to work these things out.

Judy's three young nieces were one of the few bright spots in her dreary life. Now and then they would spend Saturday nights with her, but even with her nieces in the house, Judy spent her sleepless nights reading, usually the Bible. One Saturday night little ten-year-old Amy, who was sleeping over, awakened and asked Aunt Judy what she was doing. Judy explained she was reading about the Holy Spirit.

"Who's He?" Amy asked.

Judy explained. "Aunt Judy can't run and jump and play the way you do. Yet my heart is so full of joy and thanksgiving, I just can't express it strong enough to the Lord. So the Holy Spirit takes that joy and gives the words to God."

Through her litigation cases and through contacts in the law office, Judy had met police captain John LeVrier.* Captain LeVrier, a deacon in the First Baptist Church, had become a good friend. When word came that he had been stricken with terminal cancer, Judy and Mr. McDermott went to visit him in the hospital.

Then Captain LeVrier was miraculously healed at a Kathryn Kuhlman service in Los Angeles. Well-known in Houston, he began testifying all over the city to his healing —and to the new power of the Holy Spirit in his life. It was fascinating, and for the first time Judy was aware of the possibility of healing. Yet she grew continually worse.

When she was unable to attend church any longer, she had to content herself with staying at home and watching the services of the First Baptist Church on television. As the program finished one Saturday afternoon, she turned her wheelchair and started to leave the room. Then she

* For his story see Chapter Two, "No Shortage in God's Storehouse."

heard a voice, a woman's voice, proclaim, "I believe in miracles."

"It was the most unusual voice I had ever heard," Judy told me. She was shocked as she listened to the program. She believed in prayer and felt her own life was guided by the Holy Spirit, yet miracles on a television program seemed sacrilegious. However, it was through this ministry that Captain LeVrier had been healed. At least she should approach it with an open mind. The following week she bought both of Kathryn Kuhlman's books, *I Believe in Miracles* and *God Can Do It Again*.

Judy's health was now in sharp decline. Her doctor (who had been her main physician since 1952) told her that never in his professional life had he felt so completely helpless. Because of her allergies he could not relieve her pain. All he could do was prescribe a mild medication to try to ease the violent muscle spasms that came several times a day.

Often Judy would go for two nights in a row without sleep. Then, on the third night, she would lapse into a heavy, unhealthy slumber. In the morning she was as tired as when she had closed her eyes, with no appetite, violent painful tremors, and huge black circles around her eyes. Life was draining from her.

Then Kathryn Kuhlman came to Houston for a Miracle Service. Captain LeVrier and Mr. McDermott urged Judy to attend, inviting her to accompany them. She accepted their invitation, and on June 21, 1972, they took her to Hofheinz Pavilion. It had been twenty years since her first accident.

Oddly enough, Judy's primary thoughts were not for herself. "I had been praying for my precious employer for a long time," Judy said, recalling that day, "Even more than I wanted my own healing, I wanted him to accept Jesus Christ as his personal Saviour."

Judy was not healed during the Miracle Service. Nor did Mr. McDermott accept Christ. Judy left the service, however, with a deep inner assurance that both prayers would be answered.

The very next week, Mr. McDermott walked into Judy's office, casually laying some papers on the desk, and said, "You know, Judy, I've been doing a lot of thinking. I really want to be born again."

Judy nodded, too filled with joy to speak. As Mr. McDermott walked out, however, she exploded with praise. God was already answering her first prayer.

Mr. McDermott's interest was growing. He joined with Captain LeVrier, and they made plans to take Judy to the next Miracle Service in Los Angeles. Mrs. McDermott was not going to be able to make the trip, and this meant Judy would have to ask for help from women who were total strangers. But despite her misgivings about making such a long journey away from home, she felt she was going to be healed. She made a return reservation on an airline that did not carry people in wheelchairs.

The last thing she did before leaving Houston was to call her ten-year-old niece, Amy. "Please pray for me on Sunday, Amy," she said. "Please pray that God will heal Aunt Judy."

The day before the service, Judy, Mr. McDermott, and Captain LeVrier checked into the Century Plaza Hotel. The men helped Judy to her room before going on to theirs. Once inside, she collapsed in tears, wondering how she would get through the day ahead without anyone to help her. As she trembled in anguish, her leg went into a violent spasm. Looking up, Judy caught a glimpse of herself in a full-length mirror—thin, wasting away, holding her monstrously jerking leg. "Oh Lord, have I come to this?" she moaned. "Surely this is the end unless I am healed tomorrow."

That afternoon they went sightseeing but Judy was in dreadful pain. While viewing the murals at Forest Lawn, she was forced to ask help in the ladies' room from a woman she didn't know. The rest of the day was a blurred montage, a nightmarish tour up and down twisted streets that never seemed to end.

The next morning, Sunday, the men took snapshots of Judy in her wheelchair in front of the hotel. At the Shrine

Auditorium they wheeled her backstage, where Miss Kuhlman greeted Captain LeVrier and autographed Judy's books. Mr. McDermott took more snapshots. Then the Miracle Service began . . .

Judy began praying fervently that her employer would accept Jesus. During the service she had to leave, as once again the violent spasms coursed through her body. A registered nurse helped her to the rest room and said, "You can't go back inside. You need a doctor."

"I am going," Judy insisted. "The only doctor I need is the Great Physician." Judy pushed away the nurse's restraining arms and wheeled herself back down the aisle. She had reached her end. Her entire body was in spasms. She continued to shake violently throughout the rest of the service. Even if she died, she was going to stay and pray that Mr. McDermott would accept Jesus Christ.

Finally the service was over. Mr. McDermott had resisted the invitation to come forward and accept Jesus Christ, and Judy was still the same. Captain LeVrier was crushed, but the two men pushed Judy backstage to say goodbye to Miss Kuhlman. Then, in the dressing room, Mr. McDermott finally spoke up. Despite Judy's not being healed, he told Miss Kuhlman that he wanted to make his total surrender to God. Everyone bowed in prayer. Miss Kuhlman placed a hand on Raymond McDermott's head and prayed for the Holy Spirit to bring Jesus into his heart.

"I was so happy," Judy recalled. "I looked up and felt I could actually see into heaven. I said, 'Thank You, Lord, for making it more than I ever asked You for.'

"Then," Judy told me, "I felt the strongest yet most gentle hands lifting me up out of that wheelchair. I looked behind me, and there was the chair and the empty footrest. I wondered, Where are my feet? Then I realized I was standing. I had no more pain, no pain at all. Then I felt those gentle hands on me again, and I moved forward in one complete step."

Captain LeVrier looked across the dressing room and saw Judy standing. He fell backward into a chair, dumbfounded. Miss Kuhlman wheeled around, then stood rooted in her tracks, a startled look on her face. Mr. McDermott muttered, "Praise the Lord," his first words since becoming a new man in Jesus. Judy looked down at her feet and saw that her left shoe had fallen off. Formerly her toes had curled under, but now her foot was straight.

"Look at my toes!" she cried. "They are straight!" Then realizing what had happened, she shouted, "Oh, thank You, Jesus. I'm ready. Let's go." With that she kicked off her other shoe and began to walk up and down the dressing room, never faltering once. It had been fourteen months since she had taken a step, but her walking was as natural as if she had never stopped.

Tears glistened on Miss Kuhlman's cheeks, and she kicked off her own shoes. Together they walked back and forth as the men looked on. Finally Miss Kuhlman flung open the door of the dressing room. "You want to walk, Judy? Well, go on and walk." Judy marched out into the hall in her stocking feet, with Mr. McDermott carrying her shoes, Captain LeVrier pushing her useless wheelchair, and Miss Kuhlman still in her stocking feet right behind her—all of them laughing and crying.

When they returned to the hotel the sun was still shining, and Judy ran out onto the veranda. There in the glorious sunshine, surrounded by gay pots of colorful flowers, she did stretches and bends—exercises she had not been able to do for twenty years. Mr. McDermott kept snapping pictures, while people gawked. Then Judy rushed inside to make a person-to-person call to her ten-year-old niece, Amy, in Houston.

As soon as she heard her Aunt Judy's joyful voice, little Amy began to shout, "Aunt Judy's been healed! Aunt Judy's been healed!"

"Aunt Judy," Amy confided, "I prayed for you in church this morning. I wanted to ask God to heal you, but I was so afraid I wouldn't say the right words. Then, I remembered what you told me about the Holy Spirit taking messages. So I said, 'Mister Holy Spirit, would you please tell the Lord for me that I am praying for the healing of my Aunt Judy today.' And He answered my prayers!"

Judy returned to Houston—on the airline that didn't carry wheelchair patients. The following day she kept her usual appointment with the doctor. Mr. McDermott came along as a witness. He sat in the waiting room while the doctor examined Judy. Shortly afterward, the doctor asked Mr. McDermott to join him in his office.

"Did you see this?" he asked, pointing to Judy. "She's a miracle."

Mr. McDermott laughed and said, "I'm glad you said that. I know she's a miracle. I saw it happen."

Judy sat across the room, her face beaming through the tears on her cheeks. There were tears on my cheeks, too. No longer a skeptic, I was speechless. Seeing the look on my face, Mr. McDermott grinned. "Why don't you say something?"

But all I could do was shake my head. What is there to say when you are face to face with a miracle?

I put away my note pad and pencil. Maybe I could write the story, maybe not. I was uncertain whether I should even try to record on paper what I had seen and heard that day. However, there was one thing I was sure of. God's promise, made more than twenty years before—"Judy, it will be all right"—had been fulfilled. And no skeptic, seeing Judy Lewis, could ever deny that.

FOURTEEN

The Big Fisherman

SAM DOUDS

*In my imagination I've often tried to picture what
Simon Peter must have looked like. But it wasn't until
I met Sam Douds that I think I really knew. Sam is all
man. He's six-feet-four and 250 pounds of bone and
muscle. Every commercial fisherman up and down the
Southwest Coast knew Sam. He could outdrink, out-
cuss, outfight them all. Then one day Sam was hit by
something bigger than he was—cancer. In desperation
Sam turned to God, and found that God had already
moved to meet him. Now Sam, a bachelor, has forsa-
ken his nets to follow the Master. He is living with the
Benedictine monks at St. Charles Priory in Oceanside,
California, spending the rest of his life in service to
his Lord, as Brother Samuel, O.S.B.*

I had always lived a pretty rough life. I was big enough to
outfight any man I'd ever met, and mean enough to start
the fights for no reason. Several years before I became a
commercial fisherman, I was driving one of those big highway diesels through Southern California. One morning,
after spending the night upstairs in a truck stop, I woke up
in a grumpy mood—I was always in a grumpy mood. I
heard two fellows outside, sitting in their car, talking sort
of loud. If I were still sleeping, I thought to myself, those
guys would probably disturb me. The more I thought about
it, the madder I got. So I went downstairs, slammed outside, jerked the car door open, grabbed one of the boys,

yanked him upright, and slugged him cold. I was that kind of a guy.

For the last fourteen years, Santa Barbara had been my home. Before that I didn't have a home. I spent some time as a catskinner, manhandling a bulldozer, and eight years cutting the big trees on the timberline in Washington State. If you stay with the lumberjacks for six years, statistically you're either maimed or dead. So after a while I moved to Santa Barbara, bought a sixty-six-foot ocean trawler, and started fishing commercially.

My real occupation, however, was being an alcoholic. I just fished for a living—to buy my booze and have my parties aboard the boat. I guess I was too mean and too self-centered to marry. So I drank, chased women, and fished —in that order.

One of the reasons I drank so heavily was to deaden the pain in my body. Working as a lumberjack, climbing those high trees and sawing off limbs, I had shredded the tendons in my upper arms and legs. I had been to every orthopedic doctor's office in Santa Barbara except one. All of them said the same thing—there was nothing they could do for the pain.

For eight years I had been taking heavy doses of pain pills every day. My monthly bill for narcotics ran around one hundred dollars. I wasn't able to get enough pills from one doctor, so I kept four doctors going at once, using different drugstores so they wouldn't catch on. I washed all the pills down with Beefeater gin, which made them work a lot faster.

Back in 1945, in Brawley, California, near the Mexican border, I was the driver in an automobile accident where a young fellow was killed. I was arrested, and although I was not convicted of anything, the whole town wanted to lynch me. I didn't dare go out on the streets at night, and every few days I would get in a bad fight in some bar.

With nothing else to do, I stayed in my hotel room and read the Gideon Bible. I did it partly because I was wondering if I was as bad as people said I was. One thing that really stuck with me were Jesus' words about ministering to the sick, feeding the hungry, and visiting people in jail. I figured I could make amends for killing this guy if I started bailing other guys out of jail. I didn't care how drunk a panhandler was, I'd always give him money. And if I ever heard of some guy I knew being in jail, I'd bail him out. In fact, the game warden in Santa Barbara used to accuse me of being the bail bondsman of the city, because every time he'd put somebody in jail for a fish and game violation, I'd go bail him out. The warden said they needed to stay in jail and think things over, but I had been in jail once myself and didn't like it.

The only other "religious" experience I ever had was the one time I went to a Kathryn Kuhlman meeting, back in 1967. A friend of mine, Grace, had a fifteen-year-old daughter who ran away from home. Grace was frantic to find her. I had come in off a fishing trip to complete some paperwork and stopped by Marian's Secretarial Service to get some forms run through the copying machine. While I was there, Marian MacKenzie started telling me about Kathryn Kuhlman.

"She's clairvoyant," Marian said. "She comes on the platform and closes her eyes and says, 'There's a woman out there in a white dress with blue spots on it.'"

Well, since that time, I've learned that Kathryn Kuhlman's no more clairvoyant than I am the Holy Father. But I didn't know anything about the gifts of the Spirit at the time, and I don't think Marian knew very much either. Still, there were a bunch of clairvoyant nuts in and around Santa Barbara, and some of them claimed to be preachers, too. If Grace went down to the Kathryn Kuhlman meeting in Los Angeles, I thought maybe this woman could help her find her kid. Marian knew Maude Howard, who handled the bus reservations for the meetings, so I gave her money for one ticket and called Grace on the phone.

"Hey, I've got a ticket on the bus for you to go see this clairvoyant woman in Los Angeles. Maybe she can find your kid for you."

I still don't understand why someone didn't correct me. Maybe it was God's plan that I not know the truth at that stage. For as it happened, the only way Grace would go was if I went with her.

I didn't like to take trips like that, since I knew I couldn't drink. However, I took on a big load before I got on the bus and took five 4-ounce medicine bottles full of gin along with me.

I didn't really know anything about Kathryn Kuhlman, and was half-bombed when I got to the meeting. She came on stage, and it looked like some kind of theatrical act to me. Now I know that she stays back in her dressing room and prays until she's full of the Holy Spirit. By the time she gets on the platform, she can hardly keep her feet on the ground. But when I first saw her, I was so disgusted that I got up and stomped out of the auditorium.

I got as far as the lobby and thought, Now, big boy, what are you going to do? I hadn't seen any bars near the Shrine Auditorium where the meeting was being held, and the only place I could go was to the bus. I didn't want to go sit in that stupid bus for three hours. I felt like a fool anyway, because I had forced Grace to come, and here I was, walking out. I smoked a cigarette, drank some of my gin, and went back in.

When the healings started, I stood up to leave again. It was bad enough being in a Protestant place. I wasn't much of a Catholic, but I still didn't have any use for Protestants. To combine Protestants with healing was almost more than I could stand. But then I remembered I'd just have to turn around and walk back in. So I didn't get out of the row of seats that time.

The first person Miss Kuhlman called out was an eight-year-old boy. "There's a little boy out there who's never been able to walk without braces on both legs," she said. "He can walk now. I want somebody next to him, I think it's his mother, to take those braces off and let him run up and down the aisle."

Then, without waiting, she turned quickly and pointed to another part of the auditorium. "There is a woman over here. She's about seventy years old and has deterioration of the spine. She was healed about half an hour ago. I felt it.

You haven't been able to stand unassisted for several years, but you can do it now."

Then I saw the little boy coming up on the stage. His mother was behind him, holding his full-length braces. The little boy started running back and forth across the stage, and his mother was crying. I thought, There's a real good actor for a kid. I wonder how much they paid him.

I thought I was pretty good at figuring, so I began to guess what Kathryn Kuhlman had to pay to get those two professional actors. I figured it would take about a thousand dollars apiece.

Right behind them came a seventy-year-old woman. She had her orthopedic surgeon along with her. He looked like a nice guy. There were some other doctors on the stage who recognized him. I thought, Boy, they must have really paid that sport something to make him corrupt himself. I estimated it would take at least two thousand dollars to buy him off.

The old woman said she was the one who had been healed of the spine condition, and Miss Kuhlman asked her to bend down and touch the floor. Not only did she touch the floor, but she put her palms flat on it—twelve times. She was laughing and crying at the same time.

Well, I couldn't put my hands flat on the floor and didn't know anyone else who could do it either. I thought, They've got a real seventy-year-old acrobat there. I figured out how much she must have charged to get up on the stage and pretend she'd been bad off.

Then there were others who came, and I kept figuring out how much each had to be paid. About halfway through, I thought, My gosh, they've just blown half a million dollars in payoffs! I didn't know anybody who had that much money to throw away, so I turned to the woman next to me and asked, "How often do they do this?"

She said, "Miss Kuhlman comes here once a month. She also has weekly services in Pittsburgh and in Youngstown and in some other cities around the nation."

I sat back, flabbergasted. I began adding up the figures in my head and it came out to about two million dollars a week. Wow! Nobody's got that kind of dough, I thought. Then I started thinking about how she would have to pay off all the writers in the nation who would want to do the exposés. I asked the woman if there had ever been any adverse comment written about Miss Kuhlman, and she shook her head.

I didn't like it, but I had to admit all of it was real. Even so, it just wasn't my thing. It was for weaklings and those in need, and I was neither. I returned to Santa Barbara and to my fishing, satisfied I'd seen the last of Kathryn Kuhlman.

Two years later, however, during one of my trips at sea, I stepped on a fish spine. It went nearly through my foot and hurt like crazy. When I got back to Santa Barbara I went to see the Doctors Carswell. Harold and his brother, Bowdre, who are both respected surgeons, put me in the hospital. But I stayed there only one day. When I couldn't drink I got mean, and that night I did a lot of shouting and used a lot of loud profanity, giving the nurses a pretty rough time. After ten calls from the hospital, Dr. Harold finally sent me home.

After the doctor treated my foot, I told him that I had some bad pains in my stomach. He gave me a prescription for some codeine pills, thinking the pains could be caused by a virus. I had the prescription for twenty pills filled Friday night. I washed them all down with gin and then went back and had the prescription filled again on Saturday. When I went back the third time, the pharmacist refused to fill the prescription and called Dr. Bowdre Carswell on the phone. I reached across the counter and snatched the phone away from him. "Listen, Doc, tell him to give me a few more of those pills. I'll be all right."

It was night, but the doctor insisted I come to his office for an examination. An hour later I was sitting on his table while he finished his exam. "Sam," he said, "I think you need to see an internist."

I balked but finally gave in, and he made an appointment for early the next week. The pain was increasing in my lower stomach, but after seeing the internist, I decided to go back out to sea for a few days. Maybe getting back to work would get my mind off the pain.

When I returned to port I was feeling rotten—and starved to death. I went straight to a restaurant, ordered two complete dinners, and ate them both. Then I called the internist's office. "The doctor has been trying to locate you for two days," his nurse said. "He wants you to come in immediately."

The doctor had my X ray set up for viewing when I got there. He pointed to a four-inch section of my large intestine that looked like it was plugged up. "I've got a room for you in the hospital across the street," he said sternly.

"Well, I'm not going to a hospital," I growled, getting up to leave.

The doctor turned around and flicked his pencil at the X ray. "Okay, Sam, but let me remind you, your mother died of cancer. All your aunts and uncles have died of cancer. You're going to wind up in the hospital. And until you decide to go, you better not eat anything."

"You're too late," I snorted. "I just ate two complete meals."

"Then you're going to be a very sick man," he said. "It's impossible for food to pass through the blockage."

I pulled on my jacket, gave him a mean look, and walked out into the rain. I got as far as the curb before both meals came right up. I turned around and headed back into his office.

The doctor said he would send my X rays to Dr. Carswell and that I should get in touch with him. In the meantime, he put me on clear liquids. "Don't drink anything you can't see through," he said.

The clearest thing I could think of was Beefeater gin, so I drank that. And I went fishing. I loaded the trawler up with ice and put out for sea. That night I put in at Port Hueneme, down the coast. I went to a dockside phone and called Dr. Harold Carswell. He had seen the X rays. "Sam, I want you in the hospital now. Tonight."

"But Doc, I'm not in Santa Barbara. I'm down the coast."

"Leave your boat there," he said. "Don't fool around with a bus. Get a cab. I don't care how far away you are, get a taxi and get back up here tonight. We've got to operate."

"I've got a boat full of ice and a crew that's supposed to share in the catch. Besides that, I'm supposed to take some deep-sea divers out this weekend. The operation will just have to wait." I cut him off.

The next day, however, I was really hurting. We were about fifteen miles off the coast, fishing for rock cod and sole, and I picked up the radio-telephone and called Harold's brother, Dr. Bowdre Carswell.

"Sam, what's that noise I hear in the background?" he asked.

"That's the exhaust of the boat engine," I said.

"You get that net out of the water and get right in here," he said.

"I can't, Doc. I told these fellows I would fish for a week."

"That Irish stubbornness is going to kill you," Dr. Carswell bellowed. "If your mother had gone to the hospital when we told her to, we might have saved her life. Now you're pulling the same trick."

By then I knew something was seriously wrong. I fished the next day and headed for shore. I got somebody to look after the boat when we docked in Santa Barbara, and called the hospital to confirm my room.

"We understand you are single. Is that right, Mr. Douds?" asked the woman in the business office.

"What is this?" I growled. "I want a room in the hospital and you start asking about my private life."

"Mr. Douds," she snapped back, "the operation you're facing has a high mortality rate. It's extremely difficult to collect from a single person's estate, so you'll have to put the money up before we can admit you."

By then I was mad. "Why should I give you money ahead of time? I don't get paid in advance for fish. I have to catch them first."

"Mr. Douds." Her voice was icy. "You were in here

once before, and it was a very unpleasant experience for all of us. Why don't you go to another hospital?"

"You just don't like people dying in your hospital," I shouted back over the phone. "Is that it?"

But she won out. I withdrew money from my bank account and bought my way into the hospital.

I came through the operation, but then all hell broke loose inside me. I really had a bad time. I didn't see how anybody could be that sick and still live. I knew I was going to kick the bucket, and the second night I began to pray. "Listen, dammit. I need help right now, God! Do You hear me?"

After a while I began to figure that maybe I couldn't bluff God, much less push Him around. I needed to take another tack. I talked to the hospital chaplain, a priest. I needed all the help I could get, and he seemed to be my best bet.

Then the third night I had a vision. I'm not the kind of guy who has visions, yet this was so real I could almost touch it.

I saw a rustic-type house. I could see right into the end of it. Inside, about halfway down, were two chairs, facing away from me. Jesus was sitting in the seat on my right, and Joseph was in the other chair. Mary was standing alongside Jesus. They were almost in reach. As the vision continued, I really began to pray hard. I didn't know much about asking God for help in prayer, but I figured I needed to cut out the profanity, even if it meant losing about three-fourths of my vocabulary. I was really trying to put a lot of virgin English in the prayer, but nobody in the Holy Family paid any attention to me. It looked like they had their backs turned on purpose. I was beginning to feel desperate, and really poured it on with urgency. Mary turned her head and looked back at me, but then the other two got up and all three just walked away.

I couldn't figure it out. Why had they turned their backs on me? I called for the hospital chaplain again. He came to my room, listened for a while, said "Don't worry about it," and walked out.

There was another Catholic priest in the hospital, as a patient. I paid him a visit in my wheelchair. He confirmed that I had indeed had a vision, but he didn't have any answers either.

Little by little I was able to squeeze information out of people about my case. One of the orderlies said he had seen the waste bucket in the operating room following my surgery. It was almost completely filled with intestines. But the doctors were close-mouthed. I really had to sandbag them to get them to tell me anything.

Bowdre Carswell was coming to see me every day. Each time I asked him, he said he hadn't seen the pathologist's report yet. Finally I said, "I'm fed up with that answer. If you didn't have that report by now, you'd be looking for another pathologist. Besides, I know you had the report before you ever sewed me up. I want it by tomorrow morning, and I want it in language I can understand." The next morning he came in, and I said, "Where's the report?"

He said, "How do you feel?"

I balled up my fist and began to curse pretty loud. "Get out of this room and don't come back until you have that report."

"I haven't read the report yet."

I really exploded. My insides were burning like fire, but I was ready to climb out of bed and tear that hospital apart if I didn't get some information. And I told him so.

The doctor went down the hall and returned with one of those aluminum-backed notebooks. "The pathologist's report on the tissue shows a Grade Three, Class C mass near the cecum with metastasis to the lymph nodes."

"Doc, you know I can't understand that stuff. What does it mean?"

He began to move toward the door. I knew I was forcing him to tell me something he didn't want to tell.

"Listen, Doc, just tell me how long I'm going to live."

He reached for the door handle. "Six years . . . but don't count on the last four." He stood in the doorway and told me they had found cancer and removed most of my large intestine. However, I was filled with tumors, and the cancer had extended into other tissues of my body where it was inoperable. I would be able to get up, but in a very short time I would become nonfunctional. He advised me to get all my affairs in order.

I was in the hospital for nineteen days. After I was released I spent a lot of time on my boat, sleeping. Two weeks later, during a routine office call, I spoke to Dr. Bowdre Carswell. "I keep hearing from people who want me to drink special tea and eat a bunch of herbs because their uncle or aunt got cured that way. I really don't care whether I live or die. I've got so much pain, it's not worth living. But I can't stand all these ups and downs. I want to *know*."

He got out his book and showed me in color what my tumors looked like. He told me that 85 percent of the tumors removed from me were fast-growing, malignant types. Hundreds of tumors were left in me. I had perhaps a year to live.

"Hey, wait a minute," I rumbled. "In the hospital you said two years."

He pulled off his glasses and looked me straight in the face. "Sam, in the hospital you were in no condition to be told anything. You bulldozed us into saying what we did. Now this is the truth. It will all be over in a year."

When I left the hospital the doctors had put me on a diet. I couldn't eat rice, potatoes, peas, beans, fried meats. I thought I could outdrink, outswear, outfight anyone on the Pacific Coast from Vancouver to San Diego. I had never been knocked out or even knocked down in a fight. Yet, now, about all I could do was eat Jell-O.

I could still drink, however. The doctors warned me to cut back on my smoking and drinking, but I told them the cancer would kill me before the alcohol would, so I never really sobered up—ever. I drank more than a fifth a day, and a lot more than that on weekends. But anything other than booze or Jell-O hit me like a ton of bricks. One day I drank a bottle of beer, and it took me a day and a half to get over it. Another day I ate a spoonful of rice. That took a day and a half to get over, too. Then I tried some peas.

They caused a gigantic upheaval. I was a real bonehead, but I hated diets, I hated people who were on diets, and I hated myself. I hated a lot of things.

In the meantime I kept searching for someone who could interpret my vision. I had been to five priests and even tried out a couple of Protestant ministers. Nobody had an answer for me. I had to have an answer, and since the biggest thing I had ever seen in the religious line was Kathryn Kuhlman, I decided to make one more visit down there.

I walked into Marian MacKenzie's place. I had lost seventy pounds, which made me look like a scarecrow. I was as white as a sheet. Marian took one look at me and gave me the usual greeting. "You look terrible, Sam. What's the matter?"

I told her I had cancer, had just gotten out of the hospital, and wanted to attend a Kathryn Kuhlman meeting.

"Oh, you want to go down there for a cancer healing," she said.

I got mad—I seemed to stay mad—and cursed. "I don't want a cancer healing. Furthermore, I don't want her or anybody else praying for me to be healed. I can take care of myself. I just want to find out about something."

Marian didn't ask any more questions; she just got me a ticket. Riding the chartered bus to Los Angeles, I saw somebody across the aisle praying. I reached over, shook his shoulder, and snarled, "If you're praying for me, knock it off. I'll take care of myself." I didn't want to be healed of cancer if it meant having to keep on living the way I was. I was sick of the kind of life I led, tired to death of all the fighting, drinking, and hating. Anyway, the cancer was just one of several things wrong with me. The shredded tendons in my arms and legs kept me in constant pain. I had headaches that wouldn't quit, storming up the side of my head in a path as wide as my hand.

What I really needed, and wanted, was some kind of spiritual healing. I wanted an answer to my vision. Knowing I would die within the year, I was desperate to get things right with God.

Nothing happened at the meeting, however. I returned to Santa Barbara discouraged but still determined to find the answer to that crazy vision. One day I turned to the Bible, and in the book of First Peter read: "For the eyes of the Lord *are* over the righteous, and his ears are open unto their prayers: but the face of the Lord is against them that do evil."

That was my answer, the reason why Jesus would not look at me. He had set His face against me because I was doing evil. Why hadn't those priests and ministers told me that? I knew I was bad, but how could I stop doing evil? How could I have all the hate, the meanness, the rottenness taken out of me?

Every two years or so I used to go to confession and try to get myself straightened out with the church. But the last time I went, I had sat down in the little booth and told the old priest, "Father, I've had four different women this week."

"*Four?*" he had shouted back through the little screen. "Unbelievable!" I hadn't been back to confession since.

Now I had the answer to my vision, but I was just as bad off as before. It all seemed absolutely hopeless.

Three months later, on a Friday afternoon, Marian called to say that Maude Howard had one seat left on the bus to the Shrine on Sunday and wanted me to go.

"No," I said. "I'm not going. I've been kicking myself ever since that last time. What if I had gotten healed of cancer, then had to live to be an old man with all this other junk inside me? I m not going to take another chance on going down there."

"Maybe you'll get everything," Marian said mildly.

"Not me. I've never been lucky. Why should God do anything for me? He's turned His back on me."

But Maude Howard refused to take no for an answer. She kept on holding the seat for me. The very next day a strange, good feeling about going came over me. Nobody in the world could have talked me into going, and nobody even tried. But I just began to feel good about it and knew I was supposed to be on the bus.

Something mysterious was happening inside me. I had always been the enemy of love. "Don't use that word," I would argue. "It doesn't mean the same thing to everybody. To one person it means sex, to another admiration. Nobody really loves anybody. I certainly don't want anybody loving me, and I'm not about to love anybody."

Sunday morning, however, as I parked my car and walked across the parking lot, I saw Maude Howard and Nesta Bonato standing near the bus with passenger lists in their hands. As I looked at them, a column of love engulfed me. I had never felt love for anybody before. When I got on the bus, I felt that same love flowing from the people to me, and from me to the people. I wanted to cry. Guys like me don't cry, but I wanted to. That's how strong the love was.

When we arrived in Los Angeles the bus pulled into the parking lot beside the Shrine Auditorium. I felt it again—a great love pouring out of me toward all those people waiting in front of the building. It was hard to take.

I stood in front of the building next to tiny little Nesta. I thought she was a religious nut, and sure enough, she began to preach to me. I had to bend way over to hear her. People like this have always turned me off but good. Yet even though she was spouting all this religious garbage, I felt love going out of me to her the whole time I was bending over and listening.

Ever since the bad accident I had been in thirty years before, my back had hurt like crazy when I had to bend over. I knew it was going to start to hurt pretty soon, and I started to tell the woman to shove off. Then I realized something—my back didn't hurt anymore. And when I straightened up, it still didn't hurt.

We went on into the auditorium, and I found a seat on the main floor. Again I felt love pouring through me, love for all those people.

The service began, and about halfway through, Miss Kuhlman pointed down my way and said, "There's a cancer healing down here."

The moment she said it, I felt a warm tingling going

through my body. It was exactly like that warm tingling I
had felt on the bus when all that love poured through me.
But I was determined not to be healed of cancer. I had
come for a spiritual healing.

Moments later Miss Kuhlman said it again, a little impa-
tiently. "Stand up, sir, and accept your healing."

The aisle was choked with people waiting to get up on
the ramp. Then I saw a woman who kept going up and
down the aisle looking for healings, coming toward me. I
thought she was as homely as sin—and yet the most beautiful woman I had ever seen. She was parting all those people like an icebreaker on the prow of a ship, zeroing right
in on me. I was sitting on the aisle, and there was no way
to escape.

Just about that time, I felt a hot flash in my body. Before
I could figure it out, this woman was standing beside me.
She had a look of great goodness, such a vast welcome that
I felt like I would just fall into it. When she took my hand,
I floated up out of my seat.

"That was for you, wasn't it?" she said kindly.

I was unable to speak. I just nodded my head and followed her like a little puppy. As soon as I got on stage with
all those people—some of them pushing one another—I
felt the old anger and hate trying to well up in me. I wanted to push back and curse. Then I looked up. Miss Kuhlman was reaching over the people in front of me and
touching my face with her fingertips. She asked me what
my trouble was. I started to say something, and then I was
falling backward onto the floor.

I have no idea how long I was down, but when I got up,
I knew the cancer was gone. I knew it for sure. I had always doubted those who came forward and testified their
cancer was healed. But now I understood what they meant.
I knew that I had been healed beyond any shadow of a
doubt—and it was wonderful.

When some of the ushers tried to get me to leave the
stage and go down the side aisle, I balked. I had come up
the center aisle and I wanted to go back the same way. I
felt the old anger roaring up inside me again. I was ready

to knock a few heads right there on stage, when I heard Miss Kuhlman's voice again. She was pointing at me. "Wait a minute, I want to see this one again."

She motioned for me to come to the microphone. "Did you expect a healing today?"

I can remember hearing myself say, "Thank you, thank you," as I hit the floor again.

I was still relatively thin then, less than 200 pounds, but it took three men to pick me up. Miss Kuhlman said, "Now you go back and see your doctor. You are perfectly all right now."

Well, I wasn't quite all right. When I started to walk off the stage, that foot I had stuck the fish spine through began to throb worse than ever. That was strange, because all the big pains were gone: my cancer, my back, my legs and arms, and my headaches. I also knew my alcoholism was healed. But now my foot was hurting. Then, as if somebody whispered it in my ear, I heard a voice saying, "You know, Christ had a big fat nail through that part of His foot."

All the way back to my seat I was nodding. That's right, He did. Maybe this is my crucifixion of the old rotten man, the one who couldn't stop doing evil. Maybe this is how the hate and ugliness are done away with. It's crucified. And maybe I'll be raised to be a brand-new man, born again, to start over and clean.

Back on the bus the people were praising God and saying how wonderful it was I had been healed. I just sat there, thinking to myself, What kind of silly God is this? Then I realized I shouldn't call God silly. But I looked around at all the good people on the bus, people who had always loved God and served Him. It did seem a prime piece of foolishness for Him to heal me.

Some fellow came down the aisle and asked how I felt. I said, "Well, I just think it's a piece of stupidity that God would heal a creep like me."

He looked me straight in the eye. "Sam, don't you realize God doesn't make mistakes?" That really hit me.

When we got back to Santa Barbara, Maude Howard

asked me to come over and eat potluck dinner with a group. I agreed, and the first thing they handed me was a great big casserole of chili and beans. The chili would have killed me, and so would the beans, so I passed it on. The next thing was potato salad. Potatoes, the celery, and the mayonnaise were very definitely not on my diet. I kept passing things along till somebody said, "Don't be so polite, Sam. Take some for yourself."

"I can't eat any of this stuff," I said.

Someone else said, "Don't you realize that God has healed you? He doesn't do things by halves. You can eat anything you want to eat now."

"But I've had my intestines taken—" And I stopped right in the middle of the sentence. Yeah, I thought, I guess He *doesn't* do things by halves. So I said, "Pass it all back."

I loaded that plate high, four times, with all those completely indigestible things, and wolfed them down. There was Jell-O on the table, but I never got around to it.

After I returned to Santa Barbara, I learned one of my crewmen on the *Seahawk* had quit. I took that as a sign from God that I was to shut down the whole operation until I got my boat right. I wanted it like my life, so clean I wouldn't be ashamed for Christ to come aboard.

About the third day, I was downtown and saw Marian. "Have you seen your doctor yet?" she asked.

I said, "No, and I'm not going to. I'm not going to tell the doctor a story like this. I don't think this is the kind of story that doctors like to hear."

"Well, now," she said kindly. "Kathryn Kuhlman was instrumental in your healing, and she told you to go to the doctor. I think you should go." I thought about that and finally called up Dr. Bowdre Carswell. He told me to come on by his office.

"What would you have to do to find out if I still have cancer?" I asked him.

He gave me a funny look and said, "We'd have to cut you open again."

"You're not going to do that," I said, "but—" I came to a dead stop. I couldn't think how to break into the subject.

Then I thought, Well, the heck with it, and I just hauled off and told him the whole thing.

He sat there, listening. He had my file in his hand, and when I finished my story, he began flipping through the file, like he was trying to think of the best way to answer me.

"Well, Sam," he said, stopping to clear his throat, "I could tell when you walked into the room that something had happened to you. You look better than I've seen you in ten years. My advice to you is this: Don't monkey around with it. Don't pick it apart. Don't examine it. Just live it." He paused, then looked up again. "And I say that because I don't think you have cancer anymore. I think God has healed you."

The Carswells weren't known for their religious fervor, so that really shook me. "How can you tell I've been healed?" I asked.

"I can tell by your gestures, your color, and the look in your eyes. Besides," he continued, "I have had this happen to me three times since I've been in Santa Barbara. I think God is trying to tell *me* something, too."

During the following weeks I spent much time reading my Bible. Not only had my body been healed, but that healing of the inner man had taken place, too. It was as if I had been born all over, and I was starting out fresh and new. My talk was not the same. I didn't drink anymore. There was no more need to seek love through immorality; I felt love flowing all around me.

Then one evening, lying in my bunk on the *Seahawk*, I read the story of Jesus calling His disciples. He was walking by the Sea of Galilee and saw two fishermen, Andrew and Peter: "Follow me," He said, "and I will make you fishers of men. And they straightway left their nets and followed Him."

It was like He was calling me, too. He didn't have His face turned away anymore. He was looking at me. "I will follow You, too, Lord," I said.

Three days later I was sitting across from the priest at the Catholic church, telling him my story. A faint smile played across his face. I could tell he understood. "There is an Indian orphanage in northern New Mexico that needs someone to do some carpentry," he said.

I used to do carpentry work. I knew it was God's call. I sold my boat—at a loss. I sold my house. And I took off for the wilderness of northern New Mexico to work in the Indian orphanage.

After I finished, word came that a group of Benedictine monks at St. Charles Priory in Oceanside, California, needed help in building a new bakery. They were already giving away a thousand loaves of bread each week, and with the new bakery they could do even more. I moved into the priory, and on February 2, 1973, I was taken into the Order of St. Benedict. Now I am Brother Samuel, O.S.B.

Once a month, on Sunday, I go to Los Angeles to usher at the Kathryn Kuhlman services. The last time I was there, I heard a man call me by name. I looked up. It was Dr. Harold Carswell and his wife. I could tell by the smile on his face and the twinkle in his eye that something had happened to him, too.

Our priory is located on the top of a secluded mountain overlooking the ocean. The only access is a steep, winding dirt road. The sun rises in the east over the Mission of San Luis Rey and sets into the Pacific Ocean to the west. Each day is disciplined. I'm up at five o'clock in the morning to attend the morning office with the monks. I spend each day in hard, physical work, and after a quiet supper I attend the evening office. I drop off to sleep each night like a baby.

Before my life was touched by the Holy Spirit, no one could have paid me to work as hard as I work now. Only now I do it for nothing, simply out of gratitude—and love . . . the love of Jesus.

FIFTEEN

So Much Left to Do

SARA HOPKINS

Sara Hopkins, formerly a Hollywood starlet, is best known as the co-founder of International Orphans, Inc. She lives with her two sons in Tarzana, a suburb of Los Angeles.

It was in the midst of the before-Christmas rush when I first knew I was sick. I was driving home after a board meeting of International Orphans, Inc., when the pain started—an unbreathable tightness in my chest, and shooting pains in both my arms. At first I thought I was having a heart attack. I had just read of a man who had had a heart attack while driving on the Ventura Freeway. His car had gone out of control, killing seven people. I was not afraid of dying, for I knew my relationship with Jesus Christ was secure. But I hated the thought of killing someone else. I started to pull off the road. Before I could slow down enough to leave the road, however, the pain subsided, and I was confident that I could make it to my home in Tarzana.

I parked in the driveway in front of the house and reached for the door handle of the car. The pain hit again. This time it seemed to be directly behind my heart, traveling down my side and into my arm. As before, it lasted only a moment.

I sat in the car, resting briefly, and made myself swallow my apprehensions about a possible heart attack. After all, I had been to the doctor six months ago for a routine check-

221

up, and he hadn't found anything wrong with me. There had been no cardiogram, but——

After we get home from Florida, I promised myself, I'll go to the doctor to see what this pain is all about.

My father, a dentist, was critically ill with cancer, and I was sure this would be our last Christmas together. My sister-in-law's family owned a beautiful lodge on an island off the Gulf Coast of Florida, and our family had decided to meet there to spend Christmas with Dad. John and Chuck, my two boys, ages six and ten, had been looking forward to the trip for weeks. I couldn't disappoint them, much less Daddy.

And so I didn't mention the pain to anyone in my family, even though several times it returned with great intensity. We spent the holidays in Florida, returning to California the second week in January, just as we had planned. Then I made an appointment with my doctor in Burbank.

A few days later, I sat on the examination table in his office and described my symptoms. He leaned against a white cupboard filled with gleaming stainless steel instruments, and listened intently.

"Well, Sara," he said, adjusting his stethoscope, "I know you're not a complainer. In fact, you work so hard with that orphans' group that I really have to twist your arm to get you to come in for a routine physical. I guess we had better do the works on you."

My doctor is a very methodical physician. I've always felt secure in his presence. But as he examined me this time, even though his reactions were just as noncommittal as they had always been, I had a strange feeling, a sort of sixth sense, that things weren't right. He checked me over thoroughly, asked a hundred silly questions, nodded, grunted, and made little notes on a pad from my file. He didn't seem alarmed, but something inside kept telling me that there was something wrong—very wrong.

Following the examination he said, "I can't find any external signs, Sara. No heart problem and no lumps. But I think it would be a good idea to have you go by St. Joseph's Hospital in Burbank for X rays. If there is anything wrong, they'll catch it there."

"Maybe the pain is caused from tension," I suggested.

The doctor looked at his nurse and grinned knowingly. "Ninety percent of the pain in Hollywood is caused from tension. That doesn't make it any less painful, but Sara, you're not the 'tension type.' That's why I think we had better do some further checking on you to see just where this pain is coming from."

I agreed to go over to St. Joseph's that afternoon for X rays. While I was there, they also ran a myelogram and a cardiogram. The next day I was back in the doctor's office to hear the results.

"The X rays showed up a dark shadow in your chest," he said, as I took a seat in his consultation room. "Probably nothing serious, but we need to operate to find out." He didn't make it sound very urgent.

"Well, the operation will just have to wait," I said, standing up. "I can't take time out of my schedule for surgery just now."

International Orphans, Inc., was consuming much of my time. The year before we had sponsored a fund-raising event at the Century Plaza Hotel, and most of Hollywood's top celebrities had turned out for it. Bob Hope, Roy and Dale Rogers, Martha Raye, Nancy Sinatra, Edgar Bergen (and of course Charlie McCarthy), and other well-known stars had received awards for their participation in the work. Now we were planning an even bigger affair, and it was taking all my time to get things ready. Even more important, my sons needed me, and there were some financial affairs demanding my attention.

But my doctor must have known what was going on inside my head. He reached over and laid his hand on the back of mine. "Now take it easy, Miss Activity," he smiled. "I don't think this is anything too serious—probably just a spot that we can remove. However, if we don't take care of it now, later may be too late."

Suddenly I realized he had been underplaying the part. But I wanted him to keep on underplaying it. I really didn't want the truth, not at that moment. Hollywood's a pretty worldly place, and Christians are in the minority there. But I had been active in the Hollywood Presbyterian Church, even taught Sunday school there. For years I had been rattling on about my faith in Christ. I believed in healing, in miracles, in the supernatural power of a supernatural God. Now, though faced with the specter of disease in my own body, I wanted to crawl under something and pull it in on top of me. Until that moment I hadn't realized that all my conditioning had been fatalistic: Disease leads to death. It was hard to appropriate the truth that God could heal.

The doctor was still talking. "We'll have four other doctors working on the case. You'll receive the best medical treatment in the world. But we must not wait. I would like for you to enter the hospital tomorrow."

I felt as if I were on a merry-go-round, hanging on for dear life as it whirled around and around. I nodded my head. "Whatever you say, Doctor. Just let me go home and pack and make some arrangements about the children."

Later that week, I woke up through the blurred haze of anesthesia and saw Don and Yvonne Fedderson standing beside my bed. Yvonne and I had founded International Orphans, Inc., together, long before she was married. Her husband is one of the finest producers in Hollywood, responsible for such programs as *My Three Sons* and *The Lawrence Welk Show*.

"Hi," Yvonne whispered as I blinked my eyes in awareness. I felt Don's hand in mine, his warm fingers holding me securely. "You're going to be all right," he said confidently.

"I have cancer, don't I?" I asked, looking up into Yvonne's face. "I dreamed about it just now—while I was waking up."

Yvonne nodded. She and Don were trying so hard to be cheerful, but big tears came rolling down her face. It was impossible for her to hide anything from me. "You'll be okay, though," she smiled reassuringly.

"I'll just have to go to Kathryn Kuhlman," I said.

"Who's she?" Don asked. . . .

My mind drifted back to the day I had asked the same question of an eighty-year-old carpenter who was doing some remodeling in my house.

One day he had said, "You remind me of Kathryn Kuhlman. You even talk like her."

"Who's Kathryn Kuhlman?" I asked.

He had reached into his little apron and pulled out a fistful of nails. "It would take me a hundred years to answer that question," he chuckled, kneeling down to hammer away at a baseboard. "You'll just have to go see her. Otherwise, anything I tell you will sound ridiculous." Then, pausing, he looked up. "You know, she's going to be in town next week. I go to the meetings with a busload from my church. Why don't you come alone with me?"

So we went, this eighty-year-old carpenter and I. I was awestruck by the entire service, weeping the whole time I was there. It was the deepest spiritual experience of my life. Surely, I thought, this is the way things were in the New Testament church.

Even though my work schedule and the activities at my own church had kept me from attending another Miracle Service at the Shrine Auditorium, I never doubted that God was working through Kathryn Kuhlman's ministry. Had I known I had cancer before I went to the hospital, I'd have gone to a Miracle Service first. . . .

"Who's Kathryn Kuhlman?" Don asked again, interrupting my reverie.

Remembering the answer my eighty-year-old carpenter gave me, I smiled up at Don. "It would take me a hundred years to answer that question. You'll just have to go with me to see her. Otherwise, anything I tell you will sound ridiculous."

I felt Yvonne's cool hand on my head. "You just lie still and get well," she said, "Don's going to stay here, but I have to get back to work on our orphan project."

"That's good," I said, feeling sleepy again. "I'll get well. There's too much left for me to do to die."

I had never dreamed anything would consume my life

like the work for those orphans. Back in 1959 Yvonne and I were a couple of kids, doing our bit for the USO in Japan and having a great time of it. The wild applause from the American GIs for our corny-comic act in the remote radar-site areas was the greatest reward any young Hollywood starlet could ever hope for.

Back in Tokyo we had weathered out the third heavy typhoon of the winter. After the wind died down, we went out on the streets to have a look. We hadn't gone far before we found a huddle of little kids, shivery blue, shoeless, with bloody cracked hands and hunger-racked faces. There were eleven of them, the oldest about ten and the youngest not more than two. They were all crying and saying a Japanese phrase over and over. With the help of our pocket dictionaries, we finally understood what they were sobbing out: "No mammas, no papas."

That did it. We smuggled them all up the back stairs to our plush hotel room, drew hot baths, and ordered lots of rice. Then we called our Army Colonel host and asked him what to do.

"Call the police," he exploded. The police came, shrugged, and left.

We gathered army blankets and bedded the children down for the night. The next morning we set out in an army limousine with a list of orphanages.

Not one of them would take the children. "Too full," they all explained. It was late in the afternoon before the driver, who spoke a little English, told us why. "Blue eyes, light skin." Unwanted, the kids had probably been shoved out of these very orphanages to die.

Shocked and furious, Yvonne and I took the children back to our hotel room, ordered more rice, and stormed the Colonel's office again.

"Get us an extension on our tour," we demanded. "We can't leave now. These are our children."

Someone gave us the name of the Japanese-American director of Tokyo Gospel Missions. Through him we found Mrs. Kin Horiuchi in a far corner of Tokyo. She had gathered twenty-one half-castes in a one-room shanty with no front door, no window panes, one hibachi for cooking food and for warmth, a few scraggly blankets, and only one jacket, which the oldest took turns wearing to school.

Mrs. Horiuchi took the eleven extra children, and we gave her all the army blankets we could filch, all the money we had, and a promise to raise more. Then we set out passing the hat, collecting dimes and dollars from the GIs and the brass. By the time we left for home, other urchins were being dumped a few blocks from Mrs. Horiuchi's shack with notes pinned to their tattered clothes.

Back in Hollywood, Yvonne and I incorporated ourselves under the name International Orphans, Inc.—better known as IOI—and started to work. We organized chapters in cities across the nation, and as the money began to come in, we began to build orphanages. Soon there were nine of them, a school, and a hospital.

Many famous Hollywood personalities got involved in our project. The press gave us good coverage. Mayor Yorty of Los Angeles, Lieutenant General Lewis Walt of the Marine Corps, and the Navy Chaplains Corps all supported the program. It became a full-time job for both Yvonne and me.

That was the reason I had to get well. Too many starving, homeless children depended on me. If I died, so would they. I believed with all my heart that God had called me to this task, and it wasn't completed. I knew I was supposed to remain on earth—even if it took a miracle to keep me alive.

The doctors were not at all optimistic about my chances. They told me I would be in the hospital for a long time, and that I would have many months of cobalt treatment after my release. The malignant tumor that had been pressing against my heart had caused the pain, and the doctors suspected that the cancer had already spread to my rib cage and into my glands.

The day after I got out of the hospital, I called one of Miss Kuhlman's Los Angeles representatives to find out the date of the next Shrine service.

Janice Ford, Vice President of International Orphans,

Inc. went with me to the meeting. We didn't know when
the service started, though, and arrived at the Shrine Auditorium an hour after the doors closed. Throngs of people
were waiting on the sidewalks, hoping someone inside
would leave so they could claim a seat.

I squeezed my way through the mob and banged on the
door with my fists. The door opened.

"Lady, there's no way," a woman said. "Every seat is
taken." And the door closed gently but firmly in my face.

"I just don't understand it," Janice said. "It seemed so
right that we should come today. Medically, you shouldn't
even be walking yet. You still have your stitches."

I put my hand against my side, feeling the prickling of
the stitches in my skin. "Well, I'm not going to leave," I
told her. "I believe we're meant to be here."

Janice and I walked around to the side of the building,
trying to figure out how to get in. Halfway down the block,
standing in the middle of the sidewalk talking to the people,
was one of the personal workers I had met at my earlier
visit to the Shrine Auditorium. Could it be possible that she
would remember me?

"Sara! Hi!" she called out. "Miss Kuhlman sent me out
to apologize to these people. There aren't any seats left in
the auditorium."

"I got mixed up. I thought the service began at 1:30. Is
there any way . . . ?" I pleaded.

She stood looking at me for a minute before she spoke.
"You know, Sara, I have a feeling that I'm supposed to
give you my seat. My husband is here, and he can give
your friend his seat."

I grabbed Janice's hand as I walked through the door,
thankful for the huge crowd. In the midst of it I could be
alone. Nobody knew me, I could lose myself and wait for
God to touch me.

We had no sooner taken our seats in the balcony, however, when I recognized Gloria Owen sitting beside me. She
was an old friend who had worked with me in International
Orphans, Inc. Then someone touched my shoulder. I
glanced back and saw Sister Mary Ignatius, dressed in her

Roman Catholic habit. She, too, was a dear old friend. The man in front of me turned and smiled. "Hi, Sara." He was one of the actors with whom I had worked when I was playing a role on the *Ozzie and Harriet* show. I was surrounded by people I knew!

Suddenly we were all on our feet singing "Alleluia!" Over and over we sang the chorus. I began to have the same feeling I had had when I went under anesthesia. I knew what was going on around me, but I wasn't a part of it. When we sat down, the feeling continued. I was aware that Miss Kuhlman was preaching, but I didn't hear a word she said. I was in a vacuum.

Then I saw it—a pink mist or cloud, moving across the balcony to where I was sitting. Suddenly I was completely engulfed in it. I could see out of it and wanted to reach over and touch Janice and ask if she saw it, too, but I was afraid it would go away if I spoke or moved.

Then, in the midst of the cloud, I heard Miss Kuhlman's voice coming from the stage: "There's a healing way up there in the balcony, someone with cancer."

I heard her clearly, but was afraid to hope she meant me. I began to pray, "God, if it is I, I want to know it. I don't want to wonder. I don't want to profess anything I'm not sure of. I have to know, concretely."

Instantly, something happened. It was as if I had grabbed an electrical hot line. Needles of fire surged through my body—like I was being charged with a thousand volts of electricity. I felt intense heat through my chest and midsection, and my body began to shake so hard I was afraid I would fall out of my seat.

Again Miss Kuhlman's voice saying, "The girl in the balcony with the cancer healing will know it because it's like a thousand needles going through her body."

That was it. Later I learned that all the people around me had felt the power, too. Janice, Gloria Owen, my actor-friend, Sister Mary Ignatius—all were knocked back by the shock waves of the Holy Spirit. But still I was fearful of claiming something that might not be mine. Miss Kuhlman kept on speaking.

"The girl who is being healed of cancer is sitting in the last row in the second balcony. Stand up and claim your healing."

I looked around. That was exactly where I was sitting. And there was no way Miss Kuhlman could know about me unless the Lord was revealing it to her. I got to my feet, and an usher escorted me to the platform, the pink mist still surrounding me.

I tried to tell Miss Kuhlman about my healing, but before I could say anything, she touched me. My legs buckled, and I crumpled to the floor under an overwhelming surge of power. I only vaguely remember returning to my seat.

After the service Janice and I went to the Fedderson house. When I told Don and Yvonne about my healing, they were thrilled, but I suspect that both of them would have preferred to have more evidence than just my testimony about needles going through my body.

And there *was* more evidence. That night, as I undressed, I discovered it. Earlier that day I had noticed the painful pricking of the stitches at my incision. But that night my skin felt smooth, unusually smooth, all along the eighteen-inch zigzag scar on the front and side of my rib cage. I walked to the mirror, and I could hardly believe what I saw. Skin, new skin, had grown completely over the stitches, obliterating them. Both scar and stitches had almost completely disappeared. Only by pressing firmly could I still feel the lumps of the stitches under the skin.

I was convinced. I wasted no time the next morning before calling Yvonne and asking her to go to the doctor's office with me.

We were the first ones at the office. After the doctor examined me, he left me with nurses while he went out to talk to Yvonne. I heard him through the open door. "This girl friend of yours is so kooky that her skin heals up on top of my work. We may have to perform another operation just get the stitches out." He sounded pleased but puzzled.

The nurses worked on me, trying to remove the stitches,

but with no success. Finally the doctor had to take over, using a scalpel to cut the skin and what he called a crochet needle to pull out the stitches one by one. It hurt, but it was a happy hurt.

Just a week later my father died in Tennessee, and the family gathered for the funeral. None of them, except my brother, knew I had been operated on for cancer, but all of them could tell that something wonderful had happened in my life. I knew it, too. Not only had my body been healed (later examinations proved that every trace of cancer was gone), but I had new strength, new power, new joy— enough to carry us all through my father's funeral. It was as if God had made me a living testimony to the power of Jesus Christ to keep us in times of stress.

More than a year later, looking back, I give thanks I had cancer. I realize that when Jesus reaches out and lays His healing hand on a body, that touch seeps down into the very innermost parts of the soul. His touch has caused me to completely reevaluate my life, take a look at my priorities, and determine what is important and what isn't.

The dizzy tempo of the Hollywood social activity still swirls around me. My work with International Orphans, Inc., has increased, and my energy level has grown to fantastic proportions. I am able to accomplish three times as much as before—with half the effort.

I know God has given me this victory for a purpose. It may be to enable me to bring up my own boys. It may be that I may help provide homes for hundreds of thousands of homeless children throughout the world. It may be so that I can stay on the Hollywood merry-go-round and witness about the saving, healing power of Jesus Christ. Whatever the reason, I know that each day I live is a gift from God, to be joyfully lived to its fullest, giving Him all the glory.

SIXTEEN

Something to Shout About

EVELYN ALLEN

Dying from myasthenia gravis, Evelyn Allen was carried into the Shrine Auditorium to her seat by her husband, where she reclined on two pillows, barely able to breathe. I had preached only a few minutes that Sunday when the miracles began to happen. One of the first to be touched by the power of God was Evelyn Allen. None of us will ever forget how she came up out of that seat, walking and leaping and praising God.

Myasthenia gravis is an untreatable, deadly killer. It attacks the central nervous system much as a maniac would smash a telephone switchboard with an axe. Everything is short-circuited.

Off and on during the years my husband Lee was in the Navy, I had been bothered with spells of weakness, dizziness, and fainting. I didn't think it was anything serious. Then Lee retired and accepted a responsible position with United Airlines at San Franciso International Airport. We bought a little house just across the bay in San Lorenzo, and I hoped this would be the end of my sickness.

Instead, my pain grew worse. It seemed every organ in my body was in trouble. I was in and out of the Oakland Naval Hospital several times a week as the doctors sought the cause. Three major operations did nothing to help.

One Sunday afternoon a Nazarene pastor from Alameda called to ask if I would play for a wedding in his church. I

233

agreed, although I was feeling so bad I could hardly walk. As the soloist stood to sing the Lord's Prayer, I feared I was going to black out on the organ bench. The notes of the music began to run together, and I lost control of my arms and legs. "I'll never make it through this song," I thought. "Please God, help me."

He helped, and I did get through, even though I could not see the music and didn't even know if my hands were touching the keyboard. Afterward, Lee took me right home and put me to bed. I was down for three weeks. Each time I would try to get up, it felt like my chest was caving in on my lungs, forcing all the air out of me. I had the strange feeling that I was coming apart from the inside out.

The neurologist at the Naval Hospital frankly admitted he was unable to diagnose my problem. By this time I was having two or three fainting spells a week and frequently losing control of my arms and legs. My body was filled with a raging fire of pain that seared every nerve ending. I could breathe better when I was lying down, my heart racing in my chest like an automobile engine with both the gas pedal and the clutch pushed to the floor.

Lee arranged to have full-time nursing aid around the clock. He moved my organ across the living room and set up my bed next to the wall. Our little house was transformed from a retirement nest to a nursing home for a dying woman.

I began to say prayers like, "Lord, let this next breath be my last one. I cannot stand the pain any longer." But I didn't die. All I did was waste away. The days and nights were superimposed on each other, running together in one long montage of pain.

The Navy paid all our medical expenses as long as I confined my visits to the Naval Hospital. But when they could no longer help me, I was more than ready to seek outside help. Money didn't matter. It was a matter of life or death.

In desperation I went to a civilian physician, Dr. Phelps, in San Leandro. He got all my medical records from the Navy, admitted me to San Leandro Memorial Hospital in May and immediately began an extensive series of tests.

From the very outset, Dr. Phelps knew what was wrong with me—yet no doctor wants to pronounce an irrefutable death sentence.

In August of that year I had gone to his office following a severe seizure. Normal pain relievers, even narcotics, could not help me, since they all work on the nervous system—and it was my nervous system that was being short-circuited.

"Evelyn," Dr. Phelps said kindly, "I have to level with you. There is no mistaking this diagnosis. You have familial periodic paralysis and myasthenia gravis. It probably started fifteen years ago and has grown progressively worse. I wish I could help you, but there is absolutely nothing I can do. The Myasthenia Gravis Foundation has done some research on the disease, but at this stage they have nothing to help you."

I was too sick to be surprised. For some time I had known that I was dying. All he had told me was the name of my killer.

Dr. Phelps took his time and patiently described the nature of the disease. "Familial periodic paralysis is a rare disease," he said, "that usually occurs in young people. It's marked by recurring attacks of rapidly progressive paralysis that affects the entire body. Myasthenia gravis is a chronically progressive muscular weakness affecting all the vital organs of the body. Death, when it comes, is usually from heart and respiratory failure. All I can say is that most patients in your condition aren't living now."

I nodded. "Dr. Phelps, I gave my heart to Jesus as a child back in the Wesleyan Methodist Church in Easley, South Carolina. I am thankful I grew up in a Christian home where the Bible was taught. I'm ready to go whenever He wants to take me." I could not hold back the tears, and dropped my face in my hands.

A Baptist friend of mine had given me a copy of *I Believe in Miracles* and suggested I listen to Kathryn Kuhlman's radio broadcast over KFAX. I began to look forward to the daily program. I was in total agreement with Miss Kuhlman's theology and believed that healing was part of God's plan for today. Yet it didn't seem to be His plan for me. I had prayed desperately for God to either heal me or take me. He did neither. It was as though He had forgotten all about me, leaving me to die slowly, by excruciatingly painful degrees.

Lee called my parents, Frank and Grace Knox, in South Carolina, and told them he didn't think I would last very long. Both of them were elderly and sick, but they wanted to see me one more time before I died. They flew out from Greenville, South Carolina, stayed two weeks, and returned home, promising to get everyone in the Wesleyan Methodist and Baptist churches to pray for me.

Many in our area were praying also. The pastor from the Neighborhood Church, a large Christian and Missionary Alliance Church, came by the house to see me. "Pastor, the doctor has said there is nothing they can do for me," I said, weeping when he came in.

"Well, it might be so with men," he said, "but God is still on the throne, Evelyn. His stripes are for your healing, and we're going to ask God for a miracle." Then pausing and looking around, he asked, "Do you have any oil in the house?"

"All we have is some bath oil," I answered.

"Well, God didn't say what kind," he said. "Bring it to me."

He and his companion put their hands on me and anointed me with oil. "Lord, we are praying in faith and obedience," he said. "We claim healing for this child of Yours."

September rolled around. By that time the only bright part of my day was the Kathryn Kuhlman radio broadcast. One Tuesday morning the announcer talked about the services at the Shrine Auditorium in Los Angeles. I knew it was impossible for me to make that 450-mile trip. I could hardly get out of bed to go to the bathroom. The program closed with music from the Shrine. The marvelous choir was singing, *My Hope Is Built on Nothing Less*. In the middle of the song I heard Miss Kuhlman's deep voice as she spoke to the congregation, saying, "Everybody sing it with them."

It was more than I could take. I had played the organ in church for years, and I knew I had to join in. I rolled out of bed and crawled across the floor to my organ on the other side of the living room. Clawing my way up on the bench, I flipped the switch and opened the hymnbook to the song they were singing. But as I put my fingers on the keyboard, the weakness swirled through my body. I fell forward, and the organ gave forth a bellow of discord, as though it was suffering with me.

It was hopeless. I flipped the switch to off and lay across the keyboard, weeping in pain and frustration. I couldn't even worship God.

The program was over. Miss Kuhlman was gone, and the radio shifted to some commercial announcement. When I looked up, my eyes focused on the hymnbook, and the third stanza of that grand old hymn stood out in bold relief. I had played it hundreds of times in dozens of different churches. But somehow I had never seen the words —at least had not let them speak to me. Perhaps I had to get in the position of desperation, lying across the keyboard, before the truth could come home.

> *When all around my soul gives way,*
> *He then is all my hope and stay.*
> *On Christ, the solid Rock, I stand;*
> *All other ground is sinking sand.*
> *All other ground is sinking sand.*

I put my head on the organ and said out loud, "Lord, I'm going to that Miracle Service in Los Angeles—even if I die on the way."

I crawled back to bed and had a real good cry. I continued to pray aloud. "Job came out of his suffering. The people in that book of Miss Kuhlman's came out of their suffering. Lord, I intend to come out of this, too. If You don't want me to go to that service, You had better take me now, because I'm going."

I reached for the telephone and called a friend who sometimes attended services at the Neighborhood Church. She was different from many of my Christian friends in that she prayed in a special way, "in the Spirit" she called it. If anybody would help me, she would.

"Will you go with me to the Kathryn Kuhlman service?" I cried into the phone. "I have to go, even if I die."

"Oh, yes!" she almost shouted into the telephone. "I'll go with you. I've been praying. I knew that hundreds of others had been praying also."

Lee made reservations on the special plane that would fly us down from the Oakland Airport. But on Friday, two days before we were to leave, I had a terrible attack. Lee called Dr. Phelps.

"Let me talk to your wife," the doctor said.

Lee put the phone down next to my ear, and Dr. Phelps said, "Evelyn, I'm sorry, but there is nothing anyone can do. Most patients in your condition aren't alive."

"Well, I'll tell you what I'm going to do, Doctor," I wheezed. "I'm going to a Kathryn Kuhlman Miracle Service—if I'm still living when it comes time to leave."

"Now tell me how you're going to do that," he said kindly. "I can tell by listening that you have a severe respiratory problem."

"I'll make it," I said, gasping for air. "Just wait and see."

There was a pause. "I want to see you in my office on Tuesday after you get back," he said. Then there was another pause. "And Evelyn, I'll be praying for you as you go."

The next day, Saturday, I was so weak and in so much pain, that when my friend called on the phone, I tried to back out. "I can't make it," I cried. "I can't even lift my head off the pillow without suffocating. How do you think I'll make it on the plane and into the auditorium?"

Her voice came through the telephone like the voice of God. "Oh Lord, I know You're going to use her—I know You're going to heal her—I know You're going to make her a great witness. Oh, thank You, Lord."

I was too sick to pass judgment on her type of prayer.

All I knew was she was getting through to God. I was grateful.

Saturday night I lay in bed and looked at my watch. "All right, Lord," I said. "Tomorrow night I'm going to walk back into this house, or else I'll be walking the golden streets. If I can't come back healed, I want to die right there in the Shrine Auditorium."

I wasn't bargaining with the Lord. It was more like an ultimatum. He could take me or He could heal me; it made no difference. But I wasn't willing to settle for anything halfway.

Sunday was the roughest day of my life. Lee picked me up like a sack of potatoes and put me in the car. A wheelchair was waiting at the airport and they lifted me in.

"Oh, don't push me fast. Don't push me fast," I moaned as Lee rolled the wheelchair across the ramp.

"Evelyn, we're barely creeping," he said.

They arranged seats on the plane so I could lie down. I felt myself turning blue as the weight of my muscles pulled against my respiratory system. "I can't make it," I gasped to my friend. "I'm going to die right here on the plane."

"Oh, no you're not," she said with authority. "God, don't You let her die! Oh Lord, heal her. We claim Your healing." I was convinced that God was listening to that beautiful, auburn-haired woman.

Lee had brought two pillows, and when we got on the bus at the Los Angeles Airport, they again fixed a seat so I could lie down.

We were late in arriving at the Shrine Auditorium. The building was packed, but seats had been reserved for those on our plane. Lee carried me down the aisle to my seat and propped me up on the pillows. I felt every eye in that great auditorium was on me. But when you're dying, you don't care what anyone thinks. You'll do anything to live.

I was suffering more than ever before. The choir sang the Lord's Prayer, and I whispered to Lee, "Lay me down on the floor near the door. I don't think I can sit up anymore." But before he could move, it happened.

Miss Kuhlman stepped to the microphone. "I'm not

going to preach this afternoon, because there is so much
suffering here today. The Holy Spirit is eager to move."
She started calling out healings. One, two, three—and then
I heard her say, "To my right, there is a healing of respiratory problems . . . ."

"That's me!" I whispered to Lee.

I reached out to the seat in front of me and tried to pull
myself up. I couldn't. I fell back on the pillows, my body
limp as a wet rag. I tried again, but couldn't even close my
fingers on the back of the seat.

"The Lord has passed me by," I moaned to Lee. "I'll
never make it back home."

Just then a lady dressed in a white knit dress came down
the aisle. "Has there been a healing in this section?" she
asked Lee.

Then she saw me on the pillows. "Are you receiving a
healing?"

"No," I said, "but I sure could use one."

"Will you try to walk in the name of Jesus?" she asked.

"I can't stand up."

"Will you try?" she urged.

I felt Lee's big strong arm around my waist, and before I
could answer, he hoisted me to my feet.

Then I felt it. It was a light tickle, like the tips of a feather, that started behind my left ear and with a faint brushing
feeling swept down the left side of my body, tickling,
touching ever so lightly. Suddenly I was weightless. The paralysis was gone. The pain was gone. I was strong—
stronger than I had ever been before. Before I knew it, I
was running down the aisle toward the stage. I could hear
the roar of that great crowd as they saw what was happening.

Behind me, I heard Lee shouting, "Oh, she's been
healed! God, don't let her break her leg."

I ran the length of the aisle to the platform, leaving the
personal worker far behind.

When I was on the platform Miss Kuhlman approached
me. "Have you received a healing?"

All at once I was afraid. I looked out at that great sea of

faces. I looked down at my feet, and like Peter walking on the water, I began to sink. I choked out with fear and desperation, "Miss Kuhlman, the paralysis is coming back. Please help me."

She grabbed me around the waist. "I can't help you. I have no power to help or heal. Look to Jesus." Then she turned to the congregation and said, "I want everyone here to pray that this woman's healing will be complete."

I was aware of the choir beginning to sing again, and all around me people were praying. Miss Kuhlman touched me on the forehead. I knew I felt the Holy Spirit as He flowed through my body. The feather-feeling returned, sweeping all the way from my head to my toes. I was conscious of everything. I didn't faint. But it was the greatest relaxation I had ever known. I was floating, yet I was on the floor—under the power of God.

Someone helped me to my feet, and Miss Kuhlman said, "Stomp that foot, in the name of Jesus!"

I stomped and stomped and stomped and laughed and cried and ran back and forth, splashing tears all over the platform. Then Miss Kuhlman began talking to the devil. I thought, "My word, that woman will talk to anybody."

"Satan," she said, "this girl belongs to God Almighty, and you shall never bind her again." The entire audience was on its feet, applauding and shouting praises to God.

"Is there a doctor in the auditorium who is willing to come up here and examine this woman?" Miss Kuhlman said into the microphone.

Moments later a man appeared on the stage. He introduced himself as a surgeon from Anaheim. He felt my muscles, took my pulse, listened to me breathe, and then turned to Miss Kuhlman. "I was sitting back there with three other doctors," he said. "I do not doubt her doctor's diagnosis. This has to be the power of God, for nobody with myasthenia could ever do what she is doing now." His face was awash with tears as he testified.

After the meeting the bus driver took one look at me and his face broke into a huge grin. "You've been healed!" he exclaimed. "I'll never doubt the power of God again. I saw you before, and I see you now."

When we reached the airport the people in our party grabbed Lee, holding him back. "We want to see your wife go up those steps by herself," they said.

I ran all the way to the ramp and up the steps—myself.

It was the day of the final game of the World Series, and we arrived in Oakland at the same time the Oakland A's arrived, fresh from their World Series victory over the Cincinnati Reds. Thirty-five thousand people had packed into that little airport to greet them. It took us three hours to get out of the airport.

Lee and my girl friend were both complaining of their hurting feet, but I felt I had wheels for feet. "Those A's think they have something to celebrate," I shouted above the uproar. "Nobody in the world has more to shout about than I do. I've been healed."

The next Tuesday I went to Dr. Phelps's office. His nurse immediately noticed the change in my body. "Don't say a word," I cautioned her as she helped me undress. "I want the doctor to find out for himself."

Dr. Phelps came in and looked at me sympathetically. "Evelyn, how are you today?" he asked in his deep bass voice.

"I've got trouble with my big toe," I snickered. "I think it's from wearing shoes."

He grinned slightly and started his examination. He took my blood pressure, and I noticed wrinkles across his brow. I could hardly keep from laughing. Then he checked my reflexes. For the first time in years, everything worked. Stepping back, he folded his stethoscope and stuck it in the pocket of his white coat. "Evelyn, I want to know what's happened to you."

I jumped down off the table and did a little dance right there on the floor of the examination room. "Dr. Phelps," I giggled, "you can start taking care of the sick—*I've* been healed."

"I believe it," he smiled broadly. "God did this! Now go and give Him the glory."

I left the doctor's office that morning and stood on the sidewalk breathing deeply. The seagulls were wheeling overhead as the tide from the bay ebbed seaward, leaving the exposed mudflats. My feet were not planted in mud, but on a firm foundation that would never move. I broke into song as I got in the car to drive home:

> *On Christ, the solid Rock, I stand;*
> *All other ground is sinking sand.*
> *All other ground is sinking sand.*

SEVENTEEN

God Loves Us All

CLARA CURTEMAN

Clara Curteman lives in the little Northern California community of Fortuna. She worked as a waitress in Fred Deo's restaurant and bar in Loleta before she was disabled by a paralyzing stroke. A devout Roman Catholic, she and her husband Vern, who works in a lumber mill, have five children.

It all started one evening in Fred Deo's restaurant where I was waiting on tables. As I was picking up a tray of dirty dishes, I felt a sudden wave of nausea, accompanied by shooting pains in my head and stomach. I almost collapsed, but one of the other waitresses rushed to help me while another girl told Fred of my condition. He called my husband Vern, who came and picked me up.

I got as far as the sofa in our tiny living room before I collapsed. I had never been so ill. Vern told our five children to put themselves to bed. Then he tucked me in right on the sofa, where I spent the night.

When I awoke the next morning the sun was streaming into the living room. I tried to sit up. I couldn't. My left leg and left arm wouldn't move. I tried to call Vern, but only funny noises came from my lips. I felt a wave of panic sweeping through my mind. Paralyzed! Finally my incoherent sounds woke Vern. He could tell by the terror in my eyes that something was dreadfully wrong.

It was Saturday morning, and Vern called several doctors before he found one who could see me. The doctor

245

made a quick examination and said, "I think it's probably a pinched nerve. You'll get better after some rest."

Confused, Vern took me home. My ability to speak returned slowly, but I remained in bed. The pain in my left arm and leg grew more intense.

After two weeks Vern called Dr. Dixon in Rio Dell, a small town south of Fortuna. Dr. Dixon, who had treated my grandmother, agreed to see me. The moment I hobbled through his door, he said, "I can tell right now you've had a stroke. You don't belong here, you belong in a hospital."

I objected. I have five children to take care of, and we were hard-pressed financially. Dr. Dixon reluctantly agreed to let me return home.

My condition continued to deteriorate. One night at the dinner table our six-year-old Michael said, "Dad, why doesn't my mother learn how to talk right again?"

I burst into tears. Vern tried to smooth things over. "Mother can't help how she talks, Mike. She's sick."

Even so, none of us realized just how sick I really was.

In October I entered the University of California Hospital in San Francisco. Vern drove me down, three hundred miles, and I was admitted on a Saturday night. The doctors began tests that same evening. Three days later one of the doctors came by my bed in the ward. "Mrs. Curteman, it looks like you've had a cerebral arterial occlusion. This is a medical name for a stoppage of the blood vessels in the brain. It's caused a stroke, resulting in the paralysis of your left side."

Vern came for me shortly before Thanksgiving. The doctors didn't want to release me, insisting they needed to remove part of my right lung where clots had formed. They warned me I could suffer another stroke at any moment. However, I was allowed to be home with the children for the holidays.

It was a long trip home. Even the drive through the magnificent redwood forests meant nothing to me. I had always admired those towering redwoods of Northern California, standing there since the time of Christ in mute testimony to the eternal goodness of God. Now, however, eternity seemed too close.

Back in Fortuna Dr. Dixon ordered a brace for my left leg and a cane. My foot was beginning to twist under, and the only way to hold it straight was with a special shoe and a brace that went as high as my knee.

A week before Christmas I became violently ill again. The vomiting returned, along with terrific headaches and muscle spasms in my back. Then in early January I had another stroke. I awoke one morning to see my left hand horribly twisted, looking like a claw, accompanied by a burning in my arm and hand.

Dr. Dixon examined me again and finally ordered me back to the hospital in San Francisco. One week and a hundred tests later, one of the doctors came in. "If you had a choice," he said, half laughing, "which would you rather lose—your arm or your leg?"

"You're kidding, aren't you, Doctor?" I asked.

"It's just a question," he said, smiling reassuringly. "But why don't you think about it and give me an answer one of these days?"

I tried to forget what he had said, but it kept coming back. Why did he ask it? Was he kidding, or was he serious? Did the doctors know more than they were telling me?

Three weeks later I was released from the hospital, scheduled to return every two weeks for additional treatment. Since Vern was working, and our finances were stretched to the limit, this meant I had to ride the bus back and forth.

I had a wonderful priest, Father Ryan, from St. Joseph's Catholic Church in Fortuna, who made regular calls to my house. One afternoon I was lying on the sofa in so much pain I thought I would die. "Father, what am I going to do?" I cried.

"All you can do is ask God to heal you," he said kindly. "And I shall join you in that request." Then he prayed for me.

On his way out, he met the pastor of the Foursquare

Church and his wife, who were on their way in to see me. These two precious people had ministered to my father during his illness, and continued to stop by to see me after I became ill.

I was getting progressively worse. My vision had become blurred and I had trouble focusing my eyes. My left leg was useless and my speech very hard to understand. One Sunday afternoon, after another severe attack, Vern took me back to Dr. Dixon, who insisted I be sent to San Francisco at once.

"Don't even wait to change clothes," he told Vern. "I'll call ahead and make reservations. I see symptoms I don't like."

Dr. Dixon thought I was dying. So did I.

Once again the doctors at the University Hospital ran me through a whole battery of tests. On the fourth day one of the neurosurgeons stopped by my room. "Well, Mrs. Curteman, I think we need to do a little surgery on your head," he announced, without any preliminaries.

"Why? Do I have a brain tumor?" I asked.

"It looks like it," he confessed. "But we can't be sure until we go in and look."

"You're not going to shave my whole head, are you?" I asked. It is amazing, now that I think back on it. A neurosurgeon was telling me they were going to open up my skull and look at my brain, and I was concerned about how I'd look!

He laughed, though, and it broke the tension. "I'll try to save most of your hair," he promised.

He did save it, but he made a nice-size hole in the back of my skull. Following the surgery, it was Dr. Burton who brought the news to me. "Good news and bad," he grinned. "First of all, you don't have a brain tumor. That's good. However, you do have a condition known as vasculitis, a very rare blood disease."

"And that's bad?" I volunteered.

He nodded his head. "I'm afraid so. This is a deterioration of the blood vessels in your body. It caused the strokes you've had—and can certainly cause more. Any

one of them could kill you." He then went on to say that
the disease itself could kill me and that there was no known
cure.

"What's going to happen?" I asked.

He pulled a chair up beside my bed and sat down.
"Clara, I don't know what is going to come from all this,"
he said softly. "We really can't do anything about it. I think
you should start making plans for someone to take care of
your children."

I knew he expected me to die.

Released from the hospital, I started making my every-
other-week trips back and forth. The disease progressed to
the extent that the doctors told me I could expect a massive
—even fatal—stroke any day. They began talking about
amputating my leg as a means of prolonging my life.

Then I got a call from Katherine Deo, my boss's wife.
We had been in close contact since my sickness began, but
this one day in November she called with exciting news.

"Clara, Fred's brother-in-law, Don, has just come back
from a wonderful meeting in Los Angeles. It's called a Miracle Service and it's conducted by a woman from Pittsburgh. He said he saw hundreds of sick people healed by
the power of God."

"Oh, that's wonderful!" I said.

"That's not all," Katherine continued. "Fred and I both
believe that you can be healed, too."

I knew Fred and Katherine pretty well. Neither one had
ever shown much interest in spiritual things. But Katherine
was bubbling over. "Don brought us copies of Kathryn
Kuhlman's books. I know your eyes are bad, so I thought
maybe you'd like me to read them to you over the phone."

I agreed to listen.

One night, several weeks later, as Katherine was reading
from *God Can Do It Again*—about a pitiful little clown
who had been healed even though he never got into the
Miracle Service—she started crying over the phone. Fred
picked up the phone and continued the reading. Then Fred
started crying. I heard Katherine say, "Let me finish it.
This is one story I really want Clara to hear."

Katherine did finish the story, and when it was over, I knew I was supposed to go to a Miracle Service.

I thought about my grandparents, who were wonderful Christians. As a child I could remember how my grandmother prayed for me when I was sick, and how I would be healed. I knew she was still praying for me. A feeling of excitement began to build as I lay on the sofa in my living room, thinking about how God answered her prayers—and about the healings in the Kathryn Kuhlman services.

But I couldn't afford the trip to Los Angeles. Vern and I prayed about it, believing God would provide a way. When Fred and Katherine offered to take me, I knew God had planned it.

I also knew this Miracle Service was my last chance. I had to cancel an appointment at the hospital in order to go. The doctors had wanted to begin preparations to amputate my leg. Yet I was so sure that God was going to heal me that I packed my only pair of high-heeled shoes, planning on walking out of the Shrine Auditorium as a whole person.

That's how we happened to be driving south down Highway 101 in Fred Deo's Cadillac that Sunday morning, singing and praying and crying and holding hands. We were an odd mixture. Fred had been in the liquor business for twenty-two years. Katherine was a staunch Lutheran who chain-smoked through one pack of cigarettes after another. In the back seat, beside Fred's mother and aunt, was his sister Donna, a member of a Pentecostal church in Santa Maria.

We had driven down from the northern part of the state two days before, stopping over in Santa Maria with Donna and her husband. For two nights we sat up late while they talked to us about God's healing power. As a Roman Catholic I had no problem believing in God's ability to heal and perform miracles. For centuries the Roman Catholic Church has held to such doctrines. But this was different. We were going to a specific place at a specific time, expecting a specific miracle.

Fred's brother-in-law had told us that one of the favorite

songs at the Shrine Auditorium was *He Touched Me*. None
of us knew it, but Katherine had copied down the words.
She was trying to teach them to us as we drove toward Los
Angeles.

Although the car was filled with cigarette smoke, and
Katherine's voice was hoarse and wheezing, she kept trying
to teach us the song. "No, that's not right," she would say,
stopping us in the middle of a phrase. "It goes like this . . ."
Then we would all launch into the song again.

"Let's hold hands while we pray," Katherine said, grind-
ing out her cigarette in the ashtray. So we all joined hands
and cried, prayed, and sang songs together. After a while
Katherine turned to me. "Clara, you've prayed for everybody else but yourself. Now ask God to heal you. Pray for
yourself."

For a long time I had believed that God was going to
heal me. Hadn't I brought my high-heeled shoes to wear
when I took my leg brace off and left my cane in Santa
Maria? But praying for myself was something else.

"Go on," Katherine demanded. "You Catholics beat
around the bush. We Lutherans go straight to the Big Boss,
but you Catholics go through all the saints. This time, go
straight to the Top Man."

"Dear God," I finally stammered, "I'm asking for myself
this time. Please touch me and heal me."

"Hallelujah!" Fred blubbered, tears streaming down his
cheeks. "She really means it, God. I know she does. And
we want You to heal her, too."

I closed my eyes and praised God under my breath as
the car turned into the Harbor Freeway and headed south
through the city toward the Shrine Auditorium.

The others helped me climb the stairs, and we all found
seats high up in the balcony. There we sat until the service
began, holding hands and praying for my healing.

Halfway through the meeting Miss Kuhlman said,
"There is a leg healing in the balcony." In fact, she said it
three times, and finally one of the helpers approached me
and said, "I think Miss Kuhlman is talking about you. Take
off your brace and walk."

I was shaking so badly I could hardly unbuckle my brace. All the others in our group were crying, really sobbing. I removed the brace and began to walk up and down the aisle. It felt like fire was running through my body. I turned to the helper and said, "I can't breathe. I'm so hot."

I heard someone say, "Don't touch her, she's anointed." Then I fell to the floor. Later, Donna told me that as I lay on the floor my left foot kept flopping back and forth so violently she was afraid it would break off.

The ushers finally helped me to my feet and guided me to the platform. Miss Kuhlman was smiling as they brought me forward. I was still holding my brace and shoe, and she said, "Well, now, what are you going to wear home now that you've taken your shoe off?"

"Oh, I have my other shoes in the car," I said excitedly, completely oblivious to the fact that I was standing in front of more than seven thousand people. "I knew God was going to touch and heal me."

Miss Kuhlman reached out to pray for me. "Dear Jesus . . ." and that's all I remember. When someone helped me to my feet, I heard Miss Kuhlman say, "Now what are you going to do?"

I was still flustered, but I managed to choke out, "I hope my boss gives me my job back."

"Your boss?" Miss Kuhlman chuckled. "Is your boss here in this service?"

I pointed to the balcony, and Miss Kuhlman began to call. "Boss, are you here? Come on down to the platform, and bring your wife."

They all came to the stage. Miss Kuhlman prayed, and we all fell under the power of the Holy Spirit. One of the men on the stage later told me that while I was lying on the floor that second time, he could actually see the blood returning to my face. He said it looked like a transfusion, as the color of my skin changed from its usual sickly gray to a rosy pink.

I knew my leg had been healed. Yet it wasn't until we got back in the car heading north through Los Angeles that I noticed my hand. "Look!" I screamed. "I can move my hand! My fingers are limber. They don't look like claws anymore."

"And your eyes and face!" Donna shouted. "Your eyes are healed! I can see the difference."

Everything about me was whole.

We stopped at the first gas station off the freeway so I could call home. Ten-year-old Vernon answered the phone. I could hear him shouting, "Daddy, Mamma can walk! She doesn't have her brace and cane! She's been healed!"

Vern came to the telephone, but all I could do was sob. That's all he could do, too. Fred took the phone away from me to tell Vern what had happened, but then *he* began to sob. I finally had to get back on the phone to explain to Vern. We had a revival meeting right there in that phone booth next to the gas station.

We stopped in Santa Maria where I shared my testimony in the Foursquare Gospel Church. When we finally got home, Vern and the children were waiting on the curb.

"Mamma," Vernon shouted, "run a race with me and Mike."

I dropped my suitcase and took off down the street, my two youngest sons in hot pursuit. We ran all the way to the end of the block (I think I won) and then walked back, laughing and playing.

"Daddy," little Mike said, holding me around the waist with his pudgy arms, "Mamma can run faster than me. She's not a limper anymore."

All of us were changed. Fred started making plans to get out of the liquor business. I knew deep inside that God wanted to use me to share my testimony not only among my Catholic friends but in churches of all denominations. But first I had to have my healing confirmed.

I returned to Dr. Dixon in Rio Dell. The minute I walked in the doctor's office, his nurse jumped up from her seat behind the desk. "Clara, what's happened?" Then she began to call for the doctor. "Dr. Dixon, come in here. Come see Clara."

Following an examination, Dr. Dixon said, "This is wonderful, Clara." Then he asked, "Are you still taking your medicine?"

"I flushed it all down the toilet as soon as I came home from Los Angeles," I confessed. "Since then I haven't had any need for medication."

The next month I took the bus back to the hospital in San Francisco. I made a point of wearing my best clothes, including my high-heeled shoes. After reporting to the receptionist, I took a seat in the waiting room.

Several minutes later Dr. Burton walked through the lobby. He glanced at me and kept walking, then whirled in his tracks and stared. "Clara?" he stammered, shaking his head in disbelief. "Clara Curteman?"

I grinned. "That's me, Doctor. Remember?"

"Will you come in here right away?" he asked, motioning to his office. When he had closed the door he asked, "What happened?"

"The Lord healed me."

"Tell me all about it," he blurted out. "And start from the beginning."

After I finished my story, he stepped into the hall and called one of the other doctors. "Now you tell *him* what happened," he said.

"You mean from the beginning?"

"No, I mean the part about God healing you."

The second doctor gave Dr. Burton a strange look but sat and listened. When I finished, he wrinkled his forehead and again looked at Dr. Burton.

Dr. Burton knew what he was thinking. "Psychosomatic? Forget it. I've been in on this case from the very beginning. This is the real thing."

The second doctor turned back to me. "Behind every event there is a logical reason," he said. "What do you think is the reason behind this?"

I thought of Vern and our children. I thought of my suffering. I thought of Fred and Katherine and Donna—all of us driving into Los Angeles in that car, singing and crying and praying. I thought of their love, and of God's love flowing through them to me. In my mind I kept hearing the

echo of the hymn, old to many but new to me, that I had
heard sung in the little Foursquare Church in Santa Maria:

> *Down in the human heart,*
> *Crushed by the Tempter,*
> *Feelings lie buried that grace can restore;*
> *Touched by a loving heart,*
> *Wakened by kindness,*
> *Chords that were broken will vibrate once more.*

I looked up at the doctors. They wanted a reason—a logical reason. "There is a reason," I said. "The reason is
God's love. He loves us all."

EIGHTEEN

We Tried Everything but God

DR. HAROLD DAEBRITZ

Be not wise in your own eyes:
revere the Lord and depart from evil;
it will be healing to your body
and nourishment to your bones. (Proverbs 3:7-8 Berkeley)

The tangled mess began in my childhood. I was born in Bulgaria, where my German father was an editor for a Seventh-day Adventist publication. In 1938, the year before the war began, all Germans were deported back home. I was ten years old when we settled in Schneidemühl, Pomerania, on the border between Germany and Poland.

At the time we did not know that Hitler had issued an edict that every youngster ten years of age or older had to belong to the Hitler Youth. One day there was a knock at the front door. Uniformed policemen were standing outside. "Look," the leader said to my mother, "you are keeping your children at home. That is against the law. We warn you, you are responsible to send them to the Hitler Youth meetings."

My parents had no choice. My father was drafted into the army and sent to the front. My sister and I began attending the Hitler Youth meetings. The Nazi philosophy was being thrust at us from all sides.

I advanced rapidly in the Hitler Youth. One day I found that my skills on the violin qualified me to transfer from the militant brownshirt group to the musical and cultural

257

group. As time went by I became the leader of an orchestra and band. By the time I was sixteen I was in charge of over 500 young people in an orchestra in Schneidemühl.

Hitler's Germany had abandoned God. I remember vividly the day the Hitler Youth participated in the burning of the Jewish synagogue in Schneidemühl. We were being taught through example that there was no need for God.

Of course, the war went badly for Germany. We now realize wars always go badly for those who oppose God. In honesty, though, most of us knew nothing about the things that were going on in occupied Poland. We knew very little or nothing about the horrible concentration camps or the murder of the Jews. We were content to stay at home playing Mendelssohn, Mozart, and Beethoven—and occasionally watch a Shirley Temple movie.

By the time the war was over we had lost everything. We escaped to the American sector of Germany with only two suitcases among the four of us. After the war there was a resurgence of religion, but it was primarily a matter of the intellect. I attended some small group Bible studies and was even baptized in water in a bombed-out church. The search, however, was for knowledge, rather than for the One who is the Truth. Everything was a matter of the mind.

I entered dental school. However, when I graduated and married Ingeborg, I learned it would take two years of private practice before I could qualify to practice under the national insurance program. Having no financial backing, we decided to move to the United States, where we found a whole new set of problems. The United States refused to recognize my degree in dentistry from Germany. I would have to start all over again.

About this time I began having some physical problems. On several occasions sharp, shooting pains coursed through my chest, and I felt waves of nausea, along with an awareness of a rapidly beating heart. The doctor in Detroit diagnosed my ailment as tachycardia and arrhythmia. My heartbeat would sometimes increase to 240 beats a minute from the normal 80 to 100. Whenever this happened, it could mean death unless I received immediate medical attention.

We moved to Los Angeles, thinking the climate would be better. I opened a technical dental laboratory specializing in ceramics. My health improved a little, and the local dentists were impressed with the quality of my work. Soon our business was expanding and flourishing. We had two wonderful sons. It looked as if we had achieved the American dream of financial success and security.

Then, one Friday afternoon as Ingeborg was driving home from our dental laboratory in Fullerton, a young man plowed into the back of our car. Both cars were badly damaged, and Ingeborg suffered a severe whiplash. By the next day the muscles in her back had begun to spasm and she was in terrific pain. I rushed her to the Palm Harbor Hospital in Garden Grove where she stayed for five weeks, attended by an orthopedic surgeon. Despite massive doses of medication—analgesics and barbiturates—her pain grew worse. It moved from her back into her head, and the doctors offered little hope for healing.

The next two years were an unending nightmare for us both. Even after she was released from the hospital, Ingeborg was under the constant care of a physician. Not a day went by that she did not stagger into the bathroom vomiting, because of the excruciating pain in her head. She spent much time in traction in a hospital bed we had moved into our home. Her doctors prescribed increasing amounts of drugs, until our narcotics bill was averaging $200 a month. Finally, Ingeborg was referred to a neurological group at the White Memorial Hospital in Los Angeles.

In April, 1964, two years after the accident, the doctors performed a laminectomy, removing a piece of bone from Ingeborg's hip and transplanting it into her spinal column. Three vertebrae in her neck were fused and held together with silver wires. We were hopeful the surgery would give her some relief.

The morning after the surgery, we discovered the entire procedure had failed. Her spine had not been braced sufficiently, and when it collapsed, it left exposed nerves under great pressure. Additional surgery was out of the question. The only thing we could do was to load Ingeborg with narcotics and wait it out.

Every night for the next seven years she took between eight and ten sleeping pills. During the day she was on tranquilizers. I gave her constant injections of Demerol, a synthetic morphine. I knew she was becoming addicted, but we had no choice. It was that or the unbearable pain.

The drugs and the pain began to take their toll. Sometimes at night I would sit in our living room, my heart breaking as I watched Ingeborg stagger around the house, her body jerking, her lower jaw flopping open and remaining in constant motion. She had been so young, so blonde, so beautiful when I married her. Now she was becoming a staggering wreck of a human being, like an old building that had been condemned but is still inhabited.

We consulted four other specialists—an orthopedic surgeon, a neurosurgeon, and two internists. Their final diagnosis shook me: "Your wife has Parkinson's disease and muscular dystrophy. The disease is progressing rapidly, and within two years she will be confined to a wheelchair."

I refused to accept their diagnosis. In fact, the doctors wrote into the medical record, "Husband very obstinate. Will not face facts." I knew I was stubborn. I wasn't going to rest until we had tried everything. In May, 1967, I flew Ingeborg to the Mayo Clinic in Rochester, Minnesota, for a complete examination. Although the doctors there said they saw no evidence of Parkinson's disease or muscular dystrophy, they couldn't offer any cure for her pain. Despite the danger of addiction, they advised me to continue the Demerol.

By this time Ingeborg's neck was almost immobile. The only way she could turn her head was to twist from the waist. Her once happy voice had given way to constant whimpering and crying. "There is no help for me," she said. "I am this way forever."

We tried everything man had to offer—medicine, surgery, thirty-two specialists, five different chiropractors, hot steam baths, massages, herbs and teas. I took her to a famous ethical hypnotist in hopes he could probe into her life to see if the problem was psychosomatic. He spent four and a half hours with her and came out reporting he was unable to hypnotize her. Nothing helped.

Fortunately my business was prospering and I was able to travel to various parts of the world seeking help. I heard of a large clinic in southern Germany where an orthopedic surgeon was using osteopathic treatments. Leaving the children in care of a friend, we flew to Germany, where the doctor manipulated Ingeborg's back. For the first time in almost nine years, her headache disappeared—temporarily. Eight hours later the pain was back, as severe as ever. But now we had hope. We had discovered that relief was possible, even if only for short periods of time.

Returning to the States, I heard of a famous chiropractor in Wisconsin who was having significant success with patients like Ingeborg. We talked to him on the phone, and Ingeborg flew to Wisconsin.

I didn't learn until later that she had taken sixty sleeping pills with her. She had determined that if the doctor in Wisconsin was unable to help her, she would not return home alive.

The doctor did help, though. This time, his spinal adjustments relieved the pain for thirty-two hours. When Ingeborg returned home, I decided that if chiropractic could help, I would learn it myself. That way I could give her daily adjustments, and perhaps we could return to a semblance of normal living. With my background in medicine I had a running start, already being trained in chemistry, anatomy, and physiology. I enrolled in chiropractic college in the evenings, going to class every night from 5:30 P.M. until almost midnight.

It wasn't long before I was giving Ingeborg daily adjustments instead of the constant shots of Demerol. It took more than two years before I became proficient, but finally I reached the place where I was able to relieve her pain on a temporary basis, something that drugs and surgery had been unable to accomplish.

By 1969 Ingeborg had stopped using drugs, although she was never completely free from pain. The damage caused by the unsuccessful surgery still remained, and her neck was immobile. She wore her neck brace most of the time. Even so, any slight jar, such as the car crossing a railroad track, could increase the pressure on the nerves in her neck. She would twist and cry in agony until we found a place where I could stop to help her.

After 4,480 hours of academic training I received my Doctor of Chiropractic degree. Ingeborg was my only patient. But I was still unsuccessful in bringing her lasting relief.

As a last resort we started going to church. Maybe, I thought, there was some religious power that would help. I loved the music in church, especially the liturgical music of Bach and Beethoven. But there was no "life" in the church we attended, no feeding of the lambs.

I finally said to Ingeborg, "Look, it's nice enough to go to church, and if you want to go, I'll take you. But frankly, I feel those two hours could be much better spent in bed, for at least there you get something useful—sleep."

All Ingeborg could do was cry. I determined not to pray anymore, not even to ask a blessing when we sat down to meals.

One day I realized that we had tried everything—but God. Yet how does one try God when he doesn't know Him? We tried religion, but now I understand that religion is man's search for God. Christianity is quite another matter, being God's revelation of Himself to blind people—through Jesus Christ. No man ever really finds God. He just makes himself available to God, and God finds *him*.

So it was with us. It had small beginnings, that revelation of God coming to us. Although now we can see the mighty moving of the Holy Spirit, at the time it seemed so natural. We were much like the children of Israel camped on the shores of the Red Sea. Behind us were the chariots of the Egyptians, coming to take us back into captivity. Before us was the impossible sea. Then, one night, the wind began to blow.

It was such a small breeze at first. A friend gave us a subscription to *Guidepost* magazine. We enjoyed the magazine with its brief stories of God speaking to people in various ways. Then, through the *Guidepost* book club, we received a book by Kathryn Kuhlman entitled *God Can Do It Again.* The book was filled with testimonies of people who had been healed. We didn't know it at the time, but the water was beginning to move in front of the wind of the Holy Spirit.

Ingeborg read the book. In fact, every night she read a chapter out loud to the children. Then, later at night, still unable to sleep because of the constant pain, she would get out of bed, go downstairs, and read her Bible. Sometimes she read until dawn. Like Pharaoh, however, I was stiff-necked and obstinate.

One beautiful Saturday morning I planned to stay home and work in the yard. Ingeborg stopped me as I was heading out on the patio. "Daddy, would you like to read something?"

I knew she had been poring through the Kathryn Kuhlman book. Although I wasn't interested, I hated to hurt her feelings. "Just read this one short chapter," she said. "It's about a clown who was in much pain from a back accident. God healed him."

I took the book and quickly read the chapter. Closing the book, I handed it back. "Thank you very much," I said. "Now I must go to work in the yard."

I was reluctant to look her in the face, knowing that she was crying on the inside. I knew she wanted me to become interested in spiritual things, but I was a scientist and there was no place in my intellect for a God of the supernatural. I had read my Bible many times. I knew Jesus healed people when He was here on earth. But those days were past. Jesus had returned to heaven. Now it was up to us.

Ingeborg had been unable to do heavy housework, so she had hired a cleaning man to come on a regular basis. This way she could spend what little energy she had left tending the children.

Doyle Smith turned out to be a missionary in disguise. He

knew that Ingeborg had read Miss Kuhlman's book and
was now reading the Bible. He grabbed every opportunity
he could to talk to her about the Lord. The wind was whipping into gale force.

One day he said, "Mrs. Daebritz, why don't you attend
one of the Miracle Services at the Shrine Auditorium?"

"Oh, no," Ingeborg answered. "I could never get my
husband to a meeting like that. He's too unemotional, too
intellectual."

Doyle didn't press the point, but before leaving the house
that day, he switched our radio to the station that carried
Miss Kuhlman's program. The next morning, while
Ingeborg was in the kitchen fixing breakfast, she heard
Miss Kuhlman's voice coming from the radio. As the days
went by, I found the radio constantly tuned to this station.
Not only that, Ingeborg was making it a point to be in the
kitchen every morning at just the right time to hear the
broadcast.

One morning I came into the kitchen and found
Ingeborg kneeling on the floor, with her shoes off. The
radio was playing a song, *He Touched Me*. Ingeborg
looked up. "God is real," she said. "I had to take my shoes
off, for I feel Him in this place."

Poor wife, I thought. Too many drugs have damaged
your mind.

However, the wind of the Spirit continued to blow. One
night as Ingeborg tucked our youngest son into bed, he
said, "Mommy, if Daddy would take you to one of Miss
Kuhlman's Miracle Services, maybe God would heal you."

Ingeborg shook her head. "It would take a miracle just
to get him there."

"Then I'll pray for a miracle," our son said, reaching up
and kissing his mother good night.

Two weeks later, on a Tuesday morning, I had overslept
and was late leaving the house for work. Rushing through
the kitchen on my way to the car, I heard Kathryn Kuhlman's voice on the radio. Then I heard an announcement
giving a telephone number to call for reservations on the
bus that was going to the Shrine Auditorium next Sunday.

"Well, write the number down," I said to Ingeborg, as I pulled on my coat and headed out the door. "How else will we get there?"

As I closed the door behind me and slipped into my car, it suddenly dawned on me what I had said. I sat there in silence, my hand on the key in the ignition. I knew that Ingeborg was on the telephone, making reservations. What, or Who, had made me say a foolish thing like that?

Sunday rolled around and I tried to back out. But Ingeborg had made up her mind for both of us. I found a seat for her on the bus, then took a seat beside a heavy-set woman right behind the driver.

"Young man, where do you go to church?" she demanded with authority.

"I don't go anywhere, lady," I said firmly. "And I wouldn't be going to this meeting today except that my wife put pressure on me. I would much rather be home in bed."

The lady looked shocked. I could feel her beginning to bristle. Putting her hand on my shoulder in a matronly way, she started to preach, "Young man—"

"Madam, if it is all the same to you, let's make an agreement. You don't talk to me, and I won't talk to you."

The woman withdrew her hand and remained silent the rest of the way to the Shrine Auditorium. But while we were standing outside waiting for the door to open, another woman approached me, a Bible in her hand.

"Young man, the dear Lord says in His Book that we should all repent."

"Yes, yes," I said, hoping fervently she would go away.

"Not only that," she continued, as though I had begged her to tell me more, "the Lord also says we should be born again, filled with His Spirit, forgive our enemies."

It was bad enough having to come to a Miracle Service, but to have to put up with a bunch of religious nuts was almost more than I could take. "Look, lady," I said. "Are you doing all those things yourself? Until you are perfect, don't preach to me."

I turned my back and shoved my way through the

crowd. "What's going on here?" I moaned to Ingeborg. "All I'm doing is standing here minding my own business, and those people keep picking on me."

"Maybe the Lord is trying to get through to you," Ingeborg said quietly.

Leaving the noise on the sidewalk, we walked into the auditorium where it was quiet, hushed, reverent. The huge auditorium was packed with people, and we had to find seats in the balcony. Yet even as we sat down, I sensed something special in the air. For the first time in years I wanted to cry.

The choir was on the platform. Four hundred trained voices began practicing. The director led them in a few bars, stopped, and had them do it over. Suddenly I was back in Schneidemühl, leading my own choir and singing Mendelssohn-Bartholdy. I was a child again. My adult sophistication, my intellect, my snobbery began to melt.

I tried to hold back the tears, but they just rolled down my face. I was embarrassed and glanced around. Even though the service hadn't even begun, other men around me were crying, too. It had not taken a hurricane to blow back the water, only a still small voice whispering, "God is in this place." I nodded, and cried some more. I knew it was so.

Nothing happened to me at that first meeting. But something did happen to a lot of other people. A black lady with her six-year-old son had taken a seat behind us in the balcony. The little boy was in braces from his feet to his hips. His legs were braced apart, so when he walked it was like walking on stilts. I could tell the muscles in his legs were atrophied, almost gone from disuse.

As the service progressed I heard Miss Kuhlman say, "There is a healing in the balcony. Somebody with a brace. Take it off and you will find God has already healed you."

The mother gave a gasp and started removing the child's brace.

I was shocked. I knew his little legs could not possibly support him. Yet the child stood. Not only did he stand, he walked. And when he reached the platform, he ran back and forth. The mother, overcome with joy, explained that the child had been born with the problem and had worn the braces all his life. This was the first time she had ever seen him run.

My intellect was demolished. There was no medical explanation for this. The man sitting next to me had a pair of binoculars. I borrowed them to study the child as he ran back and forth across the stage. This was no trick. The child's affliction could not have been caused by autosuggestion or hypnosis. He came in with braces and left without them. It was a miracle—and that was a word which had never before been in my vocabulary.

The monthly meetings at the Shrine Auditorium became a regular part of our lives. On the second trip we watched as Miss Kuhlman introduced a Spanish fellow named Graviel. He had come to the platform during our first meeting and testified he had been a heroin addict for twenty-two years. He had looked like it, too. His face was ashen, his body shaking, his eyes riveted on the floor. His clothes were dirty and disheveled. Miss Kuhlman had put her arm around his shoulders and led him to pray aloud, "Lord Jesus, set me free." Then the man had collapsed on the floor under the power of the Holy Spirit.

"Come back next month," Miss Kuhlman had said, "and let us hear from you."

He was back. He had been touched by God. Before, he could hardly speak. That day, Miss Kuhlman could hardly shut him up. He was dressed nicely and came with a brand-new Bible in his hand. I turned to Ingeborg. "What we are seeing is real. I now believe God can heal you, too."

When it came time for us to make our fourth visit to the Shrine Auditorium, I realized Ingeborg could no longer ride the bus. It was too painful. That Sunday morning I called the lady who handled the reservations and told her I would drive Ingeborg in our Cadillac and meet them at the Auditorium. She agreed.

As I hung up the phone, Ingeborg said, "Those people are so simple. They expect a miracle every time they enter the Shrine."

"Just what's wrong with that?" I said, still amazed at the change that was taking place in my own way of thinking.

Ingeborg sat down at the kitchen table, stirring her coffee. "I always knew Jesus died for the whole world. Now I know that means me, too. Jesus died for me." She began to cry but this time it was from joy.

Ingeborg didn't wear her neck brace to the meeting that day. She gripped my hand tightly as we took our seats in the auditorium. "God loved me so much that He let Jesus die that horrible death on the cross for me. It is so clear now. When I think of that, I know He can do something about that silver wire in my neck. He can restore my health."

I dared not look at her. I could only suck breath through my teeth. Every time I entered the Shrine, I felt like crying, but this time it was even stronger. It was like the atmosphere on one of those heavy, humid days we used to have in Germany. If just one more drop of water were added to the air, it would begin to rain. I dared not move a muscle, I was that close to tears.

Then the choir began to rehearse, singing *He Is So Wonderful To Me*. It was the drop of water I had feared, and it started the waterworks in my eyes. The power of God was falling like the latter rain, not only for me but for Ingeborg as well. I felt her hand tighten on mine and turned to look at her through my tears. She was twisting her head back and forth, at least 60 degrees in both directions, something many normal people cannot do.

"Oh, look what's happening," she cried. "He touched me. My head turns. I'm healed!"

Forgetting where I was, I leaped to my feet and began an examination of her spine. After years of adjusting Ingeborg's back, I knew where every pressure point was, every pain location. I ran my hands up and down the back of her neck and spinal column. The lumps were gone. I poked harder. There was no pain. Cervical six and dorsal two-three had always been puffy. Now they were clear. No pain! I was ecstatic with joy, and began telling the people all around us.

"She's been healed! God has healed her!"

During the service, we went to the platform and testified to the power of God. We both wound up on the floor. If there was any intellectualizing left in me, it was all washed away by the mighty outpouring of the Holy Spirit that Sunday afternoon. We had passed through to the other side of the sea, and the waters had rushed back into the void, drowning the old Pharaoh who had lived in my mind. I was a new man.

The next day, Ingeborg awakened in great pain. She tried to keep it from me, fearing I would return to my old intellectual approach. She misjudged me, however. The old man was dead and—by God's grace—would never again come to life.

Instead of giving in to the pain, Ingeborg began praising God for His perfect healing in her body. Upstairs and downstairs she went, praising God throughout the house. Her headache lasted just that one day. By nightfall it was gone. It has never returned.

While Ingeborg's pain disappeared, my old problems with my heart began to flare up. Some days at work the chest pain was so intense I could hardly bear it. My associates in the clinic became concerned about me. On several occasions they came into my lab and found me pressing my fists against my chest, my face white with pain. Two months later, with the pain growing worse all the time, I told my employees which physician to call in case I collapsed. All the symptoms of an extreme cardiac case were present. It seemed to be a matter of time.

We had joined the choir at the Shrine Auditorium. The Friday before Thanksgiving we had a special choir practice. Ingeborg begged me not to go, but I replied, "I might as well go, darling, because I will feel just as sick at home as I would there." We attended, but on several of the numbers I had to sit down because of the dizziness and pain.

The following Sunday we attended the afternoon service at the Shrine. Again Ingeborg begged me to stay home.

"No, I'm going! Why shouldn't God heal me as He did you?"

The healing service was under way, and many people with spinal problems were being touched by God. Then, in the middle of a sentence, Miss Kuhlman whirled and faced the choir. "Back here," she said, pointing toward the middle where I was sitting. "Somebody with a heart condition is being healed. Stand up."

Surely, I thought, with more than four hundred people in the choir there would be dozens with heart conditions. But no one was standing.

"Who is it?" Miss Kuhlman was saying. "Stand up and claim your healing."

I took a deep breath and stood. I was shaking and perspiring profusely. I tried to speak, but nothing came out. The pain was still there, but I was willing to step out on faith. At Miss Kuhlman's urging, I came to the microphone. People all around me were rejoicing and praising God.

"In the name of Jesus, receive your healing," Miss Kuhlman said. I collapsed to the floor. I don't know how long I was down, but as I regained my feet I felt like I had received an artificial pneumothorax—a pumping of air or gas into collapsed lungs so I could breathe again. The pain was gone. I had never felt so light, so whole. God must have taken my old heart and replaced it with a new one.

It's hard for people to understand what has happened to us. When we tell about our physical healings, some rejoice, others just shake their heads in disbelief. It makes no difference to us. We know what we were—and what we are now.

The biggest healing of all, however, was not the healing of our bodies but the healing of our souls. The Holy Spirit has filled us both, and now I feel like Moses, standing on the far shore of the Red Sea, looking back at where he had been and singing: "The Lord is my strength and song, and he is become my salvation" (Exodus 15:2).

NINETEEN

Hope for Those Who Suffer

DONNIE GREENWAY

Mrs. Zel Greenway is the wife of the fire chief in St. Petersburg, Florida. She and her husband are active members of the St. Luke's Methodist Church.

I sat at the kitchen table finishing my coffee. Little Donnie, our eleven-year-old daughter—D.J. we called her—had already left for school. It was a beautiful Florida spring morning, and the songs of the mockingbirds rode the soft tropical breeze through my kitchen window.

I glanced at the clock. It was almost eight, time to pick up Zel from the fire station. Even though Zel had been with the St. Petersburg Fire Department all our married life, and was in line for promotion to chief, I never had grown accustomed to his hours—on duty twenty-four and off twenty-four.

I gulped down my last swallow of coffee and pulled open the yellow curtains above the sink. The scent of orange blossoms from our backyard tree filled the air. I breathed a quiet prayer of thanksgiving for being alive and healthy on such a beautiful day, and I headed to the car.

God had always been very real to me. My dad had died when I was eleven, leaving my mother with twelve children. She brought us up in the Baptist church, teaching us to pray and to love Jesus. My marriage to Zel had been happy. We had a Christian home. What more could I ask?

I nosed the car out of the alley beside our house, looked both ways, and made a left-hand turn onto Twelfth Street.

Suddenly I heard the terrifying screech of tires and looked up just in time to see a speeding automobile crash into me broadside. The impact knocked my car over the curb and into our neighbor's yard. Even though the car was demolished, I didn't seem to be hurt. I called Zel at the fire station, and he arrived before the policeman had finished making out the accident report.

Zel wanted me to see a doctor, but I insisted I was all right. The next morning, however, I was black and blue and hurt in places I didn't know I could hurt. I told myself it was from being bounced around inside the car. (Cars weren't equipped with seat belts back in 1957.) I figured I'd be back to normal in a few days.

I did gradually recover from the bruises and aches, but several months later, I was running the carpet sweeper and leaned over to move a small table in the living room. As I started to lift it with my left hand, excruciating pain snatched at the lower part of my back. I gasped for breath and tried to straighten up, but I was stuck in that position. Moving just a fraction of an inch up or down sent spasms of unbearable pain through my body.

I dropped the table, let go of the carpet sweeper and, still bent over, made my way to the bedroom. Zel was at work, D.J. at school, and I was at home alone. Gradually, with tears streaming down my face, I was able to lower myself onto the bed and call my husband. It was the beginning of a sixteen-year nightmare.

Zel was a deeply committed Christian and the first thing he did, when he came in that afternoon and found me in such intense pain, was to lay his hands on me and pray, asking God to relieve the pain.

The pain did subside, enough so I could get up in the morning and go to an osteopath. I never dreamed at the time that he was only the first of more than twenty doctors I would see over the next sixteen years.

There were X rays, massages, hot baths, and other therapy. Nothing helped. Pain was my constant companion, day and night. Each morning I woke up almost paralyzed from lying in one position. The pain moved up from my back to

my shoulders, then down into my left hip. At night, as Zel
would massage my back, he said he could feel little knots
under the skin. The doctor said they were muscles convulsed with pain. Much larger knots appeared on my neck.
X rays showed a bump growing on my shoulder, which felt
like a sharp spur under the skin. My knees became covered
with callouses, not from praying but from falling. Since it
was impossible for me to bend over to reach anything or to
pick up anything, I had to fall on my knees for such simple
tasks as getting food out of the refrigerator or a pan from a
low cupboard.

After I had undergone five months of treatment without
noticeable improvement, a neighbor recommended a medical doctor who had been known to help people with back
problems. I made an appointment, and the pattern of going
from doctor to doctor was set. He examined me, said the
problem could be caused by poison in my system, and recommended an ear, nose, and throat specialist. The specialist admitted me to St. Anthony's Hospital, cut out my tonsil
tabs, and scraped the back of my throat. I left the hospital
with back problems *and* throat problems.

Another doctor said my pain could be caused by my
teeth. I was referred to a periodontist. He examined me
and said he thought I had poison in my bloodstream. He
recommended gum surgery.

This was even more painful than the pain in my back.
He cut away the gum above my teeth, peeled it back, then
covered it with plaster of Paris. The treatment lasted for
more than a month. I tried not to complain, but Zel knew
how much pain I was in. Night after night he would pray
for me, massage my back, and share my desperate frustration.

Even routine matters were becoming extremely difficult.
We had been in the habit of driving to Tampa several times
a month to see Zel's parents. However, my pain had become so intense that it was impossible for me to cross the
Gandy Bridge without having to stop so I could get out and
stretch my back.

When Zel was promoted to the position of chief of the

fire department he had better working hours, but as chief he was expected to attend various firefighters' conventions across the nation—as many as five or six a year. The men always took their wives, so I began to travel with him. If I had to sit for any length of time, I supported my back with a rolled-up towel. Pain was my inescapable bedmate every night.

One night in the Hyatt House in Atlanta, where Zel was attending an International Fire Chiefs' Conference, I woke him up in the middle of the night with my crying. I told him I wished he would just cut my left leg off, the pain was so bad. Zel rubbed me, applied hot towels, and prayed. He never stopped praying, not a single day.

Back in St. Petersburg we moved into a new house on Eighth Avenue. My mind was constantly occupied with the pain. I knew I had to get my mind on something else or I would go insane. I tried working in the yard. Sometimes, after working on my hands and knees, I would have to crawl up the steps and collapse on the carpet inside the door before I could even get up. Then I would stagger into the bathroom and sit long hours in a tub of hot water. But nothing seemed to ease the torture.

Zel was active in the St. Petersburg Rotary Club, and I worked with the Rotary-Anns. The wife of a Rotarian doctor knew of my condition. She was going to fly up to Detroit, Michigan, to be admitted to a diagnostic clinic, and she suggested I go with her for a complete examination. Zel agreed to let me go.

The clinic doctors confirmed the diagnosis of curvature of the spine, and said the vertebrae in my lower spine were deteriorating. They felt that surgery would aggravate rather than improve my condition. They also suggested that my problem could be caused by infected sinuses, so they did surgery on my face to try to correct that.

In the meantime my back problems grew more acute. I tried a new doctor every time a friend suggested one. A neurosurgeon described my spine as an electric wire with most of the insulation scraped off, the slightest movement causing extreme shocks to my system. An orthopedic surgeon fitted me with a harness to be used in traction. An internist prescribed drugs. But nothing helped.

By 1968 Zel was desperate to find me some relief from the incessant pain. He approached one of his Rotarian friends, a leading neurosurgeon, describing my symptoms, and begged him to see me.

"Well, Chief, I usually don't see patients like this," the doctor said, indicating that most of his patients were referred by other doctors. "But since she's your wife and is in so much pain, have her come in next week."

He ran a series of tests and put me in another type of traction—a neck harness that hung over the doorpost with a strap around my neck like a hangman's noose. It was like being hanged as the weights, attached by pulleys, stretched my neck. I used this contraption three times a day for two years. If I were able to accompany Zel on a trip, I took my gallows along with me.

Each night I prayed, asking God to take away the pain, then awoke in the morning to the same agony. As the years wore on I began to wish I wouldn't wake up at all.

Sometimes, when Zel was at work and D.J. at the university in Lakeland, I would sit down and try to remember what it was like when I had no pain. I could never remember how it felt to live without it.

In September, 1971, I was in St. Anthony's Hospital again for three weeks. Two orthopedic surgeons were doing everything they could do to help me. But it was the same old story. One Saturday evening, about six o'clock, one of the surgeons came into the room. Nonchalantly pulling up a chair, he loosened his tie and sat down. He grinned weakly. "Well, you've got no back left."

I couldn't believe him. I pulled the traction harness off my neck and sat up in bed. "What do you mean?"

"We've looked at your X rays from every angle. Your entire lower spine has deteriorated."

"But isn't there anything you can do?" I blurted out. "Can't you operate?"

"We've got nothing to operate on," he said, trying to

soften the blow. "You have no whole vertebra left below the waistline."

"That doesn't give me too much to look forward to, does it?" I said, a feeling of hopelessness settling down on me like night fog on a tidal basin.

He reached over and patted my arm. "No, but a lot of people live with this condition. You need to prepare yourself for a life in a wheelchair."

I think he kept on talking, but "wheelchair" was the last word I remember hearing him say. I would rather be dead than spend the rest of my life in a wheelchair.

Zel came by to see me later in the evening. I kept my head turned the entire time he was in the room, afraid I'd burst into tears.

Sunday evening the pastor from St. Luke's Methodist Church stopped in to see me. The sun had already dropped into the Gulf of Mexico, and I was lying in the semidarkness of my room, feeling lower than I had ever felt in all my life. I saw no future. I had nothing to live for. Sensitive to my wounded spirit, he told me about a prayer chain that had been started at the church. People had been praying around the clock for me. He reached over, took my hand, and prayed for me also.

Just as he finished his prayer, the phone beside my bed rang. It was Martha Bigelow, whom I had met at St. Luke's several years before. Her husband, Jimmy, had suffered a heart attack during one of the services, and Zel had ridden with him in the fire department rescue truck to the emergency room of the hospital. I had sat with Martha in the waiting room. Jimmy had recovered, and Martha and I had had occasional contact since then.

Martha had a facial condition known as tic douloureux. During surgery, a doctor had accidentally cut a facial nerve, causing her eye to droop. "I have two books on prayer I'd like you to read," she said.

"Well, Martha, I'm not much of a reader," I confessed.

"But don't you know?" she said, ignoring my disinterest. "I've been healed of my tic douloureux. My disfigurement is all gone!"

Suddenly my heart began to pound in my chest. "You don't mean it! What happened?" I knew her condition had been considered permanent.

"I was healed through prayer, and these two books helped show me the way. It started when I read *Prison to Praise*," she went on. "Then someone gave me another book about prayer. Later I went to a prayer group in Tampa conducted by a surgeon from Tampa General Hospital. He prayed for me, and I was healed. You wouldn't recognize my face."

I was so excited I could hardly talk. A wonderful, warm feeling was flowing through me. It started at my feet and flowed all the way to my scalp. All I could think about was that I might be healed, too. I wanted to get on top of the hospital and shout, *"Hope!! Hope!! There's hope, everybody!"*

Zel, D.J., and her husband Bud had been out to dinner. When they came in, I chased the men right back out. "Go right now to Martha Bigelow's and pick up two books she has for me."

Zel gave me a surprised look. He knew I didn't like to read. "But we came to keep you company," he protested.

"I don't want company. I want those books. And please hurry. I must have them."

The two men went after the books, and D.J. stayed behind with me. I told her how the people at St. Luke's had been praying; how the pastor had come in and prayed; about Martha's phone call. And then this wonderful, warm feeling that was still flowing through me.

D.J. began to cry. It had been so long since she'd seen me happy, or showing any signs of hope. "Oh, Mother, I know you're going to be all right."

Zel and Bud returned with the books, and again I chased them out. I could hardly wait to begin reading. Always before I had hated to see Zel leave the hospital. In fact, we had a little secret code. After he left I would climb out of bed and wave from the window. His fire chief's car was usually parked right in front of the hospital. When he saw me wave, he would turn on his flashing red light. That was our way of saying "I love you."

But that night I didn't even go to the window. Before they got to the elevator I was digging into the books, reading hungrily of the supernatural power of God to change lives. And hour later, the nurse came in with my sleeping pill. I didn't take it. I read through the night. It was like stumbling on an oasis after sixteen years in a parched desert. I felt I could drink forever of the fountains of hope.

The next day Zel came by and I said, "Honey, check me out of the hospital. I'm going home."

He argued that the doctor had ordered a back brace for me and it wasn't ready yet. But I knew if I ever put that thing on, I'd never get out of it. I insisted that Zel take me home. I knew that somehow, some way, God was going to heal me.

I started attending the healing services at St. Luke's Methodist Church on Tuesday and Thursday mornings. In spite of the pain in my back I always made my way up to the altar and asked for prayer. Each time, the pain would go away for a while, but it always came back. There was just enough relief, however, to let me know it was possible for God to heal me completely.

Three weeks after I left the hospital I returned to the orthopedic surgeon. He ran his hand up and down my back. "Your back is different, Mrs. Greenway," he said.

I grinned. "I know."

He continued the examination, asking me to bend over, twist, and stretch. I heard him making little grunts as he ran his fingers up and down my spine. "I can't just can't get over how much your back has improved."

"There have been so many people praying for me, it had to get better," I said.

He walked around to the head of the table where he could look me in the face. "You know," he said soberly, "we doctors need all the help we can get from the Man upstairs." I was a little taken aback by his impersonal reference to the God who had become so personal to me, but I was pleased. At least the doctor recognized that something miraculous was beginning to happen in my body.

I still had the pain, however. And with it, splitting headaches that sometimes lasted as long as thirty-six hours. Six weeks later I returned to the doctor.

"Would you consider going to a large university medical clinic in North Carolina?" he said. "They have some of the finest medical facilities in the nation. Maybe they can help you."

I felt the old hopelessness welling up inside me, even though in my heart I knew God was going to heal me eventually. "Doctor, we've spent more than $17,000 on doctors and hospitals," I said. "We just can't afford a trip like that."

He tapped his stethoscope in the palm of his hand and said, "Mrs. Greenway, I don't think you can afford *not* to go."

Zel and I prayed about it, and finally we agreed to make the trip. The doctor said he would start collecting my records from all the other doctors and send them to North Carolina. They would contact me about an appointment.

It was hot in St. Petersburg. Usually there is a breeze blowing in off the coast, but that summer the fronds on the palm trees hung motionless in the heat. My pain grew worse as July sweltered into August. I was going to prayer meetings all over the area: St. Petersburg, Clearwater, even across the bay to Tampa. Someone gave me a copy of Kathryn Kuhlman's *I Believe in Miracles,* and then I bought a copy of her *God Can Do It Again.* As I read how others had been healed of conditions even worse than mine, hope returned, and with it an increased faith that God was going to heal me, too.

Then I learned that in September, for the first time in many years, Kathryn Kuhlman was coming to Florida to conduct a Miracle Service in Orlando, just one hundred miles away. Something inside me clicked into place. I knew this was to be the time and place of my healing. That night when Zel came home, I asked him if I could go.

"We're supposed to leave on the thirteenth of September

for a fire chiefs' convention in Cleveland," he said. "Let's pray about it."

We did pray, and it seemed the answer came the next week at a prayer group where an announcement was made that there were no more seats available in the Orlando Municipal Auditorium. Only those who had reserved seats on the buses could get in. That afternoon I came home sick with disappointment and started packing to go to Cleveland. If God wanted me at the Miracle Service, He would have to get me there.

D.J. came over the next day. "Mother, Daddy doesn't seem to be very enthusiastic about going to Cleveland, does he?"

"No," I agreed, "but it's an important conference, and I'm not going to question him about it."

That night Zel was quiet at dinner, poking his food with his fork. "You know," he finally said, "I don't think we're supposed to go to Cleveland this year."

I felt that sense of excitement, accompanied by the flow of warmth, moving through my body again. "I'll be glad to go if you want," I said, in my most submissive tone. But inside I was standing up and cheering, "Oh, praise the Lord! Now I can go to Orlando."

Of course, there was still the matter of seats. The reservations on the buses were being handled by someone in the Blessed Trinity Catholic Church. They had a Friday night prayer group that met each week, and Zel took me and Martha Bigelow to the meeting. "Maybe someone will cancel out, and you can get their seats," he said.

Zel was right. There were two seats available, and they went to Martha and me. A little Roman Catholic nun from Ireland was at the meeting. When she learned of my condition, she came over, laid her hands on my head, and prayed.

On the way home, Zel remarked that I was the most prayed-for person in St. Petersburg. An entire Methodist Church had prayed all night for me, numerous prayer groups, a husband, a daughter, a son-in-law, brothers and sisters, a Methodist minister, and now a Catholic nun. "If

God doesn't heal you in Orlando, it's not because of lack of prayer," Zel laughed. I laughed too. Zel believed, just as strongly as I, that this was God's time.

Early Thursday afternoon five charter buses sat in the parking lot at Bayfront Auditorium. Their engines were running, the air-conditioners whirring. A pastor and his wife and the priest from Blessed Trinity Catholic Church were all aboard—along with two hundred others. Zel said he would be waiting when we returned, and then he put Martha and me on the bus. My pain came along too, sitting right on my shoulders all the way to Orlando.

Orlando is one of the most beautiful cities in the world. Built around a hundred lakes, many of them right in the center of the city, it gives the impression of leisure-living at its finest. As we pulled off the Interstate toward the auditorium, I could see the cars backed up for blocks. A special lane was provided for buses, and we inched our way toward the parking lot, which already seemed jammed with buses and hundreds of cars from all over central Florida.

"Look at that!" Martha whispered from the seat beside me. She was pointing to the mob of people standing in the broiling sun, waiting to get in the auditorium. "The doors won't open for another two hours, and already there must be two thousand people waiting outside."

The bus pulled around to the back door and we were permitted to go into the auditorium early. The moment we walked in, my eyes filled with tears. I saw a woman on a hospital stretcher, two ambulance attendants alongside giving her oxygen. A man I took to be her husband was standing next to her, holding her hand. I saw a little baby in a hospital crib with a nurse hovering over her. The child's head was bigger than all the rest of her body. The room seemed filled with people like this. Many of them were in wheelchairs. There were fathers holding sick children in their arms. It was as if all the hospitals in Florida had tilted up on their sides, pouring their sick into this one big room.

I began to cry. Here I was, with my only affliction a bad back. Sure, I was in pain, but nothing like these others! At least I could get up and walk around. At least I could ride on a bus and not have to be wheeled in from an ambulance. I turned to Martha, the tears pouring down my face. "Much as I want to be healed, if just one of these could be healed, I would leave with joy."

Martha couldn't answer. She was crying too.

For the next two hours (from the time we found our seats until the service started), I never again thought about myself. Instead, I spent every second praying for those around me.

Suddenly there was singing, marvelous singing from a huge choir on the stage. Then Miss Kuhlman appeared. I thought she looked like an angel, dressed in white with a glow that surrounded her as she moved across the platform.

I turned to my right and saw a woman fall to the floor. I had read in Miss Kuhlman's books about the many people who fall under the power of the Holy Spirit in her meetings. I knew this was of God. "Oh Martha, isn't this wonderful?" I whispered.

My mind was in a whirl. I tried to focus in on what was happening, but so much was going on, I couldn't comprehend it. People were being healed. Many of them were coming to the platform to testify to the power of God.

Suddenly, out of all the cacophony of sound, praise, and music, I heard Miss Kuhlman say, "There's someone in the balcony who is being healed of problems in the back, neck, and shoulders."

Before I knew it, I had leaped to my feet.

"Wherever you are—you know who you are—come on to the platform," she said.

Things rushed before me. Faces flashed by. I was running down the steps. Then, my mind still in a whirl, I found myself standing in line on the platform. I was saying, "Praise the Lord," and "Thank You, Jesus"—phrases I had never used before.

The stage was crowded, and I was being pushed back by others shoving forward to testify. I sensed the ushers were having problems controlling the crowd, yet I, too, wanted to get close so Miss Kuhlman could touch me. "Oh, if only she would touch me," I cried inwardly. "Then I would be healed." But the crowd was pushing me all the way to the back of the stage, behind the piano.

Then, very softly, I heard a sensitive masculine voice over my shoulder: "You don't need to be touched by Miss Kuhlman. It's the Holy Spirit who heals."

I turned. There, set in the midst of a handsome, black face, were the most tender eyes I had ever seen. It was Jimmie McDonald, Miss Kuhlman's baritone singer.

"Oh, thank you," I said, and turned back toward center stage. As I did, I heard Miss Kuhlman say, "Oh, there's glory over there." She was standing on tiptoe, pointing over the top of the crowd to where I was standing.

I went down. It was such a beautiful, wonderful feeling. I don't know how I got to the floor, or how I got up. All I knew was that the Holy Spirit had come upon me, in me, over me.

I staggered back down the steps of the platform in the general direction of my seat. As I reached the main floor I was aware of something falling off me, something like a cloak that had been draped around my body. I stopped and looked down at the floor, trying to see what it was I had lost, but I saw nothing. I walked on, then turned and looked back at the floor. Something *had* dropped off me; I had felt it. But there was nothing on the floor. I moved on.

I couldn't find my seat and just wandered around the auditorium. I finally stood against a side wall, basking in the glory of God's presence. Yet something was still missing. I had dropped something, left it behind. I felt incomplete.

The next thing I knew, Martha Bigelow was touching my arm. The service was over and I wasn't even aware of it. I was still saying over and over, "Praise the Lord. Oh, praise the Lord."

"You left your purse and glasses on the seat," Martha grinned. "I've got them with me."

"Oh, thank you," I mumbled, still dazed. "I knew I left something behind, but I thought I had dropped it on the floor."

It was after midnight when the buses pulled into Bayfront Park. Zel was waiting for me. I fell into his arms, and we wept all the way home. It wasn't until we were in bed, still talking, weeping, and praising God, that I realized what was missing. It wasn't my purse or my glasses. It was the pain. My constant companion for sixteen years was gone. I was free. The bondage had dropped off.

The next week, following the Tuesday morning service at St. Luke's, I spoke to the pastor. "My doctor said, 'Praise the Lord' when I told him I had been healed, but he still insisted I go on to North Carolina for the examination."

He nodded, then said, "It seems I heard Miss Kuhlman telling the people to have their healings confirmed by their doctors. Wouldn't it be wonderful if you had the medical experts confirm that you were indeed healed?"

It seemed such a waste of time and money that I didn't want to go. But I told the Lord I would go if I heard from the Medical Center. It had been three months since they had received my records.

The very next day a letter arrived. The doctors wanted to see me on October 4.

Zel and I drove up. The North Carolina hills were dressed in their most colorful costumes. The trees alongside the road were ablaze with red, orange, and yellow frocks and jackets. It was a beautiful time for praising the Lord. I knew I had been healed and could hardly contain my joy.

The security guard at the door of the Medical Center must have thought I was being admitted as a mental patient, I was so happy. I checked in at nine in the morning, and Zel went with me to the examining room. The resident orthopedic surgeon came in and did a preliminary examination. He had with him a huge sheath of files and records on my case, dating all the way back to 1957. After he finished his examination, he said, "Ah, Mrs. Greenway, just what is supposed to be wrong with your back?"

I glanced at Zel. His face was deadpan. "Well," I said, "I've been having extreme pain."

He glanced at my report. "Yes, I can see why from these records and X rays. But now I'm confused."

"Confused?" I said, having trouble keeping a straight face.

He cleared his throat. "The chief surgeon is on his way up. I'll let him look at you, and then we can tell more," he said. Moments later the chief surgeon arrived and looked over my charts. He wrinkled his forehead and looked at me over the top of his glasses. "You amaze me," he said.

"Why?" I asked.

"You are supposed to be in a wheelchair."

I tried not to smile. "Yes, I know." I lay on the examining table while he examined my back, feeling, poking, pounding.

He finally sat down in a chair and pulled off his glasses. "You know, I can't find anything wrong with your back." Then he turned to Zel. "Sir, how do you feel about coming this far and not finding anything wrong?"

"It's the best news I've ever heard," Zel answered.

"I really don't understand this," the doctor continued. "I could admit your wife and run tests on her, but it would be useless. It seems a shame you have come all this distance just to turn around and go home."

"Doctor, there isn't anything wrong with me," I said. "Since this appointment was made, I have been healed."

He stopped leafing through the papers in my folder. Looking up, he said slowly, "I'm sorry. I don't think I understand you."

"I have had a healing," I said. "I attended a Kathryn Kuhlman meeting. If I hadn't had a healing, I would be in a wheelchair. But now I am in perfect health."

The surgeon chewed on the end of his glasses. "Hmmmm. Well, I think I'll take a few X rays just the same."

After two hours of X rays we returned to the examining room and waited. Shortly afterward the doctor reappeared with two sets of X rays. Holding up one set, he asked, "Are these yours?" They were marked September, 1972, St. Petersburg. They were the last ones made before I attended the Miracle Service. I glanced at them and nodded. "I'd recognize that spine anywhere."

The doctor pointed out the mushy cloud at the base of my spine where all the vertebrae had disintegrated, the knot on my shoulder, and the S-shaped curve of the backbone. Then, holding up the other set of prints, he said, "These are the ones we have just taken. This is what you look like now."

I gazed in wonder. My spine was straight. All the lower vertebrae were in perfect shape. The knot on my shoulder was gone. The X-ray pictures were of a person with a normal back.

The doctor didn't say anything. He just stood there holding the two sets of prints. Finally he said, "It has to be a miracle. You had a classic back condition that always leads to total disability. But," he said with a crooked smile, "obviously all that has changed."

Zel put his arm around my shoulders and pulled me tight, echoing the doctor's words. "Obviously."

The security officer opened the front door of the Medical Center as we left. "What did they find wrong?" he asked.

"Not a thing," I bubbled over. "Not a thing in the world."

He just shook his head. "I stand at this door eight hours a day. I see people bringing their loved ones, and leaving under the sentence of death. They come and go in ambulances, wheelchairs, on crutches. Sometimes they come and never leave. But I've never seen anyone like you. Why did you come to begin with?"

"I came because once I was in so much pain I could hardly walk. I had been sentenced to a life in a wheelchair. Then Jesus Christ, the Great Physician, touched me in the power of the Holy Spirit. Now I am perfectly well."

The guard turned and looked at the fading sunset. A cold wind was whipping around the edge of the hospital, but it wasn't the wind that was making his eyes water. "That's wonderful," he said in a faraway voice. "I'm glad to know there is still hope for those who suffer. It will make things easier as I stand here at the door."

TWENTY

Yet in Love He Sought Me

PATRICIA BRADLEY

I'll never forget the little girl in the big boots running across the stage in Dallas, Texas. Nor will I forget her mother, a strikingly beautiful young woman with a West Virginia drawl who bubbled over with the excitement of having been born again and filled with the Holy Spirit.

Pat Bradley was born and raised in Kenova, West Virginia. At the age of fifteen she left home with her husband. Three years later a daughter, Gina, was born. It took thirteen years for the circumstances to get so bad that she finally turned to the Lord.

The muted roar of the night traffic outside the dimly lighted Catholic church formed a background for my desperate sobs echoing through the empty sanctuary. It was almost midnight and I had been kneeling at the altar rail for two hours, weeping. My eight-year-old daughter, Gina, sat quietly on the front pew.

I had been a topless nightclub dancer in Dallas. I was divorced, lonely, and desperate. I had worked as a stripper in such clubs as Little Egypt and The Landing Strip in the bawdy part of town. My former husband was deep into drugs and alcohol. Three times he had beaten me so badly I had to go to the hospital. The last time, it required plastic surgery to restore my nose and cheekbones.

There are some who think the life of a striptease dancer is fun. I knew better. Lonely, pawed over by men, expected to enter into all kinds of perversion for money, I finally broke under the strain and my world collapsed around me.

I knew that back home in West Virginia, my folks, especially my mother, were praying for me. I had been brought up in an evangelical church and had gone to Sunday school as a child. But when I married at the age of fifteen, I had turned my back on God and plunged headlong into a hell on earth.

First it was the world of drinking and drugs. Then, after we moved to Dallas from Oakland, I started working as a stripper. Our marriage fell apart. One of my friends offered to murder my husband, and I encouraged him to go ahead. But my husband found out about it and hired killers to murder Gina and me. We fled for our lives.

I moved into a small apartment and took a job as a waitress in a German restaurant. With my life crumbling around me, I began reading the Bible, hoping God might intervene and save me. My boss, the other strippers, and my friends all thought I had lost my mind. They didn't understand. All they could see was a young divorcée with a pretty face and a sexy body. They couldn't see into my heart—the torment, the guilt, the gnawing hunger to be more than an object.

"Wrestle a live nude girl," said one sign in front of a club in Dallas, as if a girl were an animal like a chained bear. Some of the clubs put the topless dancers in cages and suspended them above the audience, where they twisted and gyrated to the deafening beat of the acid rock music. Oh, God, didn't they know we were creatures of God— made in His image and longing to be persons, not objects or animals?

One December night after spending the evening in my tiny apartment, weeping and trying to read my Bible, I snatched Gina by the wrist and headed out the door onto the sidewalk. I would walk the dark streets of Dallas until I found a church. There, I knew, I would find God.

It was just a few days before Christmas and many of the stores were still open. But the only church I could find still unlocked at ten o'clock was a huge Roman Catholic one. It was back off the sidewalk, dark and foreboding in the shadows. A small light burned over the door of the sanctuary, and we gingerly made our way up the steps and slipped inside.

Gina clung to my hand as we walked down the dimly lighted aisle. On the sides were statues with cold melted wax around their feet. A robed priest appeared from a side room, moving silently in my direction.

"I'm Protestant," I said, my voice shaking. "But I need to pray."

He looked at Gina, who had crawled up onto the front pew and was sitting, frightened, her hands squeezing together in her lap. He glanced back at me, knowing the kind of girl I was from my dress and makeup. He nodded, waved his hand toward the altar rail, and disappeared through a door in the shadows. I collapsed at the altar, and my sobs bounced through the hollow stillness of the empty building.

I had forgotten how to pray. I could remember the first few words of the childhood formulas—"Now I lay me down to sleep" and "God is great, God is good"—but the rest had faded from my memory, obliterated by the years of rebellion. All I could do was sob convulsively and cry out to God to help me. It never dawned on me that this was prayer in its finest form. "I don't want to be like I am," I sobbed. "I want to be pure. I want to be clean. Please, God, please."

It was almost midnight when I finally quieted down. Exhausted, my tears drained dry, I leaned my head on the altar rail. The statues stared down, their lips sealed, their eyes unseeing, their hearts stony. But Someone had heard.

Gradually I became aware of a light in the sanctuary. It was soft and quiet, filling every corner. Where was it coming from? The only lights were the artificial ones burning behind the Communion table. But there was another source of light there, one I couldn't see. I could feel it, however. It was like warmth and peace. It seemed to soak into me, bringing its illumination into the darkest corners of my heart, chasing away the darkness. Like a tiny child who crawls out of bed in the middle of the night and snuggles in between her father and mother, I felt secure and loved. All my fears drained away. My yesterdays no longer pressed down, causing me to stagger, to want to hide. All the dirt, and shame, and guilt were gone, covered by an ocean of love and peace. I was free.

I knew almost nothing about spiritual things, but I knew I had cried out to God, and He had answered me. "Lord," I whispered, "I don't have a son to give You, like You gave me. But I give You my little girl, more precious to me than my own life. Use her for Your glory." I was to forget that prayer in the months that followed, but God remembered it.

When we came out of the church, the Christmas lights still blinked in the streets. The December wind still stung my face. Gina still gripped my hand tightly, looking up into my face, wondering what she saw there. But I was no longer the same. It was as though I had been born for the first time.

Wafting up through the mist of memory came the words to an old country hymn I had heard sung in Mamma's West Virginia church.

> Perverse and foolish, oft I stray'd,
> But yet in love He sought me,
> And on His shoulder gently laid,
> And home, rejoicing, brought me.

We returned to the church the next night at the same time. As before, the church was empty. This time there was not even a priest to greet us. Gina and I sat down on the front pew.

But something was different, something was wrong. The peace of the night before was gone, replaced by some sinister sense of foreboding. I felt a chill. Involuntarily, I shuddered. Gina huddled up against me as though she felt the same ominous threat. Her short, dark hair framed the fright in her round child's face.

"Don't be afraid, honey," I said, trying to reassure her and myself. "This is God's house."

Suddenly we heard a noise, like the opening of a trap door. It came from somewhere behind us, down the aisle. Gina whirled to look. Her little arms reached out and grabbing me around the neck, her eyes widening in terror. "Mommy!" she screamed.

I looked back over my shoulder. Coming down the aisle were two grotesque figures. Apparitions! They were walking like puppets, arms and legs jerking stiffly, yet they seemed to be floating.

"Mommy!" Gina screamed again. We jumped and backed against the altar rail, clinging together.

The man had Mexican features, but his skin was bloodless gray, his face the mask of death. The woman, jerking along beside him, had pale white hair falling alongside colorless cheeks. Their eyes, unseeing, stared straight ahead. They were like walking corpses.

I was petrified with fear. They approached within arm's reach, and the female, her face still expressionless, reached out and touched Gina on the shoulder. Then they were gone. I began to scream. Holding Gina by the hand, I raced down the long dark aisle and out onto the sidewalk.

Back at the apartment, I continued to scream. A neighbor called friends who came and tried to calm me.

"I saw them!" I screamed. "I saw them!"

One of my friends called the police. I tried to tell them what I had seen, but like my friends, they just looked at one another and shook their heads. Gina and I were put in the police car and taken to the hospital.

"She's seeing things," one of the officers told the psychiatric nurse. "We'll take the little girl down to the Juvenile Department at the station."

"No," I pleaded. "You can lock me up—but not Gina. Let me call my sister. She lives close by and works at Baylor Hospital. She'll take care of Gina."

The officers agreed, and my sister Faye came by and picked up Gina. I was locked in the psychiatric ward for observation.

"Oh God, what is happening?" I moaned as they put me in bed and gave me a shot. "Yesterday everything was so beautiful. Now this. Were those demons? Why did they touch Gina?" I drifted off to sleep, crying softly, my questions hanging in the air.

I didn't know then that during my years of alcohol, drugs, sex, and sin, I had been opening my life to the power of Satan. When I invited Jesus into my life the night before, He had cast out all the demons. But they had come back—to touch Gina. The results of that creature's touch were about to break into the open in a nightmare too horrible to describe.

I was in the mental hospital in Terrell, outside Dallas, for six weeks. One psychiatrist said I had a nervous breakdown. Another said I was hallucinating. I tried to argue that I was sane, but they didn't believe me. Instead, they kept pumping me full of drugs.

Faye brought Gina to see me each Saturday for a while. On the third visit, when we were alone, Gina whispered, "Mommy, those two people meet me every Friday after school and walk home with me. They say I am going to die. I'm too scared to say anything to anybody about them. They might put me in the hospital, too." Her eyes had a haunted look, deep inside.

"Just pray to God, honey," I wept, holding her close. "He'll see us through this."

I was released from the hospital the first week in February. Faye came to pick me up. A "blue norther" had blown in out of the Texas panhandle that morning, and the temperature had plunged below freezing, accompanied by a dry, biting wind that whined through the branches, hurtling bits of twigs against the side of the car. We sat in the parking lot for a few moments, waiting for the car to warm up.

"How's Gina?" I finally shivered out, my nose still stinging from the cold wind.

Faye didn't reply. She just sat looking at the steering wheel. I thought she hadn't heard me, and started to ask her again, when she looked up; fear was written across her face.

"What's wrong?" I asked, my voice shaking, remembering that Gina hadn't come to see me last Saturday.

"We were afraid to tell you, Pat," Faye said, her eyes brimming with tears.

"What are you talking about? Where is Gina?" I grabbed her arm, my fingers biting through her coat.

"Two weeks ago, on Friday afternoon, she came home from school complaining of a pain in her left ankle," she explained. "We took her to the doctor, thinking it might be a sprain, but he could find nothing wrong. Then, Saturday morning, when my kids tried to get Gina out of bed to watch cartoons on TV, she couldn't move. Her whole body was stiff and swollen, and she could barely talk. We rushed her to Baylor Hospital."

I sat stunned. It was like a horrible dream.

"How is she?" I finally asked.

Fays shook her head. "Not good. She's been transferred to another hospital, and the doctors don't know yet what's wrong with her. But it's serious, Pat. She's mighty sick."

We went straight to the Children's Medical Center, where things were even worse than Faye had described them. Gina was lying naked on a bed in an isolation room in the children's section. Her body was swollen out of shape, her joints so stiff she couldn't move. Her head was drawn back, the muscles in her neck standing out like ropes. Saliva drooled from the corners of her mouth as she moaned in pain. A nurse was beside her, checking the I.V. tubes that dripped their colorless liquid into her arms. Twice, the nurse told me, they had to pack Gina's body in ice to reduce the raging fever.

I bent over Gina. Although conscious, she was unable to speak. Her eyes searched my face for help and comfort, but I was too shocked to give her anything. Even as I watched, her eyes slowly rolled back into their sockets until only the whites showed.

I was horrified. The nurse just shook her head. "We can't put clothes on her, because she screams in pain when anything touches her body," she told me.

Then she pointed out that Gina's hands and feet were

beginning to draw up. "It's some outside force that the doctors haven't been able to identify yet," she said. "They're doing all they can, though."

I believed her. But I also feared that no medical treatment would ever be able to release Gina. I could tell her pain was increasing. Days and nights blended together in one long nightmare. I stayed with Faye during the day and spent the nights beside Gina's bed.

It was during one of those long, lonely night sessions that the convulsions began. Gina's little body began to bend backward, twisted by some invisible hand of cruelty. Her eyes rolled back and she began to gag.

The nurse rushed in, took one look, and gasped, "She's swallowing her tongue!"

Grabbing a cloth, she pushed her fingers deep into Gina's mouth. She was able to keep the air passage open, but Gina's breathing rapidly became faster and more shallow. Then it stopped.

We stood looking in silence for a fraction of a second. Gina's body was jerking involuntarily, much as a snake or chicken twitches after its head has been chopped off. But from somewhere behind me, I heard a gentle voice, speaking ever so softly. "Do not be afraid. I am right here with you."

Who had spoken? Turning, I saw no one, but at the sound of the voice I felt the fear drain out of me. Gina's body relaxed immediately. The nurse began mouth-to-mouth resuscitation. In seconds, Gina was breathing again. A doctor rushed into the room and started oxygen. The nurse put her arm around my waist and guided me out into the hall. I looked back over my shoulder at the little form on the bed as the doctor reinserted the tubes that had been pulled out during her convulsive thrashing. I wondered how she could survive such a convulsion.

She did survive it, however. Not just that one, but many more. Several times she stopped breathing, and the doctors finally told me that she had suffered irreparable brain damage from being deprived of oxygen.

By this time Gina had lost control of her bodily functions. We had to change her diapers and tend to her as if she were an infant. The first week of April, Gina began to scream with pain. She didn't stop. She screamed for a week and a half before the doctors increased the drugs sufficiently to bring the pain under control. They still had not been able to fully diagnose her illness.

Even though Gina was a welfare case, the doctors and nurses at the Children's Medical Center were kind and patient toward us. They pulled a cot into Gina's room so I could sleep during the long night watches. One morning I noticed a lot of loose strands of hair on Gina's pillow. I gently ran my hand over her head, and the hair came loose in my fingers. In days she was completely bald. Then black hair began growing on her arms, legs, and back. The doctors said it was caused by a hormonal change.

Dr. Chester Fink, a pediatrician who specialized in blood disorders, asked permission to perform surgery on Gina's legs. He wanted to open her thighs and take a biopsy of the muscles. I consented, and the procedure was successful, leading to the diagnosis of a rare blood disease called periarteritis nodosa.

One evening I picked up a pad of paper and sat down to write my mother a letter, bringing her up-to-date on Gina's condition. I knew she had been praying for both of us. The pad was one that Faye had used previously, and I was flipping through the pages to find a clean sheet on which to write my letter when I ran across a note in Faye's handwriting: *Pat doesn't know this yet*, it read, *but the doctor called yesterday from the hospital and said Gina could not live. He told us to begin making arrangements for her funeral.*

I sat staring at the words, as if I were reading a novel. They were unreal. Yet they were in Faye's handwriting. I knew I had stumbled upon an unfinished letter to my mother.

Faye was sleeping in the other room, and I ran in and awoke her. "I've got to know what is going on. You have been hiding the truth from me, afraid I'll have another breakdown. Tell me everything."

Faye reached out and put her hand on my arm. "I'm sorry, Pat," she said. Then she admitted what the doctor had said. There was no hope. Gina was dying.

I went to the hospital to spend the night. The next morning when the doctors made their rounds, I cornered one of the physicians—a young doctor, very feminine and very pretty—and asked her if Gina was going to die. Looking me straight in the face, she said, "Mrs. Bradley, there's no sense in trying to kid ourselves. Gina cannot live. She's too sick. The disease is getting worse. At the most she has six months to live—maybe only three." She continued to look deep into my eyes. Just a trace of moisture formed around her own pale blue ones. "There's nothing we can do," she said. Then, squeezing my hand, she turned and walked out of the room.

In July the doctors finally regulated Gina's blood pressure and gave in to my constant nagging, saying I could take her home, even though she was taking drugs fourteen times a day. I moved into an apartment, the Welfare Board increased my allowance, Buckner Baptist Benevolences helped me with some food, and a special nurse came over every morning from the hospital to help with Gina's medication and feeding. I was hoping for those six months.

While she was in the hospital I had been praying for Gina and talking to her about Jesus, but her mind was so confused that I was not sure she understood. After she got home, I sat down beside her bed and told her again about the Jesus I had met. I knew she had brain damage, but I had decided that Jesus died for retarded children just as much as for normal ones—maybe even more. Satan might kill her body, but Jesus could save her soul. She understood, and asked Jesus to come into her life. In the midst of sorrow, it was a joyful moment.

One day while Gina was sleeping, I went through the yellow pages of the phone book until I found the name of a funeral home in our neighborhood. The director gave me prices on embalming, casket selection, and transportation of the body back to West Virginia for burial. Then I called my father and asked him to see about a cemetery lot and to make arrangements with a local funeral home in Kenova. Then Daddy asked me if there were any way I could bring Gina home for a visit before she died. He too was dying of cancer. He wanted to see us one last time.

I wanted to try to take Gina to see him, even though I knew it would be an ordeal. I talked with the airlines and with the doctors. Scottish Rite Hospital in Dallas furnished me with a wheelchair, and with the attendants helping at airports along the way, we were finally able to get home.

I could tell that Daddy didn't have long to live. He had lost so much weight, he didn't even look like himself.

One warm summer afternoon he drove me out to the cemetery to show me the lots he had bought. I was crying so hard it was difficult for me to see. "Daddy, this is the hardest thing I've ever had to do," I sobbed.

We got out of the car and started walking across a grassy space toward the woods. "Nothing in life is easy," he said, his voice shaky with pain. " 'Yet man is born into trouble, as the sparks fly upward.' Job said that, and it is still true. But he also said something else we both need to remember: 'Though He slay me, yet will I trust Him.' "

I put my arms around Daddy's waist and held on. The sun was slipping behind the clouds, casting shadows across the grave sites. A soft breeze blew out of the woods, and I could hear, behind it, the sound of birds singing in the trees. Everything spoke of life. But we were here on death's business.

Mother really ministered to me. I had known for years that there was something different about her. Even while I was dancing in the strip clubs, Mother would write or call and say she loved me and was praying for me. She never looked down on me. She just loved me with more love than I could imagine. While I was at home, I asked her about it.

"We don't have much of this world's goods," she said, sitting down beside me on the old worn sofa. "We've had to work mighty hard just to have food on the table. But I've got something that's worth more than all the money in the world. It's the Holy Spirit."

"I thought we all had the Holy Spirit when we accepted

Jesus," I said, quoting the last sermon I had heard in the Baptist church in Dallas.

Mother smiled and raised her wrinkled hands over her head. "Oh, we do, honey," she said. "But it's the *Baptism* in the Holy Spirit that gives you the power."

I didn't understand what she was talking about, but I knew that for Mother, it was real. She said something else that was so far out I just let it slip through my mind at the time. She said, "Patricia, God can heal Gina. Take her to a service where the power of God is falling, and she'll be healed." I couldn't believe that, because I knew that Gina was under a death sentence from medical science. It was beyond me to even consider anything else.

We flew back to Dallas amid many tears. The next time I returned to West Virginia, it would be to bury Gina.

Faye met us at the airport and drove us to our apartment. Gina was terribly weak and crying out with pain as we picked her up and carried her into the house. After we got her into bed and filled her with drugs, Faye pulled me aside.

"Pat," she said hesitantly, "a friend of mine, Diane Smith, gave me a book. I read it and think maybe you should read it, too. I don't want to get your hopes up, because we all know that Gina is dying, but this is a book about healing. It's called *I Believe in Miracles,* by Kathryn Kuhlman."

I read the book, and the next week I met Diane. An active worker in the First Baptist Church of Dallas, she told me that Kathryn Kuhlman was going to be speaking in a large Methodist church the next week. She urged me to take Gina. My mind backtracked over Mother's words— "Patricia, God can heal Gina"—and I agreed to go.

It was hot that day in Dallas. The August sun burned down on the concrete streets and bounced up in shimmering heat waves that seemed to make the sidewalks move up and down. For two hours we stood in line outside the huge Methodist church, waiting for the doors to open. Gina was in a wheelchair in front of us. I kept expecting her to cry out in pain, but she seemed content just to sit and look around at the other people.

Finally the doors opened and we went inside. Diane helped us to our seats. "I can hardly believe it," I said to her. "Gina has not been able to sit up for more than fifteen minutes at a time. Look how well she's doing now."

Diane smiled, as though she knew something I didn't, as though she couldn't see how pitiful Gina looked.

I had bought Gina a wig to hide her baldness before we went to West Virginia, and it was difficult to keep it on straight, since she had no hair to fasten it to. Her feet were so twisted they no longer fit in her old shoes. The only thing she could wear was a pair of my old knee boots that laced up the front. They were many times too big, but by lacing them tight I was able to make them stay on. I knew Gina looked strange, sitting there in the big wheelchair with those oversize boots, her wig askew, and such a pathetic look on her blank face. But I was desperate enough that I didn't care what people might think. I just did what I had to do.

It was a beautiful meeting. I had never attended anything like it. Throughout the afternoon Miss Kuhlman kept using the same term my mother had used, "the Baptism in the Holy Spirit." My heart responded. I knew this must be the secret to power in the Christian life.

Gina grew restless. The ushers kept bringing us water so I could give her more medication. But something was happening. As Miss Kuhlman started the healing portion of the service, I heard her say, "Satan, I command you, in the name of Jesus Christ, to release the captives in this audience."

At the same time, I heard an inner voice saying to me, "Gina is healed."

I turned and looked at Gina. She seemed the same, but I knew I had heard the voice. It was the same voice that had spoken to me in the hospital room. Suddenly I knew whose voice it had to be—and I believed it.

Partway through the healing service the people stood and broke into spontaneous singing. It was so beautiful.

The tears washed down my face as I sat and listened, deeply touched. I glanced at Gina again. Her lips were moving, and she was making strange sounds. I bent over, knowing that her confused brain often caused her to do odd thngs at unpredictable times. But this wasn't odd. Gina was singing. The sounds coming from her lips were not very musical, but there was no doubt as to what was happening. She was singing along with the crowd, making up her own words and music as she went.

Then, very slowly, she reached out and grabbed the back of the seat in front of her. With great effort she pulled herself up out of the wheelchair and stood with the others. It had been seven months since she stood up. She couldn't walk, and had to hold onto the seat in front of her to keep from falling, but here she was, on her feet. Her head was up, and her lips were moving in time to the song.

When the other people took their seats, Gina sat down, too. She didn't try to stand again, but I knew that her healing had begun.

During the next two weeks I noticed remarkable improvement in every area of her life. She began to talk with understanding. Before, her eyes looked dead and blank. Now they sparkled—as though someone had turned on a light behind them. Not only that, Gina was getting out of her wheelchair. By holding onto the wall or a table, she was able to take steps.

A group of Christians I had met at the Berean Fellowship started coming to the house. One couple, in particular, meant much to me. They were Negroes whom I knew only as Brother and Sister Phillips. Gina and I lived in a mixed neighborhood and were not accepted by some of our neighbors. I knew this wonderful couple was running a great risk in coming to see us, but they insisted God wanted them to visit and bring encouragement.

One afternoon Sister Phillips looked at Gina and said, "You can walk. I know you can. Why don't you just get up out of that chair and walk across the room?"

Gina looked at me. "Mommy, give me your boots again."

I pulled them out from under the bed and helped her put them on. Then, slowly but with deliberation, Gina rose up out of the wheelchair, without holding onto anything, and took a step toward Sister Phillips, then another and another.

I felt the tears again, splashing down my face onto my blouse.

"That's right, honey," Sister Phillips encouraged. "That's right. Praise the Lord. Thank You, Jesus."

She was crying, too. Brother Phillips was crying also. Everyone was crying but Gina. She had the biggest grin on her face I had ever seen.

After the Phillipses left, Gina returned to her wheelchair. The next day, when she tried to walk again, she fell. Instead of getting up and trying again, she crawled back toward the chair.

"No, Gina!" I insisted. "You can walk. You can't give in to fear."

"I can't walk, Mommy," she said. "I can't walk anymore. I want my wheelchair back."

I pushed it away, across the room. Gina went after it, sliding along on her bottom. "Please, Mommy, give it back. I can't walk."

Finally I let her return to the chair. Once again, discouragement descended on the house.

In September Miss Kuhlman returned to Dallas to speak at a meeting sponsored by the Full Gospel Business Men's Fellowship International. New friends from Berean Fellowship called to tell me about it. Time was short, but we made it to the meeting, getting there just before it started.

This time an usher met us at the door and took us by elevator right into the auditorium. Several thousand people had already been packed inside, but he rolled the chair right down near the front and found a seat for us. As he left, he whispered, "I'll be praying for you during the meeting."

It was a needed gesture. I felt loved again.

I looked at Gina. She was sitting transfixed. Then I heard Miss Kuhlman say, "There is somebody here with a

fatal blood disease. God has healed you, and every bit of
that disease is burned out of your body. Satan made you
sick, but the Great Physician has made you well. Stand and
claim your healing."

Gina was struggling with her boots again. She finally got
them on, and straightening her wig, she stood to her feet.
One of the personal workers came quickly down the aisle.

"Has she been healed?"

Before I could say anything, Gina moved past me and
into the aisle. "Yes, ma'am," she said, in perfectly clear English. "Satan made me sick, but God has made me well."

"Come with me," the worker said, tears running down
her face. "Let's go up there and tell Miss Kuhlman all
about it."

As Gina walked to the platform, the entire congregation
broke into thunderous applause. Many of them had seen
Gina come in, riding in her wheelchair. Miss Kuhlman
asked her a few questions, and then began walking with
her, back and forth across the stage. Faster and faster they
went, until Gina broke into a run.

"Look at her go!" Miss Kuhlman shouted to the audience. "Those of you who believe that's the power of the
Holy Spirit say, 'Praise the Lord!' "

"Praise the Lord!" The building thundered. *"Praise the
Lord!"*

Back in her seat, Gina was radiant. She could hardly
hold still. I reached over and put my hand on her arm—
and noticed something else. The long black hairs on her
arm were just brushing off and falling to the floor.

"See, Mommy," she grinned. "I'm well all over."

She was well in every way. That night we had a great
service in the bathroom—pouring all her pills down the toilet. The doctors had told me that rapid withdrawal from
the cortisone could have disastrous effects, but I figured
that since God was taking care of everything else, He could
certainly take care of that, too.

Within a week I noticed stubble appearing on Gina's
head. Her hair was growing back. And as it grew longer, I
saw God had given her a bonus. Instead of coming in

straight as it had been before, her hair was coming in curly. Her face, once chalky white, was now rosy pink. She never again returned to the wheelchair.

Sometime later, I took her back to the Children's Medical Center. After a brief examination, the doctor looked up at me quizzically.

I knew he was Jewish, but I also knew I had no choice but to tell him what had happened. "Do you believe in God?" I asked him.

"Did you take her to a faith healer?" he asked, without otherwise acknowledging my question.

I remembered what Miss Kuhlman had said. She was not a faith healer. She had no power to heal anyone. Only the Holy Spirit healed. "No, I didn't take her to a faith healer," I said. "But I did take her to a Miracle Service."

The doctor bit his lower lip and shook his head.

"Well, I believe it!" I heard a woman's voice say.

I looked up to see the woman doctor with the pale blue eyes. "I've seen others healed in just the same way," she said. "And there is no explanation for it except the power of God. This child was ready to die. Look at her now."

We went into her office and she gave Gina a thorough examination. "We really don't need an examination to see that she's been healed," she said. "But there are always some people who have to be shown the facts on paper. Even then they don't want to believe."

On our way out of the office we were stopped by one of the other doctors who had previously treated Gina and had heard of her healing. "Mrs. Bradley, Gina will get sick again if you withdraw her medication—especially the phenobarbital. That's the only thing that is preventing her from having a fatal seizure."

I looked at him straight in the eye. "Doctor, I thank you for your concern. You folks have been wonderful to me here. But the phenobarbital is not what's keeping Gina alive. It's the Holy Spirit."

Two weeks later we returned to West Virginia. There was no need for a wheelchair this time. When we got out of the car in front of the old house, Mother came running down the walk to meet us, her arms in the air, her face shining with the glory of God.

"I had a vision," she wept as she embraced me. "I had a vision of Gina out in the backyard playing under the apple tree. Her cheeks were rosy, and she had a head full of long, curly dark hair. Oh, praise the Lord!"

Three months later, Daddy died. His sins, like mine, had been washed away in the blood of Jesus. We buried him in the plot that had been picked out for Gina. That afternoon, when we returned from the cemetery, we sat quietly around the living room. Mother got up and stood at the window. Beckoning to me, she said quietly, "Patricia, come here. I want to show you something."

I stood beside her and looked out in the backyard. There was Gina, her cheeks rosy, her glossy hair blowing in the winter wind, standing under the apple tree.

Mother reached for the old Bible beside the lamp on the table. Picking it up, she leafed through it until she found a verse of scripture in the Old Testament.

"Your Daddy's in heaven," she said, brushing away a tear with the back of her hand. "But Gina's still here." Then she read: "The Lord giveth and the Lord taketh away. Blessed be the name of the Lord."